Computational Models of Language Evolution

Editors: Luc Steels, Remi van Trijp

In this series:

1. Steels, Luc. The Talking Heads Experiment: Origins of words and meanings.

2. Vogt, Paul. How mobile robots can self-organize a vocabulary.

3. Bleys, Joris. Language strategies for the domain of colour.

4. van Trijp, Remi. The evolution of case grammar.

5. Spranger, Michael. The evolution of grounded spatial language.

ISSN: 2364-7809

The evolution of case grammar

Remi van Trijp

language science press

Remi van Trijp. 2017. *The evolution of case grammar* (Computational Models of Language Evolution 4). Berlin: Language Science Press.

This title can be downloaded at:
http://langsci-press.org/catalog/book/52
© 2017, Remi van Trijp
Published under the Creative Commons Attribution 4.0 Licence (CC BY 4.0):
http://creativecommons.org/licenses/by/4.0/
ISBN: 978-3-944675-45-9 (Digital)
       978-3-944675-84-8 (Hardcover)
       978-3-944675-85-5 (Softcover)
ISSN: 2364-7809
DOI:10.17169/langsci.b52.182

Cover and concept of design: Ulrike Harbort
Typesetting: Sebastian Nordhoff, Felix Kopecky, Remi van Trijp
Proofreading: Benjamin Brosig, Marijana Janjic, Felix Kopecky
Fonts: Linux Libertine, Arimo, DejaVu Sans Mono
Typesetting software: X∃LATEX

Language Science Press
Habelschwerdter Allee 45
14195 Berlin, Germany
langsci-press.org

Storage and cataloguing done by FU Berlin

Language Science Press has no responsibility for the persistence or accuracy of URLs for external or third-party Internet websites referred to in this publication, and does not guarantee that any content on such websites is, or will remain, accurate or appropriate.

To Elise

Contents

Preface		ix
1 Case and artificial language evolution		**1**
1.1	Introduction	1
1.2	Case and the grammar square	2
	1.2.1 Overview	2
	1.2.2 The functions of case systems	2
	1.2.3 Stage I: no marking	3
	1.2.4 Stage II: specific marking	4
	1.2.5 Stage III: semantic roles	6
	1.2.6 Stage IV: syntactic roles	8
	1.2.7 Further developments	9
1.3	Modeling language evolution	10
	1.3.1 Overview	10
	1.3.2 Three models of artificial language evolution	10
	1.3.3 The do's and don'ts of artificial language evolution	13
1.4	A brief history of prior work	16
	1.4.1 Overview	16
	1.4.2 The emergence of adaptive lexicons	17
	1.4.3 Towards grammar	18
	1.4.4 Other research avenues	20
2 Processing case and argument structure		**23**
2.1	Introduction	23
2.2	Representing and linking meanings	24
2.3	A brief introduction to Fluid Construction Grammar	27
	2.3.1 Overview	27
	2.3.2 Unify and Merge	28
	2.3.3 Structure building	30
2.4	Parsing 'Jack sweep dust off-floor'	32
	2.4.1 Overview	32
	2.4.2 Unifying and merging lexical entries	33

		2.4.3	A syntactic case marker	39

       2.4.3   A syntactic case marker 39
       2.4.4   The caused motion construction 40
   2.5 Producing 'jack sweep floor' 43
       2.5.1   Overview 43
       2.5.2   Unifying and merging lexical entries 44
       2.5.3   The agent-acts-on-surface construction 45
   2.6 Networks and conventionalization 47

3 Baseline experiments   49
   3.1 Introduction 49
   3.2 Experimental set-up 49
       3.2.1   Overview 49
       3.2.2   Key abilities and self-assessment criteria 50
       3.2.3   Description games 52
       3.2.4   The world, sensory-motor input and conceptualization . 54
       3.2.5   Additional assumptions and scaffolds 59
   3.3 Baseline experiment 1: no marking 62
       3.3.1   Overview 62
       3.3.2   An inferential coding system 64
       3.3.3   Results and discussion 68
   3.4 Baseline experiment 2: specific marking 70
       3.4.1   Overview 70
       3.4.2   Speaker-based innovation 70
       3.4.3   Results and discussion 79
   3.5 Baseline experiment 3: semantic roles 86
       3.5.1   Overview 86
       3.5.2   Generalization as a side-effect 86
       3.5.3   Results and discussion of set-up 3a 95
       3.5.4   Results and discussion of set-up 3b 97
       3.5.5   Results and discussion of set-up 3c 101
       3.5.6   Results and discussion of set-up 3d 104
       3.5.7   Conclusions and future work 107

4 Multi-level selection and language systematicity   111
   4.1 Introduction 111
   4.2 Pattern formation 112
       4.2.1   Overview 112
       4.2.2   Pattern formation in language 112
       4.2.3   Operationalizing pattern formation 116

4.3		Experiment 1: individual selection without analogy	120
	4.3.1	Overview	120
	4.3.2	Experimental set-up	120
	4.3.3	Results and discussion	121
	4.3.4	The problem of systematicity in other work	127
4.4		Experiment 2: multi-level selection without analogy	132
	4.4.1	Overview	132
	4.4.2	Experimental set-up	133
	4.4.3	Results and discussion	134
4.5		Experiment 3: multi-level selection with analogy	141
	4.5.1	Overview	141
	4.5.2	Experimental set-up	141
	4.5.3	Results and discussion	143
4.6		Towards syntactic cases	152
	4.6.1	Overview	152
	4.6.2	A first experiment	152
	4.6.3	The grammar square: a roadmap for further work	159

5 Impact on artificial language evolution and linguistic theory — 163

5.1		Introduction	163
5.2		Pushing the state-of-the-art	164
	5.2.1	Overview	164
	5.2.2	Experiment 1: A primitive case system?	164
	5.2.3	Experiment 2: dealing with variation	168
	5.2.4	Experiment 3: implementing communicative pressures	171
	5.2.5	Experiment 4: more innate knowledge	172
	5.2.6	Summary: case markers serve communication	175
5.3		Argument structure and construction grammar	176
	5.3.1	Overview	176
	5.3.2	Argument structure in BCG and SBCG	177
	5.3.3	An example: the ditransitive construction	178
	5.3.4	Discussion and comparison	179
5.4		Analogy, multi-level selection and the constructicon	184
	5.4.1	Overview	184
	5.4.2	The organization of the linguistic inventory	185
	5.4.3	Construction grammars	186
	5.4.4	The inventory in Fluid Construction Grammar	188

Contents

5.5	Linguistic typology and grammaticalization		191
	5.5.1	Overview	191
	5.5.2	The status of semantic maps	192
	5.5.3	Thematic hierarchies in case systems	198
	5.5.4	A redundant approach to grammaticalization	200

Postscriptum   207
    Artificial language evolution   208
    Acknowledgements   209

Appendix: Measures   211

References   215

Index   229
    Name index   229
    Subject index   231

Preface

This book is dedicated to the study of case – an inflectional category system for marking the relations between events and the roles of their participants. However, I have to confess that it wasn't exactly love at first sight between case marking and me. Or second. I can still recite the complete Latin case paradigm without batting an eyelash because me and my fellow pupils were drilled to do just that: *-us -a -um -i -ae -a*. Later, at the age of sixteen, I had an unpleasant encounter with what Mark Twain described as *"that awful German language"*. One time you had to say *den* and the other *dem* without any obvious reason. When I asked the teacher about it, I was literally told to just learn the dialogues in the book by rote and trust him that I was saying the right thing. In the meantime, English and French were stealing my heart because they opened new worlds to me without making a fuss about what seemed to be tiny little details at the time.

And yet, here I am presenting a book about the origins and evolution of case systems. You may interpret this as an unhealthy tendency towards masochism, but I am in fact making amends for my early prejudices against case. While working on my doctoral research, it dawned on me that case systems are very elegant solutions to a very complex communicative problem. Case markers turn out to be grammar's Swiss army knife: they can be used for expressing event structure, spatial and temporal relations, gender and number distinctions, and many other subtle grammatically relevant meanings. I marveled at this unexpected display of functionality and I got intrigued by the rise and fall of case paradigms.

The research in this book therefore tries to be a new step in unravelling the secrets of case systems by modeling *how* such systems may emerge as the result of the processes whereby language users continuously (re)shape their language in locally situated communicative interactions. Since these processes are virtually impossible to grasp in natural languages, this book offers additional evidence through agent-based models in which a population of embodied artificial agents self-organize a case-like grammar with similar properties as found in case languages such as German, Latin and Turkish.

More specifically, two innovative experiments are reported. The first experiment offers the first multi-agent simulations ever that involve polysemous linguistic categories. Here, the agents are capable of inventing grammatical markers for indicating event structure relations, and of generalizing those markers to semantic roles by performing analogical reasoning over events. Extension by analogy occurs as a side-effect of the need to optimize communicative success. In the second experiment, agents are capable of combining case markers into larger argument structure constructions through pattern formation. The results show that languages become unsystematic if the linguistic inventory is unstructured and contains multiple levels of organization. This book demonstrates that this problem of systematicity can be solved through multilevel alignment. All the experiments are implemented in Fluid Construction Grammar (FCG), and use the first computational formalization of argument structure in a construction-based approach that works for both production and parsing.

Even though the experiments involve the formation of artificial languages, the results are highly relevant for natural language research as well. This book therefore engages in an interdisciplinary dialogue with linguistics and contributes to some currently ongoing debates such as the formalization of argument structure in construction grammar, the organization of the linguistic inventory, the status of semantic maps and thematic hierarchies and the mechanisms for explaining grammaticalization.

1 Case and artificial language evolution

1.1 Introduction

The more than 6.000 languages in the world each have their unique way of offering their speakers an astonishing range of expressivity. We can just as easily engage in hair-splitting philosophical debates as we can start gossiping about as soon as somebody leaves the room. At the heart of the grammar that allows us to communicate all these complex meanings lies the way in which relations between words are organized. If you want to hear about juicy facts such as who kissed whom, grammar can help you finding out using various strategies such as word order, verbal agreement and case marking.

Among all the possible strategies employed by language users, only few have seduced linguists so skillfully as grammatical case has done. Ever since Pāṇini(4th Century BC), case has claimed a central role in linguistic theory and continues to do so today. However, despite centuries worth of research, case has yet to reveal its most important secrets, as can be gleaned from the many recent monographs (Blake 1994; Butt 2006), collections (Kulikov, Malchukov & de Swart 2006; Barðdal & Chelliah 2009; Malchukov & Spencer 2009) and projects ("Case and thematic relations", Davidse (1996); PIONEER, Amberber & de Hoop (2005); "Indo-European Case and Argument Structure in a Typological Perspective", Barðdal (2009)). Among the many open questions, the following two are explored in this book:

1. Why do some languages evolve a case system?

2. How can a population self-organize a case system?

Both challenges have proven to be problematic and even controversial in the literature on case. The first question is answered differently by each linguistic theory – if answered at all. The second one has largely been out of reach of linguists due to insufficient historical data, which makes that changes in a language can often only be detected once that change has already propagated and become acceptable in a population (Croft 1991: 34–35).

1 Case and artificial language evolution

This book proposes that case categories are *culturally* constructed (as opposed to being innate), and that a case system may emerge spontaneously as language users try to optimize their communicative success in locally situated interactions while at the same time minimizing the cognitive resources required to do so.

The validity of this hypothesis is demonstrated through agent-based modeling – a research methodology that is well-established in fields such as biology and economics, but which is still relatively unknown in linguistics. One reason is that experiments in artificial language evolution have so far mainly focused on simple one-to-one mappings between meaning and form, whereas all natural language systems are highly complex and ambiguous phenomena. As the experiments in this book will show, however, it is perfectly feasible to tackle such intricate phenomena as well if we use more sophisticated tools for handling linguistic representations and processing.

1.2 Case and the grammar square

1.2.1 Overview

Before delving into methodological issues, however, let us first look at the empirical domain that needs to be modeled in order to have a clear appreciation of the complexity of case systems and the problem of "argument realization" (i.e. the relation between event structure and its morphosyntactic realization in language).

1.2.2 The functions of case systems

Most case systems are used as a device for marking what the role of a participant is in a particular event. Consider the following example from Turkish:

(1) Mehmet   adam-a elma-lar-ı ver-di.
    Mehmet.NOM man-DAT apple-PL-ACC give-PST-3SG
    'Mehmet gave the apples to the man.' (Blake 1994: 1, example 1)

The case markers make it clear to the hearer that Mehmet was the giver of the apples, not the recipient. Marking the roles of participants in an event has some serious advantages: it allows the hearer to interpret the utterance correctly without actually observing the scene (i.e. "displacement" becomes possible) because it rules out ambiguities, and it reduces the semantic complexity of parsing because the hearer does not have to infer who was the giver and who was the receiver from other contextual cues. So one of the basic functions of case marking is **to indicate event structure**.

Secondly, case markers are also used **for packaging information structure**. In example 1.2.2, the suffix *-ı* not only marks the accusative case, but it also indicates that the apples are "specific" (as opposed to undetermined). Many languages also exploit case markers for marking the topic and focus of an utterance, for marking new vs. given information, and so on.

Finally, case marking can be used for indicating various other grammatical distinctions such as number and gender, as shown here for German:

(2) ein klein-er   Man
     a   little-M.SG man
     'a little man'

(3) drei klein-e Frau-en
     three little-PL woman-F.PL
     'three little women'

This book focuses on the first function of case systems: indicating event structure. More specifically, it reports on experiments in artificial language evolution that show how a primitive case system may emerge in a multi-agent population. In order for the experiments to have any scientific value, they must be compatible with what is known about the evolution of real-life case systems, which I will summarize in the following sections.

1.2.3 Stage I: no marking

Many languages do not have a case system at all, but rather employ a different strategy such as word order (e.g. English). There are even languages that hardly use any marking whatsoever for indicating "who did what to whom" to the hearer. For instance, the language Lisu generally does not mark event structure. Li & Thompson (1976; quoted from Palmer 1994:23) give the following two examples:

(4) a. làma nya ánà khù-a.
         tigers TOP dog bite-DECL
         'Tigers bite dogs.' / 'Dogs bite tigers.'
     b. ánà xə   làma khù-a.
         dog NEW TOP tigers bite-DECL
         'Tigers bite dogs.' / 'Dogs bite tigers.'

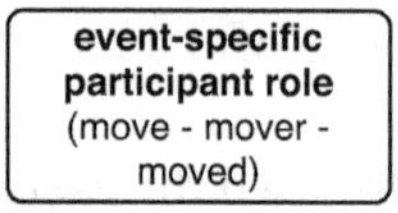

1 Case and artificial language evolution

> **event-specific participant role**
> (move - mover - moved)

Figure 1.1: In the first stage, the experiments start with a lexicon but without any grammar. The lexicon may contain words such as *move*, whose event structure may include participant roles such as "mover" (i.e. the one who did the moving) and "moved" (i.e. the thing that is being moved). However, the language has no means of marking those participant roles explicitly, hence the hearer has to infer the intended interpretation from the context.

In both sentences, there is only a topic marker ("known topic" versus "new topic"), but the correct reading depends on the context in which the sentence was uttered. Another example is Riau Indonesian (Gil 2008), which only marks event structure in extremely rare cases. While such examples seem odd for speakers of most other languages, Palmer (1994: 23) notes that even English does not always mark event structure. For example, the famous phrase *the shooting of the hunters* does not indicate whether the hunters did the shooting or whether they got shot themselves.

The experiments in this book therefore start from the point where a population of language users have already evolved a lexicon, but **no grammar yet** (see Figure 1.1). This point of departure is not only justified by the empirical observation that new case markers evolve from existing lexical items (see further below), but also by the fact that experiments on artificial language evolution have already shown how vocabularies may emerge in a population of grounded embodied agents (e.g. Steels 1996b,a; 1997c). In this way we can better isolate the features that are hypothesized to be formed in the experiments. Of course, once the dynamics of these experiments are better understood, a series of integrated experiments must be carried out to confirm the results.

1.2.4 Stage II: specific marking

Attested examples of the emergence of modern case markers show that they are recruited from existing lexical items and that they start out in very restricted use scenarios. Blake (1994: chapter 6) gives examples of how verbs, nouns and even adverbial particles can develop into case markers. Blake writes that a predicate like COME is a two-place predicate implying a "comer" and a "destination". A predicate like LEAVE mirrors this implication by having a "leaver" and a "source". A predicate like FLY, however, only implies a "flier". If speakers then wish to produce utterances such as *he flew to/from Bangkok*, pairs of predicates can be used. Blake gives the following examples from Thai:

(5) a. thân cà bin maa krungthêep
he will fly come Bangkok
'He will fly to Bangkok.'

b. thân cà bin càak krungthêep
he will fly leave Bangkok
'He will fly from Bangkok.'
(Blake 1994: 163–164)

Such languages are known as "serial verb language languages". The second verb is (usually) non-finite and cannot be marked for tense, aspect or mood independently of the first verb, and it takes no expressed subject or it implies the same subject as that of the first verb. Blake writes that functionally speaking, these second verbs are equivalent to prepositions. Serial verb language constructions are in fact very frequent and their development into adpositions and case markers has been widely attested, especially in the languages of West Africa, New Guinea, Southeast Asia and Oceania (ibid., at 163; also see Givón (1997), section 7, for more on serial verb language constructions and similar examples).

The recruitment and evolution of a lexical item into an adposition and eventually a case marker is a long and complex process. For reasons that I will explain later on in this book, this crucial step in grammaticalization is "scaffolded" in the experiments. Rather than reusing an existing lexical item in a more grammatical way, the artificial agents will be capable of inventing a new form which already acts as some kind of adposition or verb-specific case marker, as shown in Figure 1.2. The experiments thus simplify stage II in order to focus first on the function of such markers and how they can be propagated in a speech community. It is needless to say, however, that this part of the grammaticalization

Figure 1.2: In the second stage, a specific marker arises in order to solve a communicative problem. In natural languages, this marker is often a lexical item which is recruited for a new use. In the experiments, this stage involves the invention of a new marker.

chain remains on the research agenda for future experiments and first steps towards grammaticalization of existing lexical elements have already been taken by Wellens, Loetzsch & Steels (2008).

1.2.5 Stage III: semantic roles

When verb-specific case markers propagate successfully in a speech community, they often extend their coverage to other verbs as well. To come back to example 5, this would mean that *maa* 'come' evolves from the marker of the destination of a flight to a general allative case role (i.e. the destination of motion events). Extension of the use of a marker would in this case be *semantically motivated* and can occur by analogical reasoning over events. This is also the strategy that is employed in the experiments.

Figure 1.3 illustrates the new mapping between meaning and form when case markers become generalized semantic markers. Instead of directly mapping a particular participant role (e.g. the "mover") onto a case marker, a **semantic role** (such as Agent) mediates between this mapping.

Since case markers in natural languages usually carry more than one function, it is hard to say what the semantic roles are that underlie a syntactic pattern. We can however look at "agnating structures" (Gleason 1965). Agnation illustrates a structural relationship between two grammatical constructions which have the same (major) lexical items, but different syntactic structures. If the alternation between these two structures is recurrent for groups of constructions, then this can be seen as a pattern in the language. An example of agnating structures is the alternation between the English ditransitive (as in *I gave him a book*) and its prepositional counterpart (as in *I gave the book to him*).

Differences in the semantic categorization of verbs can come to surface if small but regular variations show up between these agnating structures. Compare the groups of agnating structures in the following examples:

(6) I gave him a book.   I gave the book to him.
    I sent him a letter.   I sent the letter to him.

(7) I baked him a cake.   I baked a cake for you.
    I bought him a present. I bought a present for him.

Both groups of verbs can occur in the ditransitive construction, but they select a different preposition in the agnating prepositional construction. The choice for either *to* or *for* is semantically motivated: the verbs listed in example 6 entail an *actual* transfer of the direct object (= recipient), whereas the verbs in (7) indicate

1.2 Case and the grammar square

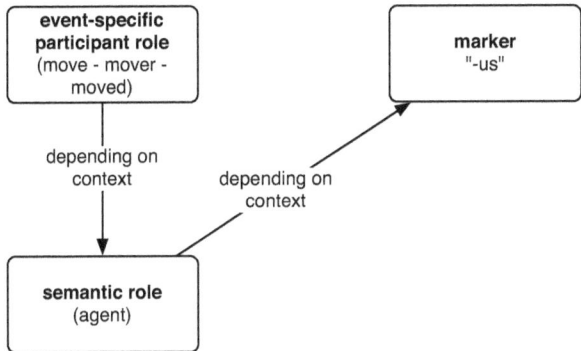

Figure 1.3: Specific markers may get extended through analogy in stage III. They now start to act as semantic roles.

that there is an *intended* transfer (= beneficiary). This is confirmed in the fact that sentences such as *?I gave him a book, but he refused it* feel awkward, whereas sentences such as *I baked him a cake, but he refused it* are perfectly acceptable. So it seems that both groups of verbs belong to different subclasses.

The extension of specific markers to semantic roles is useful for communication in several ways. First of all, semantic roles increase the potential for generalization in a language: by extending the functionality of a semantic role, there is a higher chance that it will be reused for categorizing new and similar participant roles as well. Instead of having to negotiate a different marker for each new instance, speakers of a language can thus make a semantically motivated innovation which increases the chance that the hearer will understand the speaker's intention. Second, and related to the first point, semantic roles increase the expressiveness of a language because they allow speakers to profile different aspects of the same event. For example, semantic roles can focus on the relation between an agent and a patient as in *he broke the window*, but also profile exclusively the resulting state of one of the participants as in *the window was broken*. Finally, semantic roles can significantly reduce the inventory size by grouping together larger classes of verbs.

The model proposed in this book predicts that the conventionalization of a mapping between verb-specific arguments and semantic roles (even though semantically motivated) is neither a determined nor a straightforward one. The choice depends on the conventions that are already present in the language, on a speaker's previous experience, frequency, etc. Moreover, the model predicts that there will be several varieties in the population which compete with each other

1 Case and artificial language evolution

for becoming the dominant semantic role of a particular argument. Thus we can expect that languages come up with very divergent classifications. For example, Italian features dative subjects with verbs such as *like* (Palmer 1994: 27), whereas English doesn't:

(8) Gli   piacciono le   ciliege.
    they.DAT like   DET cherries
    'They like cherries.'

Linking similar events can also be reversed from language to language. For example, when French speakers want to say *I miss you*, they literally say something like 'you are missing to me':

(9) Tu me manque-s.
    you me miss-2SG.PRS
    'I miss you.'

So semantic roles seem to be language-specific, which fits our assumption that they have to be constructed and learned. But once they become part of a language, are they an affair of 'take it or leave it', or is it possible that the same verb-specific participant role can be mapped onto multiple semantic roles? The answer seems to be that this mapping too is indirect and dependent on the context. For example, the 'sneezer' in *he sneezes* seems to be a patient, whereas it is (also) a causer in *he sneezed the napkin off the table.* All the above observations are reflected in Figure 1.3 and more evidence is provided in the next chapter.

1.2.6 Stage IV: syntactic roles

Languages typically have thousands of verbs and semantic roles. However, case languages tend to have streamlined case systems with only a dozen cases or less. As Croft (1991) states

> surface case marking imposes structure on thematic relations to an even more abstract degree than verb roots impose structure on the human experience of events. (Croft 1991: 158–159)

We know that a case marker has evolved into a *syntactic* marker once it can be dissociated from a particular semantic role (Givón 1997: 2–3). For instance, the German nominative case can be used for covering virtually all semantic roles of the language.

1.2 Case and the grammar square

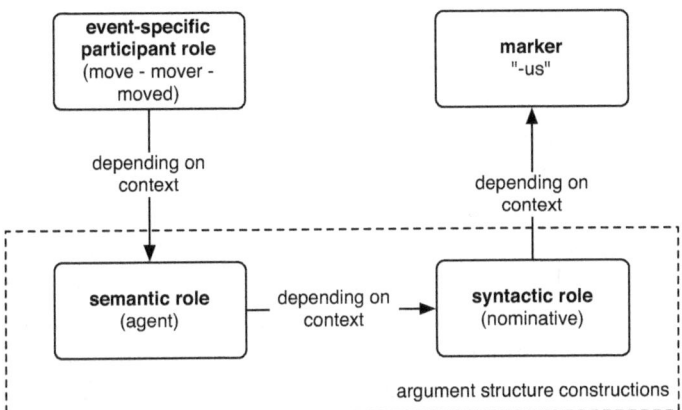

Figure 1.4: In the next step, even more abstractions occur through syntactic roles. The mapping between semantic roles and grammatical cases is hypothesized to be handled by argument structure constructions which can combine several semantic roles into a larger pattern.

Figure 1.4 shows an updated mapping between event structure meaning and its surface form, which is now mediated by an abstract and hidden layer of semantic and syntactic categories. I will from now on refer to this picture as the **grammar square**. Each mapping in the square can vary according to the communicative and linguistic circumstances, so the relation between a participant role and its morphosyntactic realization is multilayered and indirect.

The picture presented here however has the danger that case markers are considered in isolation, whereas they can only be understood in relation to the other parts of the pattern in which they occur. Indeed, the mapping of semantic roles onto syntactic roles (and vice versa) is hypothesized to be taken care of by **argument structure constructions** (Goldberg 1995). These constructions may be schematic, verb-class-specific or even verb-specific. I will come back to this point in the next Chapters that introduce the formalization of such constructions.

1.2.7 Further developments

Stages I–IV described the possible evolutionary pathway of a case marker which resulted in an inflectional category that groups together various semantically related roles. This is also the endpoint of the experiments described in this book because they focus only on case marking as a way to express event structure in a grammatical way. There are, however, other functions which may be performed by case markers such as packaging information structure, marking perspectivization and other grammatical distinctions such as gender and number (as argued in §1.2.2). Especially information structure seems to be the most important pressure for case markers to extend their coverage and become even more dissociated from their previous meaning.

Finally, case markers eventually decline and even whole grammatical systems of case may get lost and replaced by other grammatical devices. This is apparent in the (almost) complete loss of case marking in languages such as English, French and Dutch, which replaced it with word order constraints. Individual case markers may disappear because they are "merged" with another case such as the merger of the instrumental and locative case in Middle Indo-Aryan (Blake 1994: 176). Whereas merger seems to be relatively common in the life cycle of case systems, case split is quite rare. Merger of case markers means that the case system is reduced unless new members are recruited. With the loss of cases and further developments in the grammaticalization of case markers, the different cases of a language may become insufficiently differentiated from each other. This allows other strategies, such as word order complemented with prepositions in English, to become more popular and eventually the new conventions of a language. The decline of entrenched and conventionalized grammatical units falls beyond the scope of this book.

1.3 Modeling language evolution

1.3.1 Overview

The experiments reported in this book are models of *artificial language evolution*, in which computational and mathematical models and robotic experiments are used for evolving (new) artificial languages that have similar properties as found in natural languages. As such, the methodology provides possible and operational explanations for those properties. Experiments typically involve a *population of artificial language users* (henceforth called *agents*) that engage with each other in communicative interactions.

1.3.2 Three models of artificial language evolution

There is a wide consensus in the field that language has evolved because there is a *selectionist* system underlying it. Despite this consensus, there is disagreement on how linguistic variation and hence the potential for change is caused, and which selectionist pressures are operating to retain a particular variation

1.3 Modeling language evolution

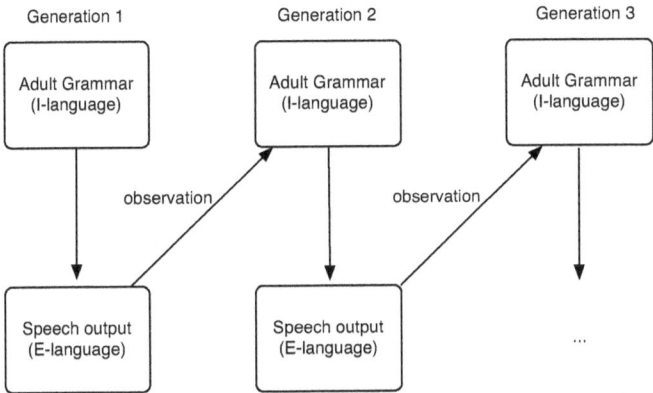

Figure 1.5: Iterated learning models assume that languages evolve because children are faced with a learning bottleneck when observing and reconstructing the language of the previous generation.

in a language. There are basically three different perspectives based on genetic evolution, cultural transmission, and problem-solving respectively.

Models of genetic evolution (e.g. Briscoe 2000; Nowak, Komarova & Niyogi 2001) investigate the biological evolution of the *language faculty* (i.e. our ability to acquire and use language). These models put the selectionist pressure at the level of fitness (i.e. the ability to survive and reproduce), which is assumed to be directly related to communicative success. Agents are endowed with an artificial genome that determines their communicative behavior. Depending on how much of language is assumed to be innate, the genome may include which concepts can be employed by the agents for structuring their world, which types of categories are to be used, and so on. Potential innovation takes place when this genome is transmitted from parents to children. Because genome copying involves crossover and possibly mutation, variation is inevitable, and some of it will lead to higher or lower success.

Iterated Learning Models (ILM, Brighton, Kirby & Smith 2005; Kirby 2001; Kirby & Hurford 2002; Kirby, Smith & Brighton 2004; Smith, Kirby & Brighton 2003) investigate what happens when language is culturally transmitted from one generation to the next without any interference from functional pressures, as illustrated in Figure 1.5. Each cycle, an adult generation (typically represented by a single agent) produces speech output based on its internal grammar, which is observed by a new generation (also typically a single agent) for reconstructing the language. The model assumes that there is a learning bottleneck (i.e. the child cannot observe all utterances in the language), hence the learner agent may overgeneralize the input based on innate learning biases. When the adult agent "dies" and is replaced by the child, the mistakes in learning become the new convention and the language changes. The ILM shows strong affinity for child-based theories of language change as found in generative linguistics (King 1969).

The third class of models views the task of building and negotiating a communication system as a kind of problem-solving process. Agents try to achieve a communicative goal with maximal success and minimal effort. This problem-solving process is definitely not a rational but an intuitive one that is seldom accessible to conscious inspection. It is not an individualistic problem-solving process either, but a collective one, in which different individuals participate as peers. According to this view a communication system is built up in a step by step fashion driven by needs and failures in communication, and it employs a large battery of strategies and cognitive mechanisms which are not specific to language but appear in many other kinds of cognitive tasks, such as tool design or navigation. Recent experiments by Galantucci (2005) on the emergence of communication in human subjects provide good illustrations of these problem-solving processes in action. Variation and innovation in problem-solving models are common because each individual not only tries to converge to the shared communication system, but can also contribute innovations to it. In fact the main challenge is rather to explain how agreement between individuals and thus a globally shared population language can ever arise. This approach to language evolution is closely related to cognitive-functional theories of language and utterance-based models of linguistic change (Croft 2000; 2004).

The three models are of course not mutually exclusive: it is clear that the models of cultural evolution expect a rich cognitive-linguistic system, which can only be explained through the genetic endowment of the agents. Similarly, problem-solving models can be modeled using a generation turnover as well (Vogt 2007). However, one particular advantage of the problem-solving approach is that it attempts to explain as many linguistic phenomena as possible in terms of functional and communicative pressures. This means that innate mechanisms are only used as a last resort, which arguably avoids putting all the explanatory burden on the shoulders of biology. This book therefore subscribes to the problem-solving approach.

1.3.3 The do's and don'ts of artificial language evolution

The question of the origins and evolution of language is notoriously difficult because there are no fossil traces or written accounts left of the first languages, and there are no data available about the biological changes that enabled language. These facts have led Christiansen & Kirby (2003) to pose the provocative question: is language evolution the hardest problem in science?

Without attempting to answer that question, it actually *is* possible to come up with solid theories despite the lack of real-life data: in various other disciplines, such as the origins of the universe, significant advances are made using mathematical models and computational simulations. Another example is Artificial Life where computational models, robotic experiments and biochemistry are used as techniques to develop artificial phenomena that may help to explain processes of evolution in natural phenomena.

(i) Creating natural language-like phenomena. Let me start by debunking a myth about modeling language evolution that seems to be lingering in the minds of some people: computational simulations and robotic experiments can never lead to the emergence of an actual natural language like English or Russian. There are just too many factors that have shaped these languages and modeling them would require to model the entire state of every speaker and every interaction *ever*. The "languages" that emerge in this kind of experiments should thus not be *directly* linked to natural languages: they are novel artificial constructs and hence **the methodology only offers a "proof of concept" of what results can be achieved within the specific set-up of a given experiment**. However, these constructs may be natural language-*like* and thus offer a possible and working hypothesis for how similar phenomena could have come about in natural languages.

Secondly, even in abstraction, we cannot model every aspect of language at once, just as it is impossible to perform controlled psycholinguistic experiments that take every detail about language processing into account. The key is therefore to pick a phenomenon observed in natural languages and try to isolate this feature into a controlled simulation or experiment. Focusing on smaller problems is standard practice in many scientific disciplines. As Stephen Hawkin writes in his *A Brief History of Time*:

> It turns out to be very difficult to devise a theory of the universe all in one go. Instead, we break the problem up into bits and invent a number of partial theories. Each of these partial theories describes and predicts a certain limited class of observations, neglecting the effects of other quantities, or

1 Case and artificial language evolution

> representing them by simple sets of numbers. It may be that this approach is completely wrong. If everything in the universe depends on everything else in a fundamental way, it might be impossible to get close to a full solution by investigating parts of the problem in isolation. Nevertheless, it is certainly the way we have made progress in the past.
> Hawkin (1988: 12)

In problem-solving models of artificial language evolution, the researcher therefore first chooses a topic of interest that is common to most if not all languages, such as tense, aspect and mood. Investigating such a feature involves the following steps (Steels 2006):

1. The researcher selects a feature of language to investigate;

2. The researcher hypothesizes which set of cognitive mechanisms and external pressures are necessary for the emergence of this feature:

    a) These cognitive mechanisms are operationalized in the form of computational processes, and a population of simulated or embodied agents is endowed with these mechanisms;

    b) The external pressures are operationalized in the form of an interaction pattern embedded in a simulated or real world environment;

3. Systematic computer simulations are performed demonstrating the impact of the proposed mechanisms. If possible, results should be compared between simulations *with* a proposed mechanism and simulations *without* this mechanism in order to show that it is not only a sufficient but also a necessary prerequisite for the emergent feature.

Even if the simulations show that the investigated feature only emerges if certain mechanisms are included, this still does not prove anything about similar features in natural languages because different evolutionary pathways are possible. However, the simulations then at least show one possibility and may provide an additional piece of the puzzle next to evidence from linguistics, archeology, biology and other fields.

(ii) Clarifying the scaffolds and assumptions. Computational simulations and robotic experiments are at the same time blessed and cursed with the fact that every detail of the hypothesis has to be spelled out completely, otherwise the system does not work. "Blessed" because this may reveal effects of the hypothesis that were overlooked or not expected by the verbal theory; "cursed" because there is a danger of "kludging" something together to get the system off the ground. There is often a fine border between significant results and quirks resulting from a kludge, so it is crucial that it is crystal clear which features of the model are supposed to be "emergent" on the one hand, and which features are "assumed" or "scaffolded" on the other.

Assumptions and scaffolds are unavoidable in computational simulations because it is simply impossible to explain everything at once. Drawing the line between what is "assumed" and what is "scaffolded" is not always an easy decision. I define "assumed features" as those aspects of the simulations that we cannot explain using the methodology described here. One example is the assumption that agents are social and cooperative beings that *want* to reach communicative success. Another example is the capacity for building composite structures. I define "scaffolded features" as those aspects of the simulations that in principle could be evolved using the methodology but are given so that not every simulation or experiment has to start from scratch. An example of a scaffold is the space of possible phonemes: in none of the experiments in this book, agents had to learn the distinctive sounds of their language. These "scaffolded" features may be brought in at a later stage or form the subject of other experiments, such as work on the emergence of vowel systems (de Boer 2000; Oudeyer 2005).

(iii) **Global versus local measures**. Another important dichotomy is that of global versus local measures. In experiments that study language from a usage-based point-of-view, only local measures which can be observed by the agents themselves within the local interaction may have an influence on the linguistic behaviour of the agents. Typical local measures are:

- Success of the language game: the agents that are involved in a language game can experience whether the game was a success or not. This may influence the confidence with which they employ certain linguistic items;

- Search and difficulty: An agent can "measure" for example the ambiguity of an utterance because it causes an elaborate search space during processing;

- Cognitive effort: Agents can "measure" the cognitive effort needed during parsing and production, such as how much processing time they need, how many times they need to add information from their world model to the linguistic data, how many times they need to perform additional operations such as egocentric perspective reversal, etc.

Global measures, then, are measures which are used by the experimenter solely for analyzing the simulations. These measures should by no means have an in-

1 Case and artificial language evolution

fluence on the linguistic behaviour of the agents. For example, if an agent should decide between two competing forms for a meaning, it has to make the appropriate choice based on its *individual* past experiences and on the local information in the language game. A global measure such as how many agents share one of the competitors would require an overview of the complete population, which no speaker ever has. Convergence has to come about in a distributed, self-organized fashion without external guidance or central control.

1.4 A brief history of prior work

1.4.1 Overview

This book is part of more than a decade worth of research on language as a complex adaptive system. The research itself is rooted in prior work in Artificial Intelligence and robotics in the mid-eighties, which involved home-made robots of all shapes and sizes – driving around on wheels, flying with balloons and propellers, or waggling their tails in the rough waters of the Brussels' university swimming pool. These creations were the result of a break with mainstream research in Artificial Intelligence: whereas most work in AI tried to formalize human intelligence, Luc Steels and his students at the Artificial Intelligence Laboratory (VUB, Brussels) investigated how "intelligence" might evolve in a community of physical agents as they autonomously interact with each other, their environment, and humans. They thus developed a bottom-up, behaviour-oriented approach to sensori-motor intelligence, which was at the same time also being explored by Rodney Brooks at the MIT Artificial Intelligence Lab (Steels & Brooks 1995).

Even though fascinating results were obtained, something was missing that could ever lead the experiments to other, more human-like intelligent behaviour than was displayed by the robots. The research then shifted its focus from behaviour-based robotics to embodied language in the autumn of 1995 when Steels had the following two ideas: first of all, language may have been the missing link in the initial experiments. Language may be a necessary step that enables the human cognitive system to bootstrap itself in tight interaction with the world and in a population of social cooperative agents (Steels 2003a). Second, the same principles and mechanisms that had since 1985 proven to be relevant for the work in robotics also had to be relevant for bootstrapping intelligence and language. These principles included self-organization, structural coupling, level formation and other (mainly biologically inspired) mechanisms (Steels 1998b). In this section I will give an overview of the research efforts at the AI Lab in Brussels and

1.4 A brief history of prior work

SONY Computer Science Laboratory Paris (which adopted the work on language as one of its founding research topics in 1996).

1.4.2 The emergence of adaptive lexicons

The first breakthrough experiment investigated how self-organization could explain the emergence of coordinated vocabularies (Steels 1997c). Self-organi-zation is a phenomenon in which coupled dynamical systems form a structure of increased complexity without guidance by an outside source or some central controller. Standard examples of self-organization are the formations of termite nests or paths in an ant society. The process has been used successfully for describing phenomena in various scientific disciplines: physics (e.g. crystalization), chemistry (e.g. molecular self-assembly), economy (catallaxy), etc. Language is also an example of a complex system that is shared by a speech community without central control (although some "watchdogs" such as the *Académie française* do their utter best to have people speak according to their set of standards).

In the experiments reported by Steels (1997c), agents engage in communicative interactions about a set of predefined meanings. If the speaker has no word for a meaning, he will invent a new one which may be adopted by the hearer. The agents assign a **success score** to the form-meaning mappings based on success in the interaction. After some rounds of negotiation, a shared set of form-meaning mappings emerges without the need for central control. Similar experiments using neural networks were reported by Batali (1998).

The notion of a **language game** was first introduced by Steels (1996; also see Steels 2001 for an introduction). Language games are routinized local interactions or scripts. An example of a language game in natural languages is a speaker who asks *Can you pass me the salt, please?*. The language game is a success if the hearer passes the salt or even if he responds that he refuses to do so (but at least he understood the message). The game is a failure if the hearer passes the pepper instead of the salt or if he just shrugs her shoulders. The speaker can then point to the salt, which gives the hearer some additional clues as to what he meant with *salt*. An iteration of language games is called a **dialogue**, but this more complex interaction pattern has not been studied anymore since Steels (1996a).

In these first experiments, the meaning space of the agents was predefined. However, since no concepts or categories are assumed to be innate in this line of work, several experiments have been conducted investigating how agents can create their own concepts and meanings. The first breakthrough was reported in Steels (1996c), in which agents created perceptual categories through **discrimination games**. In a discrimination game, an agent tries to discriminate a certain object from the other objects in the context by creating or using a set of one or more distinctive features for that object. In the next breakthrough experiment, discrimination games and language games were coupled to each other so that agents did not only self-organize a lexicon, but also used the lexicon for sharing concepts or perceptual distinctions (Steels 1997a,d; 1998a; 1999a,b). In a next step, it was shown how these ideas can be grounded in actual robotic agents (Steels 2001b; 2002a; Steels & Vogt 1997; Vogt 2000). The structural coupling of concepts and lexicons has also been successfully applied to the domains of colour (Belpaeme 2002; Belpaeme & Bleys 2005; Steels & Belpaeme 2005) and space (Loetzsch et al. 2008b; Steels & Loetzsch 2008).

The research on lexicon emergence steadily grew and touched upon topics such as how lexicons can continue to change and evolve because of language contact and population dynamics (Steels 1997b; Steels & McIntyre 1999) and stochasticity in cultural transmission (Kaplan, McIntyre & Steels 1998; Steels & Kaplan 1998a,b). The experimenters also developed the notion of a **semiotic landscape**, a powerful framework to study the **semiotic dynamics** involved in the language games (Steels & Kaplan 1999a,b). The research culminated in the Talking Heads experiment which involved thousands of agents travelling over the internet in order to play language games with each other (Steels 1999c; 2000b; 2001a; Steels & Kaplan 1999a,b; 2002; Steels et al. 2002).

The research on lexicon emergence is still being pursued today. For example, the Naming Game, which first appeared in Steels (1997c), has recently been implemented in humanoid robots that autonomously have to recognize objects as individuals and then agree on names for them. The Naming Game has also been picked up by scientists from statistical physics and complex systems who search for scaling laws and who investigate the long-term behaviour of the system using mathematical models (Baronchelli et al. 2006; De Vylder 2007). Other recent work using computational modeling investigates how word meanings can be more flexible and how the emergence of lexicons can scale up to much larger worlds (Wellens, Loetzsch & Steels 2008).

1.4.3 Towards grammar

Even though the first decade has been largely spent on investigating the properties of emergent adaptive lexicons, the emergence of grammar has always been on the research agenda with first attempts as early as 1997 (Steels 1997e). The research strategy involves moving all the insights gained from the experiments on lexical languages to the domain of grammar and identify which additional mechanisms and ideas are needed for the emergence of languages featuring grammatical properties (Steels 2005a).

The first steps towards grammar involved a pregrammatical stage of **multiple**

1.4 A brief history of prior work

word utterances, which was first investigated by Steels (1996b). In this experiment, multiple word utterances emerge naturally as the set of distinctive features for talking about objects expands and the agents have to adapt to cope with it. Van Looveren (2005) then showed how a multiword naming game can yield a more efficient communication system because a smaller lexicon could be used for naming objects. However, none of these experiments involved any grammar.

At the end of the nineties, a significant breakthrough was achieved which resulted in the general roadmap for investigating the emergence of grammar that is still being followed today (Steels (1999c): 44–47; Steels (2000a)). Whereas lexical languages are perfectly suited for language games involving only one object, grammar becomes useful when agents have the possibility of communicating about multiple objects because the search space becomes exponentially larger. Grammar thus emerges not in order to reduce inventory size or to become more learnable (as is proposed by genetic and Iterated Learning Models), but rather to **reduce the complexity of semantic parsing** for the hearer (this idea has been formalized and operationalized by Steels 2005b). Luc Steels then worked on systems for studying the emergence of **compositional meanings** (see §1.4.4) and for the emergence of grammar to take care of these compositional meanings.

Van Looveren (2005) applied these ideas to his experiments on multiple word games and lifted the agents' assumption that multiple words always refer to the same object. For example, the utterance *yellow ball* might refer to one object (a yellow ball) or at least two objects (some yellow thing and a ball). When faced with this referential uncertainty, the agents can exploit a simple syntax for indicating to the hearer which words refer to the same object. Referential uncertainty has also been investigated from the viewpoint of pattern formation (as another pregrammatical stage, Steels, van Trijp & Wellens 2007) and as a trigger for introducing additional syntax (Steels & Wellens 2006).

Another key issue in the emergence of grammar is the question of how agents can autonomously detect when additional constraints or grammar might become useful in order to improve their communicative success. The answer is "re-entrance" (Steels 2003b), a strategy which was already present in the experiments on the emergence of lexicons but which had to be developed further to fit into a grammatical framework. Re-entrance can be seen as some kind of self-monitoring in which the speaker first simulates the effect of his utterance on the hearer by taking himself as a model. If he detects problems such as ambiguity or an explosion of the search space during parsing, he will adapt his linguistic behaviour by adding more constraints or choosing a different verbalization. Similarly, the hearer can perform re-entrance for learning novelties in the speaker's utterance.

1 Case and artificial language evolution

A similar mechanism called "the obverter strategy" can be found in other negotiation-based models as well (Smith 2003a). Another way to increase the autonomy of the agents is to offer them strategies for self-assessing what kind of communicative goals they can attain given their present linguistic experience (called the "autotelic principle", Steels 2004b,c; Steels & Wellens 2007).

Most of the above ideas were put to practice in 2001 in the first "case experiment", which I will describe in Chapter 3 and of which some results were published in Steels (2004a) and to a lesser extent in Steels (2003b; 2007). Luc Steels implemented a unification-based grammar formalism to support the experiment, which ultimately led to the first design of Fluid Construction Grammar (FCG, also see Chapter 2). FCG is under constant development to meet the demands and requirements of new experiments such as the following:

- A bidirectional and uniform way of language processing (Steels & De Beule 2006). This feature is needed for allowing agents to act both as a speaker and as a hearer; and for allowing the agents to perform re-entrance;

- A way to deal with compositional semantics and to link meanings to each other (Steels, De Beule & Neubauer 2005).

The name "Fluid Construction Grammar" comes from the fact that FCG has many features in common with (vanilla) construction grammar (Croft 2005) and that it aims at investigating the "fluidity" of language emergence (i.e. various degrees of entrenchment of linguistic units). A software implementation of FCG, incorporated in a more general cognitive architecture called "Babel2", has been made freely available at *www.emergent-languages.org*.

Fluid Construction Grammar has already been used for investigating the emergence of compositionality (De Beule & Bergen 2006), recursion and hierarchy (Bleys 2008; De Beule 2007; 2008), structures for expressing second-order meanings (Steels & Bleys 2005) and semantic roles (Steels 2004a; van Trijp 2008c).

1.4.4 Other research avenues

The above account of the history of the research on language as a complex adaptive system did not refer to the experiments on the emergence of vowel systems and phonology (de Boer 2000; Oudeyer 2005). I also left out the work performed on event recognition, but I will come back to this in Chapter 3. Another area that I left largely uncovered is the research into conceptualization and the emergence of complex meanings.

Together with the key insights on the triggers and functions of grammar at the end of the ninetees, Steels developed a constraint-based system for studying

1.4 A brief history of prior work

the emergence of compositional meaning (Steels 2000a) which uses constraint propagation both for conceptualization and interpretation. In the system, a set of constraints can be composed into some kind of semantic program that the speaker wants the hearer to perform. For example, if the speaker wants to draw the hearer's attention to a particular ball in the context, he has to conceptualize a network of meanings or constraints that will help the hearer to correctly identify this ball. For example, the utterance *the red ball* indicates to the hearer that he has to (a) filter the objects in the context and retain those that match with the prototype [BALL], (b) filter this set of balls and retain the red ones, and (c) pick out the one remaining object (its uniqueness was indicated by the determiner *the* in combination with the singular form *ball*). The system allows for the composition of second-order semantics (e.g. *the bigger ball*) and context-sensitive meanings (e.g. a "small" elephant is still bigger than a "big" mouse).

Even though at that time there was already an operational system, the research on compositional meanings was put on a hold to first develop a grammar formalism that could support it. With the recent advances in Fluid Construction Grammar, the research got picked up again and first experiments have already been reported that couple meanings produced by the system to FCG and vice versa (Bleys 2008; Steels & Bleys 2005). The system has also been completely re-implemented and improved upon (see Van den Broeck 2007; 2008: for an introduction).

2 Processing case and argument structure

2.1 Introduction

The mathematical properties of case and argument structure have been extensively studied in the tradition of formal grammars such as Combinatorial Categorial Grammar (CCG; Steedman 2000), Lexical-Functional Grammar (LFG; Bresnan 1982) and Head-driven Phrase Structure Grammar (HPSG; Pollard & Sag 1994). The focus of those studies has been the development of *competence models* (i.e. knowledge representations), thereby treating *linguistic processing* as a problem that can be dealt with separately. However, if our artificial agents have to use their linguistic knowledge in communicative interactions, we need a strong integration of both processing and competence.

One family of linguistic theories that is particularly interesting for achieving such an integration is *construction grammar*, because it is explicitly concerned with how meanings can be mapped onto forms and vice versa. Unfortunately, *computational* construction grammars are scarcely out of the egg: the formalizations of Construction Grammar (CxG; Kay & Fillmore 1999) and Sign-Based Construction Grammar (SBCG; Boas & Sag 2013) have not actually been implemented (yet), and Embodied Construction Grammar (ECG, Bergen & Chang 2005) only has a parsing model but cannot handle production.

In order to conduct the experiments presented in this book, I therefore implemented a bidirectional processing model for argument structure and case in Fluid Construction Grammar (FCG). To the best of my knowledge, this implementation is the first (and currently the only) constructional account of argument structure that handles both parsing and production. This Chapter discusses the operationalization in more detail, which is necessary for appreciating the structures that the artificial agents evolve in the experiments. I will discuss the operationalization's relevance for linguistic theory in more detail in Chapter 5, where I compare my solution to a recent proposal on argument realization in Sign-Based Construction Grammar.

2 Processing case and argument structure

2.2 Representing and linking meanings

The operationalization follows a proposal by Steels (2005; also see De Beule (2007); Steels, De Beule & Neubauer (2005); Steels & Wellens (2006)) and uses a logic-based representation for meaning. For example, the utterance *box and ball* may be represented as follows:

(1) box(?obj-x) ∧ ball(?obj-y)

As is standard practice in first order predicate calculus, variables (i.e. all symbols that start with a question mark) are used for referring to objects. The variable '?obj-x' thus has to be bound to the object [BOX] and the variable '?obj-y' has to be bound to the object [BALL]. Suppose that we want to say that the box is big and that the ball is blue, then the meaning may be represented as:

(2) big(?obj-x) ∧ box(?obj-x) ∧ blue(?obj-y) ∧ ball(?obj-y)

Note that 'big' and 'box' share the same variable '?obj-x' because they both refer to the same object; and that 'blue' and 'ball' also share the same variable '?obj-y' because they both refer to [BALL]. The speaker may then express this meaning as *(the) big box and (the) blue ball.* Now imagine that the hearer is a non-native-speaker of English who has learned several words, but hasn't acquired the grammar yet. In other words, he does not know that English uses word order in an Adjective-Noun Construction to indicate which adjective modifies which noun. If he just uses his limited linguistic knowledge of English, he would come up with the following parsed meaning:

(3) big(?obj-w) ∧ box(?obj-x) ∧ blue(?obj-y) ∧ ball(?obj-z)

In this parsed meaning, there are neither shared variables between *big* and *box*, nor between *blue* and *ball* because lexical meanings do not specify which words go together. So there may be several hypotheses possible: each word may refer to a different object (i.e. in some languages adjectives can be used as heads of a phrase as well as nouns), *blue* may refer to [BALL] but also to [BOX] (as it is possible to put adjectives in French both before and after a noun as in *un grand ballon bleu* 'a big blue ball', lit. 'a big ball blue'), etc. So the hearer has to witness the scene if he wants to disambiguate the possible interpretations of the speaker's utterance, which may even not be possible if there are other big and blue objects available.

One of the primary functions of grammar is therefore marking which meanings should be *linked* to each other. In the present formalization, this means that

2.2 Representing and linking meanings

the grammar has to take care of **variable equalities**. Variables are said to be equal if they refer to the same object. In the meaning in example 3, there is an equality between '?obj-w' and '?obj-x' because they both refer to [BOX], and there is an equality between '?obj-y' and '?obj-z' because they both refer to [BALL]. These variable equalities can be resolved by the English Adjective-Noun Construction, which leads to the meaning of example 2.

This book is concerned with how case systems indicate who's doing what in an event. This can be easily operationalized using the same formalization of linking meanings through variable equalities. I will illustrate this for examples 4 and 5, which are two different argument realization patterns of the verb *sweep*.

(4) He sweeps the floor.

(5) He sweeps the dust off the floor.

If we consider *sweep* to be a verb of surface contact and motion (such as *wipe, rub,* and *scrub*; see Levin & Rappaport Hovav (1999)), then *sweep* can take at least three participant roles: a sweeper, something being swept, and the source from where the motion starts. One could imagine other roles as well, such as the instrument used for sweeping (a broom or a hand) or the destination of the motion, but they are not necessary for this discussion. In a logic-based representation, the meaning of *sweep* can be represented as follows:

(6) sweep(?event-x) ∧ sweep-1(?event-x, ?object-a) ∧ sweep-2(?event-x, ?object-b) ∧ sweep-3(?event-x, ?object-c)

Note that the meaning does not only contain a logic predicate for the event, but also explicit predicates for the participant roles themselves. Instead of using the labels *sweeper, swept* and *source*, the more neutral labels *sweep-1, sweep-2* and *sweep-3* are used. These are in fact arbitrary labels which can be mapped by robotic or software agents onto their sensory experiences. The meanings of the words *jack, floor,* and *dust* can be represented as:

(7) jack(?object-u)

(8) floor(?object-v)

(9) dust(?object-w)

These meanings are introduced by the lexical entry of each word, but it is not yet specified how the meanings should be linked to each other. This is again taken care of by the grammar through variable equalities, which is illustrated

2 Processing case and argument structure

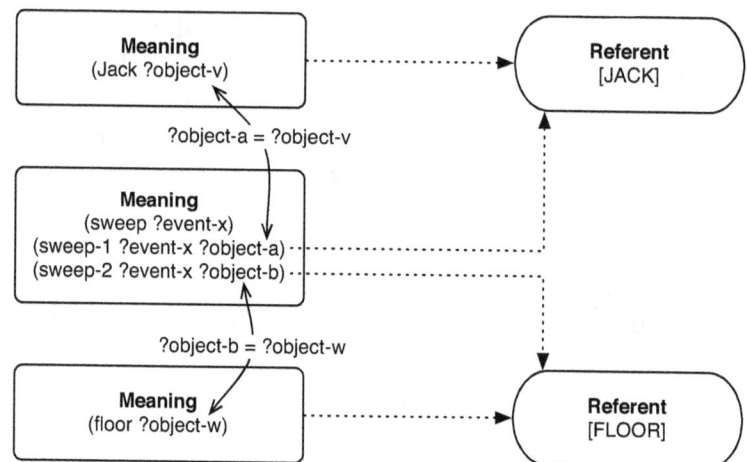

Figure 2.1: One of the primary functions of grammar is to indicate how different meanings should be linked to each other. In the present formalization, this is represented through variable equalities: the variables '?object-u' and '?object-a' should be made equal because they both refer to [JACK]; and the variables '?object-v' and '?object-b' should be made equal because they both refer to [FLOOR].

in Figure 2.1. Here, the variables ?object-u and ?object-a should be made equal because they both refer to [JACK]. The equality between ?object-v and ?object-b should also be identified because they both refer to [FLOOR]. After making the coreferring variables equal, the hearer can parse the following meanings for examples 4 and 5:

(10) ∃ ?object-a, ?object-b, ?object-c, ?event-x: jack(?object-a) ∧ floor(?object-b) ∧ sweep(?event-x) ∧ sweep-1(?event-x , ?object-a) ∧ sweep-2(?event-x, ?object-b) ∧ sweep-3(?event-x, ?object-c)

(11) ∃ ?object-a, ?object-b, ?object-c, ?event-x: jack(?object-a) ∧ dust(?object-b) ∧ floor(?object-c) ∧ sweep(?event-x) ∧ sweep-1(?event-x, ?object-a) ∧ sweep-2(?event-x, ?object-b) ∧ sweep-3(?event-x, ?object-c)

2.3 A brief introduction to Fluid Construction Grammar

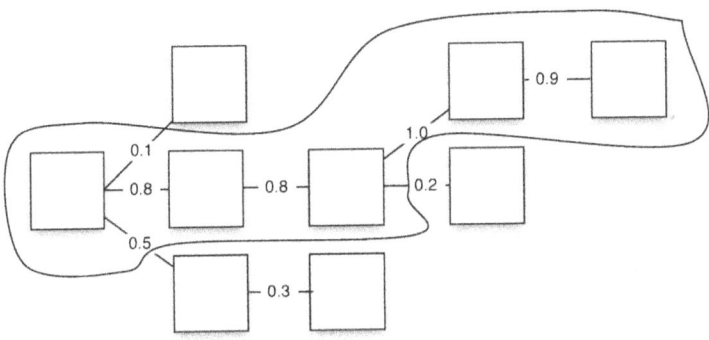

Figure 2.2: During processing, the language user builds up a reaction network by trying out constructions. The pathway with the highest confidence scores is selected for producing or parsing an utterance.

2.3 A brief introduction to Fluid Construction Grammar

2.3.1 Overview

As already mentioned before, Fluid Construction Grammar is a computational grammar formalism for bidirectional language processing, learning and evolution. During linguistic processing, the FCG-system is either provided with a meaning that needs to be verbalized (production) or an utterance that needs to be analyzed into a meaning (parsing). The FCG-system then builds up a 'reaction network' (or search tree; see Figure 2.2) in which each node represents a stage in the build-up of the semantic and syntactic structure of an utterance.

Traveling from one node to the next can be achieved by applying a construction (i.e. a conventionalized mapping between meaning and form). Since there may be several hypotheses given a certain context, each link between the nodes has a 'confidence score' to guide the search. This score is based on (a) the (linguistic) context in which constructions can be applied, and (b) how successful the applied constructions have been in previous communicative situations. The system will in the end choose the chain with the highest estimated success.

FCG uses many well-known techniques from computational linguistics such as term unification and feature structures to represent linguistic knowledge. In fact, all linguistic knowledge (including constructions) is represented as **coupled feature structures**, which couple a semantic pole to a syntactic pole. All feature structures are organized in units which are used by the basic operators of FCG

2 Processing case and argument structure

for retrieving and adding new feature-value pairs. Thus, all linguistic knowledge is represented according to the following pattern:

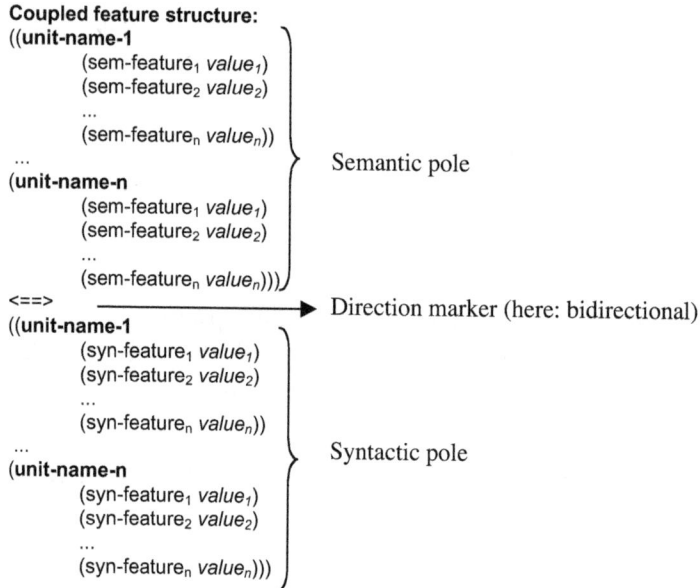

2.3.2 Unify and Merge

The two basic operations performed in FCG are called 'unify' and 'merge' (Steels & De Beule 2006: not to be confused with 'merge' in Minimalism). These operators decide whether or not a construction can be applied in order to obtain a new node in the reaction network. 'Unify' means that – depending on the direction of processing – the feature structure of one of the poles of a construction acts as a set of constraints that have to be compatible with the corresponding pole of the current node in the reaction network. If all the constraints are satisfied, the other pole is 'merged' with the corresponding pole in the current node (unless merging fails because of conflicts in both poles). The combination of the unify and merge operations leads to a new coupled feature structure, which is the next node in the reaction network (see Figure 2.3).

Constructions can be applied bidirectionally using the same operations, so parsing and production use the same linguistic knowledge but in opposite directions. Achieving both production and parsing is a non-trivial problem, and some formalisms therefore focus exclusively on either production or parsing (e.g. Em-

2.3 A brief introduction to Fluid Construction Grammar

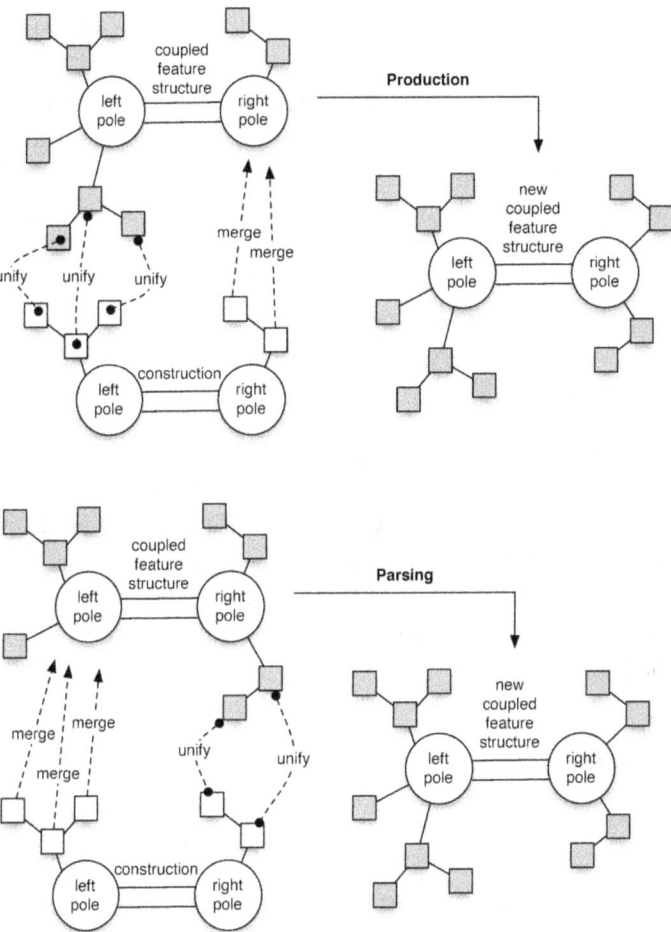

Figure 2.3: During production, the feature structures (squares) in the left pole of a construction (bottom left in top figure) are unified with those of the current coupled feature structure (top left in top figure). If unification is successful, the right pole is merged with the coupled feature structure. This yields a new coupled feature structure, which is a new node in the reaction network (right). During parsing, the same operation is performed but this time the right pole of the construction is unified and the left one is merged with the current node.

2 Processing case and argument structure

bodied Construction Grammar). FCG makes no claim that *all* linguistic knowledge is bidirectional, but uses bidirectional application of constructions for coupling input to output so that agents equipped with FCG can act both as speakers and as hearers.

When in production mode, the FCG-system unifies the left pole of a construction (typically the semantic pole) with that of the current node; and if successful it merges the right pole (typically the syntactic pole) with that of the current node. During parsing, exactly the same linguistic items are used, but this time in the opposite direction: here, the right pole has to unify with the corresponding pole in the current node after which the left pole can be merged with its corresponding pole in the current node.

2.3.3 Structure building.

FCG has a special operator – called the 'J-operator' – for specifying hierarchical relations between units. Roughly speaking, all units marked with a J-operator are ignored during the unification phase, but are added or merged during the merge operation. I will limit my discussion here to the functions of the J-operator that are relevant for the constructions in this chapter. For a more technical specification, see De Beule (2007: chapter 4) and De Beule & Steels (2005). The basic syntax of the J-operator is shown in example 12.

(12) a.
```
((J ?unit ?parent (?child-1 ... ?child-n))
 (feature-1 value-1)
 ...
 (feature-n value-n))
```

In this syntax, the variable '?unit' has to be bound to some unit in the coupled feature structure. If the unification phase did not yield a binding for this variable yet, a new unit will be built. This unit is then made a sub-unit of the unit that matches with the second argument of the J-operator. In this example this is the unit that is bound to the variable '?parent'. The J-operator can also take an optional third argument, which is a list of the units which have to be made sub-units of the unit that is bound to the first argument of the J-operator (?unit). Next, additional feature-value pairs can be listed which are merged to the structure by the J-operator. I will illustrate the J-operator through an example. Suppose that we only have the top-unit on one of the poles in the coupled feature structure and that there is a construction containing the following J-unit:

2.3 A brief introduction to Fluid Construction Grammar

(13)
```
((J ?new-unit ?top-unit))
```

Since there is no unit yet which could have been bound to the variable ?new-unit during the unification phase, a new unit is created. This unit is then made a sub-unit of the unit that is bound to the second argument of the J-operator so that we get the following structure:

(14)
```
Top-unit
   |
New-unit
```

Suppose now that another construction applies which contains the following J-unit:

(15)
```
((J ?another-new-unit ?top-unit (?new-unit)))
```

Let's assume that the variable ?top-unit was bound by the unifier to 'top-unit' and that the variable '?new-unit' was already bound to 'new-unit' (which depends on the unification of the units that were not marked by the J-operator). The variable '?another-new-unit' does not have a binding yet so a new unit is built, which is made a sub-unit of 'top-unit'. This time there is also a third argument of the J-operator. All the units in this list are made sub-units of the newly created unit so we get the following structure:

(16)
```
    Top-unit
       |
Another-new-unit
       |
    New-unit
```

Another use of the J-operator that is adopted in this thesis is the possibility of merging additional feature-value pairs to an existing unit. This can be done as follows:

(17)
```
((J ?unit NIL)
 (feature-1 value-1)
 ...
 (feature-n value-n))
```

2 Processing case and argument structure

If the second argument of the J-operator is an empty list (NIL), no structure building operation needs to be performed. In this case, the J-operator will only try to merge the feature-value pairs that are specified with the structure of the unit which is bound to the first argument of the J-operator (?unit). This functionality is needed because it allows the merging of new feature-value pairs on the same pole after successful unification rather than only merging the other pole of the construction to the coupled feature structure. In other words, it allows a construction to add both semantic *and* syntactic feature-value pairs to the coupled feature structure.

It should be noted that the above tree-like representation of hierarchical structure is only a visualization. The units of a construction or coupled feature structure are only elements of a flat list and are themselves not hierarchically organized. Instead, hierarchical relations in the linguistic structure are explicitly represented as feature-value pairs using the feature 'sem-subunits' on the semantic pole and the feature 'syn-subunits' on the syntactic pole.

2.4 Parsing 'Jack sweep dust off-floor'

2.4.1 Overview

With the meaning representation and FCG overview in mind, we can now dive into more details of the operationalization. This section illustrates parsing using the sentence *Jack sweep dust off- floor* is parsed, which is a simplification of the sentence *Jack sweeps the dust off the floor*. Obviously, this section does not provide a description of an actual English utterance, but only highlights the problem of argument realization while ignoring issues such as agreement, determination, and so on.

At the beginning of the parsing process, the FCG-system creates a first node in a reaction network, which is a coupled feature structure with an empty semantic and syntactic pole. I assume here that the utterance is segmented into the separate strings "jack", "sweep", "dust", "off-" and "floor". These strings are all lumped together along with the observed word order (i.e. the 'meets'-constraints) into the form-feature of one unit on the syntactic pole, which I will call the top-unit. The label 'top-unit' is arbitrary but makes interpretation easier for human readers. On the semantic pole, the corresponding unit (also called 'top-unit') is still empty:

(18)
```
<Node-1: coupled-feature-structure
  ((top-unit))
```

2.4 Parsing 'Jack sweep dust off-floor'

```
<==>
((top-unit
  (form
    ((string jack-unit "jack") (string sweep-unit "sweep")
     (string dust-unit "dust") (string off-unit "off-")
     (string floor-unit "floor") (meets jack-unit sweep-unit)
     (meets sweep-unit dust-unit) (meets dust-unit off-unit)
     (meets off-unit floor-unit)))))>
```

2.4.2 Unifying and merging lexical entries

In the next step, the FCG-system performs a lexical look-up for all the words in the utterance. For this, we need a lexical entries (also called lexical constructions). The lexical entry for *jack* looks as follows:

(19)
```
<Lexical entry: jack
((?top-unit
  (meaning (== (jack ?object-1))))
 ((J ?new-unit ?top-unit)
  (referent ?object-1)
  (sem-cat animate\is{animacy}-object)))
<==>
((?top-unit
  (form (== (string ?new-unit "jack"))))
 ((J ?new-unit ?top-unit)
  (syn-cat (== (pos noun\is{noun})))))>}}
```

Note that the lexical entry for *jack* contains variables not only for the meaning but also for the unit-names. The unification engine of FCG can use these variables to match them against the unit-structure of the current node in the reaction network. Since we're in parsing mode, the right pole of the entry (under the directional marker <==>) needs to be unified with the right-pole of node-1. The right pole specifies that there has to be some unit (?top-unit) which must contain the feature form, which itself must contain in its value the feature-value (string ?new-unit "jack"). These constraints are indeed satisfied: the variable ?top-unit can be bound to the unit top-unit in the current node because it fulfills all the necessary conditions.

Since unification is successful, the left pole, which contains the meaning of the lexical entry, can be merged with the left pole of node-1. The units that are marked with the J-operator were ignored during the unification phase, but are now integrated: the J-operator pulls the lexical information for *jack* down into a new

2 Processing case and argument structure

unit and specifies that this new-unit is a sub-unit of the top-unit. The J-operator also merges additional features with this new unit concerning its referent and its semantic and syntactic categorization. One could devise many other categorizations and features for *jack*, but they are not necessary for understanding the example here so they are left out for convenience's sake.

Since both unification and merge were successful, a new node is created in the reaction network. Here we see that the other words are still in the top-unit, but that there is a new unit for *jack* (which I conveniently label 'jack-unit' here but this may be any arbitrary symbol) both in the semantic and in the syntactic pole:

(20)
```
<Node-2: coupled-feature-structure
 ((top-unit
    (sem-subunits (jack-unit)))
  (jack-unit
    (meaning ((jack ?object-1)))
    (referent ?object-1)
    (sem-cat animate\is{animacy}-object)))
 <==>
 ((top-unit
    (syn-subunits (jack-unit))
    (form
      ((string sweep-unit "sweep") (string dust-unit "dust")
       (string off-unit "off-") (string floor-unit "floor")
       (meets jack-unit sweep-unit) (meets sweep-unit dust-unit)
       (meets dust-unit off-unit) (meets off-unit floor-unit))))
  (jack-unit
    (form ((string jack-unit "jack")))
    (syn-cat ((pos noun\is{noun})))))>
```

The lexical entries for *dust* and *floor* look almost exactly the same, apart from their semantic categorization and meaning. Both entries also unify and merge successfully with the current node and build new nodes in the reaction network:

(21)
```
<Lexical entry: dust
 ((?top-unit
    (meaning (== (dust ?object-2))))
  ((J ?new-unit ?top-unit)
    (referent ?object-2)
    (sem-cat moveable-object)))
 <==>
 ((?top-unit
    (form (== (string ?new-unit "dust"))))
  ((J ?new-unit ?top-unit)
    (syn-cat (== (pos noun\is{noun})))))>
```

2.4 Parsing 'Jack sweep dust off-floor'

```
<Lexical entry: floor
((?top-unit
    (meaning (== (dust ?object-3))))
 ((J ?new-unit ?top-unit)
    (referent ?object-3)
    (sem-cat surface-object)))
<==>
((?top-unit
    (form (== (string ?new-unit "floor"))))
 ((J ?new-unit ?top-unit)
    (syn-cat (== (pos noun\is{noun})))))>}}\\
```

The lexical entry for *sweep*, however, is a bit more complicated. Its main function is the same as for the other lexical entries: given the string "sweep", it will merge the meaning of this word with the semantic pole of the current node in the reaction network. The main difference with the other words lies in the semantic and syntactic categorization of *sweep*. Take a look at the features 'syn-frame' in the syntactic pole and 'sem-frame' in the semantic pole:

(22)
```
<Lexical entry: sweep
((?top-unit
    (meaning (== (sweep ?event-x)
                 (sweep-1 ?event-x ?obj-x)
                 (sweep-2 ?event-x ?obj-y)
                 (sweep-2 ?event-x ?obj-z))))
 ((J ?new-unit ?top-unit)
    (sem-frame (== (sem-role-agent ?unit-a ?obj-x)
                   (sem-role-surface ?unit-b ?obj-y)
                   (sem-role-moveable ?unit-c ?obj-y)
                   (sem-role-source ?unit-d ?obj-z)))))
<==>
((?top-unit
    (form (== (string ?new-unit "sweep"))))
 ((J ?new-unit ?top-unit)
    (syn-cat (== (pos verb\is{verb})))
    (syn-frame (== (syn-role-subject ?unit-1)
                   (syn-role-object ?unit-2)
                   (syn-role-oblique ?unit-3)))))>}
```

At first glance, it seems that the lexical entry contains a predicate or case frame that lists the valence of a verb as in traditional lexicalist approaches. The big difference with most other approaches is however that these frames do not directly list the argument structure of the verb but only its **potential valents**. For example, the syn-frame only states that *sweep* can occur in an argument structure in

2 Processing case and argument structure

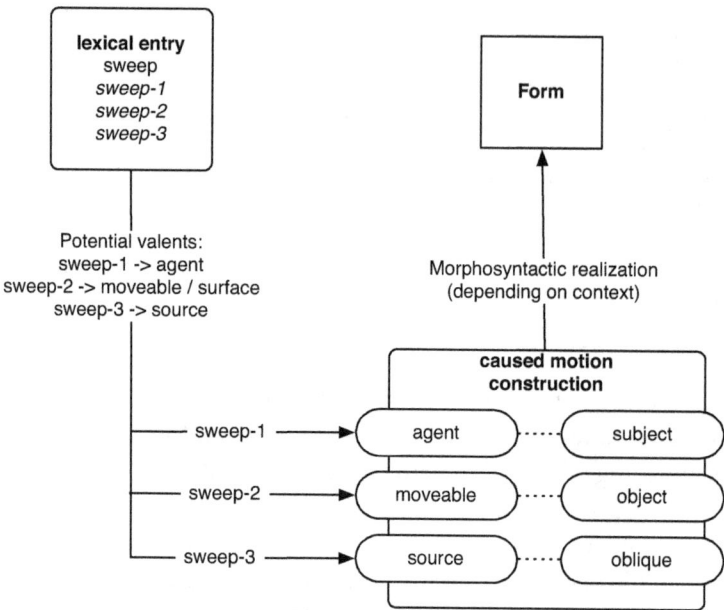

Figure 2.4: The relation between the meaning of an event and its morphosyntactic realization is indirect and multilayered. This figure shows how a lexical entry introduces its 'potential valents' from which the construction selects the actual valency combination. The construction then maps this meaning onto a syntactic pattern, which in itself is realized as a certain form (depending on linguistic and extra-linguistic context)

which there may be some unit playing the role of subject, some unit playing the role of object, some unit playing the role of oblique, or several units playing a combination of these roles. None of these roles are however obligatory: the verb remains agnostic as to which of these valents actually should be realized or what the possible combinations may be. I will show later that it is the construction that will select from the potential valents what the **actual valency** of the verb is or will be in the utterance (also see Figure 2.4).

This architecture of potential valents is mirrored in the semantic frame. Here too, the verb only lists all its potential valents: there may be an agent role, a surface role, a moveable role, or a source role. The sem-frame does not specify which of these roles actually have to be realized, nor what the possible combinations are. It does specify, however, how these potential valences should be

2.4 Parsing 'Jack sweep dust off-floor'

linked to the verb-specific participant roles in the meaning feature. For example, 'sem-role-agent' is linked to 'sweep-1' because they share the variable '?obj-x'. 'Sem-role-source' is linked to 'sweep-3' because they share the variable '?obj-z'. The participant role 'sweep-2' is even linked to two different potential valents: 'sem-role-surface' and 'sem-role-moveable'. The lexical entry thus allows participant roles to be mapped onto different semantic roles.

Both the sem- and syn-frame also contain variables that have to be bound to the unit-names of the arguments to which the roles may be assigned later on. For example, the variable '?unit-1' should be bound to the unit that plays the role of subject (if present). Notice, however, that this variable is not the same one as the variable name of the unit that may play the agent role (if present): '?unit-a'. In most other grammar formalisms, such as HPSG, a direct link between 'agent' and 'subject' is assumed and alternating argument structures such as passives are *derived* through lexical rules. **I do not assume such a link between subject and agent**: having two different variable names reflects the fact that both can be bound to different units as is the case in the passive voice. I therefore consider the passive as an alternative argument structure construction instead of a derivational one. An active construction links agent and subject to each other by making their variables equal, whereas the passive construction features a different pattern by making other variables equal (e.g. those of the subject and the surface role as in *The floor was swept*). Here again, it is the construction that decides and not the verb. I will return to this matter in Chapter 5.

The next two Chapters will demonstrate how these potential valents can be gradually acquired and constructed through language use. They should therefore not be seen as a rigid set of possibilities or as some set of innate categories. Instead the potential uses of a verb can be extended (and shrunk) if needed for communicative purposes, and each possibility may become conventionalized or become obsolete in the speech community.

Unifying and merging the lexical entries for *sweep*, *floor* and *dust* (the ordering does not matter) will lead the hearer to a fifth node in the reaction network:

(23)
```
<Node-5: coupled-feature-structure
  ((top-unit
    (sem-subunits (jack-unit sweep-unit dust-unit floor-unit)))
  (jack-unit
    (meaning ((jack ?object-1)))
    (referent ?object-1)
    (sem-cat animate\is{animacy}-object))
  (sweep-unit
    (meaning ((sweep ?event-x))
```

2 Processing case and argument structure

```
                    (sweep-1 ?event-x ?obj-x)
                    (sweep-2 ?event-x ?obj-y)
                    (sweep-3 ?event-x ?obj-z)))
       (sem-frame ((sem-role-agent ?unit-a ?obj-x)
                   (sem-role-surface ?unit-b ?obj-y)
                   (sem-role-moveable ?unit-c ?obj-y)
                   (sem-role-source ?unit-d ?obj-z))))
  (dust-unit
    (meaning ((dust ?object-2)))
    (referent ?object-2)
    (sem-cat moveable-object))
  (floor-unit
    (meaning ((floor ?object-3)))
    (referent ?object-3)
    (sem-cat surface-object)))
<==>
((top-unit
   (syn-subunits (jack-unit sweep-unit dust-unit floor-unit))
   (form
     ((string off-unit "off-") (meets jack-unit sweep-unit)
      (meets sweep-unit dust-unit) (meets dust-unit off-unit)
      (meets off-unit floor-unit))))
 (jack-unit
   (form ((string jack-unit "jack")))
   (syn-cat ((pos noun\is{noun}))))
 (sweep-unit
   (form ((string sweep-unit "sweep")))
   (syn-cat ((pos verb\is{verb})))
   (syn-frame ((syn-role-subject ?unit-1)
               (syn-role-object ?unit-2)
               (syn-role-oblique ?unit-3))))
 (dust-unit
   (form ((string dust-unit "dust")))
   (syn-cat ((pos noun\is{noun}))))
 (floor-unit
   (form ((string floor-unit "floor")))
   (syn-cat ((pos noun\is{noun})))))>}}
```

The meanings in the above coupled feature structure are however still unlinked (see §2.2). In other words, the hearer knows at this stage the meaning of the individual words, but not who is doing what in the sweep-event: the variables that accompany the meaning of *sweep* ('?obj-x', '?obj-y' and '?obj-z') are not shared by any of the arguments ('?object-1', '?object-2' and '?object-3'). We therefore need to unify and merge the correct construction that is able to handle the unresolved variable equalities.

2.4 Parsing 'Jack sweep dust off-floor'

2.4.3 A syntactic case marker

Before that construction is applied, there is still the string "off-" in the top-unit that needs to be parsed. In this example I analyze *off-* as some kind of simple case marker that assigns the oblique case to the argument that immediately follows it. By treating *off-* as a case marker I can immediately illustrate how markers are represented in the experiments as well.

In line with its definition in §1.2.6, a syntactic case marker is dissociated from a particular semantic role. I therefore implement case markers in a morphological rule or construction (a "morph-rule") in which both the left and the right pole are syntactic (so both poles operate on the syntactic pole of the current node in the reaction network). One could say in this approach that a case marker has a syntactic or grammatical meaning rather than a semantic one. The notion of potential valents can also be applied to capture the polysemous nature of case markers, but for simplicity's sake I will assume here that there is a one-to-one mapping between the syntactic role 'oblique' and the marker *off-*.

The morph-rule specifies that, during parsing, there needs to be a unit which contains in its form-feature the string "off-" and a word order constraint that says that the marker immediately precedes ("meets") some other unit. If this unifies (and it does with the right pole of node-5), the left pole merges with the syntactic pole of the current node in the reaction network. The information added here is that the role of oblique is assigned to the other unit (which immediately followed the marker). Note that this other unit should already be present in the current node as a sub-unit of the top-unit. This is indeed the case: the variable '?some-unit' can be bound to 'floor-unit' which was already present after unifying and merging the lexical entry of *floor*.

The morph-rule also contains a two-legged operation using the J-operator: in a first step, a new unit is created for *off-*, and in a second step the J-operator specifies that the newly-made unit must become a sub-unit of the other unit that immediately followed it (floor-unit). Without repeating the entire coupled feature structure, the syntactic structure now looks as in Figure 2.5.

The morphological rule itself looks as follows:

(24)
```
<Morph-rule: off-
  ((?top-unit
    (syn-subunits (== ?some-unit)))
   (?some-unit
    (syn-role syn-role-oblique)))
  <==>
  ((?top-unit
```

2 Processing case and argument structure

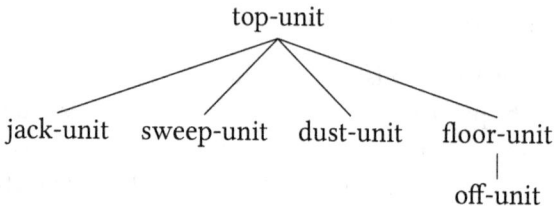

Figure 2.5: Syntactic structure.

```
(form (== (string ?marker-unit "off-")
          (meets ?marker-unit ?some-unit))))
((J ?marker-unit ?top-unit))
((J ?some-unit ?top-unit (?marker-unit))))>}}
```

2.4.4 The caused motion construction

The utterance *Jack sweeps the dust off the floor* is a typical example of the caused motion construction (Goldberg 1995: chapter 7), which here carries the meaning of 'X causes Y to move Z by sweeping'. In the semantic pole, the construction selects from the verb the semantic roles of agent, moveable patient and source. On the syntactic pole it assigns the syntactic roles of subject, object and oblique to the arguments. The construction looks as follows:

(25)
```
<Construction: caused-motion
((?top-unit
  (sem-subunits (== ?unit-a ?unit-b ?unit-c ?unit-d)))
 (?unit-a
  (sem-frame (== (sem-role-agent ?unit-b ?obj-x)
                 (sem-role-moveable ?unit-c ?obj-y)
                 (sem-role-source ?unit-d ?obj-z))))
 (?unit-b
  (referent ?obj-x)
  (sem-cat animate\is{animacy}-object))
 (?unit-c
  (referent ?obj-y)
  (sem-cat moveable-object))
 (?unit-d
  (referent ?obj-z)))
<==>
((?top-unit
  (syn-subunits (== ?unit-a ?unit-b ?unit-c ?unit-d))
  (form ((meets ?unit-b ?unit-a) (meets ?unit-a ?unit-c)
```

2.4 Parsing 'Jack sweep dust off-floor'

```
              (meets ?unit-c ?unit-d))))
       (?unit-a
         (syn-cat (== (pos verb\is{verb})))
         (syn-frame (== (syn-role-subject ?unit-b)
                        (syn-role-object ?unit-c)
                        (syn-role-oblique ?unit-d))))
       (?unit-d
         (syn-role syn-role-oblique))
       ((J ?unit-b NIL)
         (syn-role syn-role-subject))
       ((J ?unit-c NIL)
         (syn-role syn-role-object)))>}}
```

Since the hearer is parsing, the right pole needs to be unified with the current node in the reaction network. The right pole here demands there to be some unit with at least four sub-units and with a certain word order among them (i.e. the "meets"-constraints). The last argument also has to have the syntactic role of oblique. The right pole of the current node satisfies all the constraints: jack-unit receives subject status and dust-unit becomes the object. The unit for *floor* was already marked as oblique by the morphological rule that was shown in the previous section.

Thanks to the word-order constraints, the construction can unambiguously bind the variables '?unit-b' to 'jack-unit', '?unit-c' to 'dust-unit' and '?unit-d' to 'floor-unit'. The construction then links the syntactic roles to the semantic roles by making the necessary variables equal: the subject jack-unit is assigned the role of agent, the object dust-unit is assigned the role of moveable (object) and the oblique floor-unit is assigned the role of source. By doing so, the construction can also link the meanings to each other: sem-role-agent shares the variable '?obj-x' with sweep-1 and the referent of jack-unit, sem-role-moveable shares the variable '?obj-y' with sweep-2 and the referent of dust-unit, and sem-role-source shares the variable '?obj-z' with sweep-3 and the referent of floor-unit. This leads to the following node in the reaction network:

(26)
```
       <Node-7: coupled-feature-structure
         ((top-unit
           (sem-subunits (jack-unit sweep-unit dust-unit floor-unit)))
         (jack-unit
           (meaning ((jack ?obj-x)))
           (referent ?obj-x)
           (sem-role sem-role-agent)
           (sem-cat animate\is{animacy}-object))
         (sweep-unit
```

41

2 Processing case and argument structure

```
      (meaning ((sweep ?event-x)
                (sweep-1 ?event-x ?obj-x)
                (sweep-2 ?event-x ?obj-y)
                (sweep-3 ?event-x ?obj-z)))
      (sem-frame ((sem-role-agent jack-unit ?obj-x)
                  (sem-role-surface dust-unit ?obj-y)
                  (sem-role-moveable dust-unit ?obj-y)
                  (sem-role-source floor-unit ?obj-z))))
 (dust-unit
   (meaning ((dust ?obj-y)))
   (referent ?obj-y)
   (sem-role sem-role-moveable)
   (sem-cat moveable-object))
 (floor-unit
   (meaning ((floor ?obj-z)))
   (referent ?obj-z)
   (sem-role sem-role-source)
   (sem-cat surface-object)))
  <==>
 ((top-unit
   (syn-subunits (jack-unit sweep-unit dust-unit floor-unit))
   (form ((meets jack-unit sweep-unit)
          (meets sweep-unit dust-unit)
          (meets dust-unit off-unit))))
 (jack-unit
   (form ((string jack-unit "jack")))
   (syn-role syn-role-subject)
   (syn-cat ((pos noun\is{noun}))))
 (sweep-unit
   (form ((string sweep-unit "sweep")))
   (syn-cat ((pos verb\is{verb})))
   (syn-frame ((syn-role-subject jack-unit)
               (syn-role-object dust-unit)
               (syn-role-oblique foor-unit))))
 (dust-unit
   (form ((string dust-unit "dust")))
   (syn-role syn-role-object)
   (syn-cat ((pos noun\is{noun}))))
 (floor-unit
   (syn-subunits (off-unit))
   (form ((string floor-unit "floor")))
   (syn-role syn-role-oblique)
   (syn-cat ((pos noun\is{noun}))))
 (off-unit
   (form ((string off-unit "off-")
          (meets off-unit floor-unit)))))>}}
```

2.5 Producing 'jack sweep floor'

Now we can extract the following meaning from the semantic pole of the coupled feature structure:

(27) ∃ ?obj-x, ?obj-y, ?obj-z, ?event-x: jack(?obj-x) ∧ dust(?obj-y) ∧ floor(?obj-z) ∧ sweep(?event-x) ∧ sweep-1(?event-x , ?obj-x) ∧ sweep-2(?event-x, ?obj-y) ∧ sweep-3(?event-x, ?obj-z)

As can be seen in the meaning, all variables that refer to the same referent have been made equal by the construction. The hearer thus knows that *jack* was the sweeper, that *dust* was the thing being swept, and that the *floor* was the source of the motion. In the experiments reported in this book, the agents will then match this parsed meaning against their world model.

2.5 Producing 'jack sweep floor'

2.5.1 Overview

This section gives an overview of how an utterance such as *jack sweep floor* can be produced in Fluid Construction Grammar. In this case, the caused motion construction is not used, but a construction which maps the semantic frame 'X acts on surface Y' onto the syntactic frame 'Subject-Verb-Object'. The speaker starts with the following meaning (in which NIL stands for 'empty' or 'not profiled'):

(28) ((jack object-1) (floor object-2) (sweep event-1)
(sweep-1 event-1 object-1) (sweep-2 event-1 object-2)
(sweep-3 event-1 NIL))

In order to verbalize this meaning, the speaker constructs a reaction network. The first node in the network is a coupled feature structure in which the entire meaning is placed into one unit in the semantic pole, and in which the syntactic pole is still empty:

(29)
```
<Node-1: coupled-feature-structure
  ((top-unit
    (meaning ((jack object-1) (floor object-2)
              (sweep event-1) (sweep-1 event-1 object-1)
              (sweep-2 event-1 object-2) (sweep-3 event-1 NIL)))))
  <==>
  ((top-unit))>}}
```

2 Processing case and argument structure

2.5.2 Unifying and merging lexical entries

Next, the speaker builds new nodes in the network by unifying and merging the lexical entries that cover these meanings. Suppose that the speaker has the same lexical entries as given in the previous section and that all three of them (*jack, sweep* and *floor*) are a successful match, then the new coupled feature structure looks as follows:

(30)
```
<Node-4: coupled-feature-structure
 ((top-unit
    (sem-subunits (jack-unit sweep-unit floor-unit)))
  (jack-unit
    (meaning ((jack object-1)))
    (referent object-1)
    (sem-cat animate\is{animacy}-object))
  (sweep-unit
    (meaning ((sweep event-1)
              (sweep-1 event-1 object-1)
              (sweep-2 event-1 object-2)
              (sweep-3 event-1 NIL)))
    (sem-frame ((sem-role-agent ?unit-a object-1)
                (sem-role-surface ?unit-b object-2)
                (sem-role-moveable ?unit-c object-2)
                (sem-role-source ?unit-d NIL))))
  (floor-unit
    (meaning ((floor object-2)))
    (referent object-2)
    (sem-cat surface-object)))
 <==>
 ((top-unit
    (syn-subunits (jack-unit sweep-unit floor-unit)))
  (jack-unit
    (form ((string jack-unit "jack")))
    (syn-cat ((pos noun\is{noun}))))
  (sweep-unit
    (form ((string sweep-unit "sweep")))
    (syn-cat ((pos verb\is{verb})))
    (syn-frame ((syn-role-subject ?unit-1)
                (syn-role-object ?unit-2)
                (syn-role-oblique ?unit-3))))
  (floor-unit
    (form ((string floor-unit "floor")))
    (syn-cat ((pos noun\is{noun}))))))>}}
```

Since the speaker knows which meaning he wants to express, there are no unresolved variable equalities in the meanings in the semantic pole. However, so far no semantic or syntactic roles have been assigned yet: the lexical entry of *sweep* has merely introduced its potential valents, but not its actual valency. This is reflected by the fact that the arguments do not have the feature 'sem-role' or 'syn-role' yet and that there are still variables left for the unit-names in both the syn- and sem-frame. It is also still undecided which participant should be mapped onto subject and which onto object or oblique.

2.5.3 The agent-acts-on-surface construction

Trying to unify the caused motion construction leads to a failure: first of all, *floor* is categorized as a static surface-object and thus violates the construction's constraint that the patient has to be moveable, and second, the source argument is missing. So a different construction needs to be unified and merged to travel to the next node in the network. The following 'agent-acts-on-surface' construction would do the trick:

(31)
```
<Construction: agent-acts-on-surface
((?top-unit
    (sem-subunits (== ?unit-a ?unit-b ?unit-c)))
 (?unit-a
    (sem-frame (== (sem-role-agent ?unit-b ?obj-x)
                   (sem-role-surface ?unit-c ?obj-y))))
 (?unit-b
    (referent ?obj-x)
    (sem-cat animate\is{animacy}-object))
 (?unit-c
    (referent ?obj-y)
    (sem-cat surface-object)))
<==>
((?top-unit
    (syn-subunits (== ?unit-a ?unit-b ?unit-c ?unit-d))
    (form ((meets ?unit-b ?unit-a) (meets ?unit-a ?unit-c))))
 (?unit-a
    (syn-cat (== (pos verb\is{verb})))
    (syn-frame (== (syn-role-subject ?unit-b)
                   (syn-role-object ?unit-c))))
 ((J ?unit-b NIL)
    (syn-role syn-role-subject))
 ((J ?unit-c NIL)
    (syn-role syn-role-object)))>}}
```

First the speaker tries to unify the semantic pole with that of the current node in the reaction network. This is a success because all the constraints are satisfied: the construction expects some unit with three sub-units, one of which is an animate-object and one of which is a surface-object. The construction also selects

2 Processing case and argument structure

the semantic roles of 'agent' and 'surface' from the verb's potential valents and assigns them to the correct arguments. Next, the right pole of the construction is merged with the right pole of the current node. Since it is specified that the agent maps onto subject and the surface maps onto object in this construction, the correct syntactic roles are assigned to the arguments, including their word order. The new node looks as follows:

(32) ──────────────────────────────
```
        <Node-5: coupled-feature-structure
         ((top-unit
           (sem-subunits (jack-unit sweep-unit floor-unit)))
          (jack-unit
           (meaning ((jack object-1)))
           (referent object-1)
           (sem-role sem-role-agent)
           (sem-cat animate\is{animacy}-object))
          (sweep-unit
           (meaning ((sweep event-1)
                     (sweep-1 event-1 object-1)
                     (sweep-2 event-1 object-2)
                     (sweep-3 event-1 NIL)))
           (sem-frame ((sem-role-agent jack-unit object-1)
                       (sem-role-surface floor-unit object-2)
                       (sem-role-moveable floor-unit object-2)
                       (sem-role-source ?unit-d NIL))))
          (floor-unit
           (meaning ((floor object-2)))
           (referent object-2)
           (sem-role sem-role-surface)
           (sem-cat surface-object)))
         <==>
         ((top-unit
           (syn-subunits (jack-unit sweep-unit floor-unit))
           (form ((meets jack-unit sweep-unit)
                  (meets sweep-unit floor-unit))))
          (jack-unit
           (form ((string jack-unit "jack")))
           (syn-role syn-role-subject)
           (syn-cat ((pos noun\is{noun}))))
          (sweep-unit
           (form ((string sweep-unit "sweep")))
           (syn-cat ((pos verb\is{verb})))
           (syn-frame ((syn-role-subject jack-unit)
                       (syn-role-object floor-unit)
                       (syn-role-oblique ?unit-3))))
          (floor-unit
           (form ((string floor-unit "floor")))
```

```
(syn-role syn-role-object)
(syn-cat ((pos noun\is{noun})))))>}}
```

The speaker has no other constructions or linguistic items that could unify and merge, so he is almost done processing. In the final phase, he takes all the formal constraints specified in the syntactic pole of the last node and renders them into the utterance *jack sweep floor*.

2.6 Networks and conventionalization

The previous two sections showed how lexical and constructional meanings can integrate through the potential valents of the verb on the one hand, and the selection of the actual valency by the constructions on the other. I also suggested that the list of potential valents can be extended if needed for communication. However, this solution is too powerful because it does not explain why speakers of English prefer not to use *sweep* in for example the ditransitive construction as in **he swept him the dust*. We therefore need an additional strategy to restrict the powers of the proposed representation.

Utterances such as **he swept him the dust* are perfectly intelligible but somehow speakers (usually) refrain from using words in constructions that they are not conventionally associated with. Convention or entrenchment can intuitively be captured in a network as illustrated in Figure 2.6. The basic idea is the following: we never observe words in total isolation but always in language use. We can therefore keep links between constructions that reflect their past co-occurrences. For example, *sweep* has a link to the intransitive construction, the caused motion construction, etc. The link reflects conventionalization through a confidence score: the higher this score, the more confident the speaker feels integrating the lexical entry with the construction. The lower the score, the more "strain" there is to go ahead and fuse the lexical entry with the construction. Scores in the network can be changed each time the lexical entry and the construction co-occur: the score increases if they are used in successful communication, but decreases if co-occurrence leads to communicative failure. Each interaction also yields the possibility of adding new links. I will come back to the exact nature of this network in the following chapters.

2 *Processing case and argument structure*

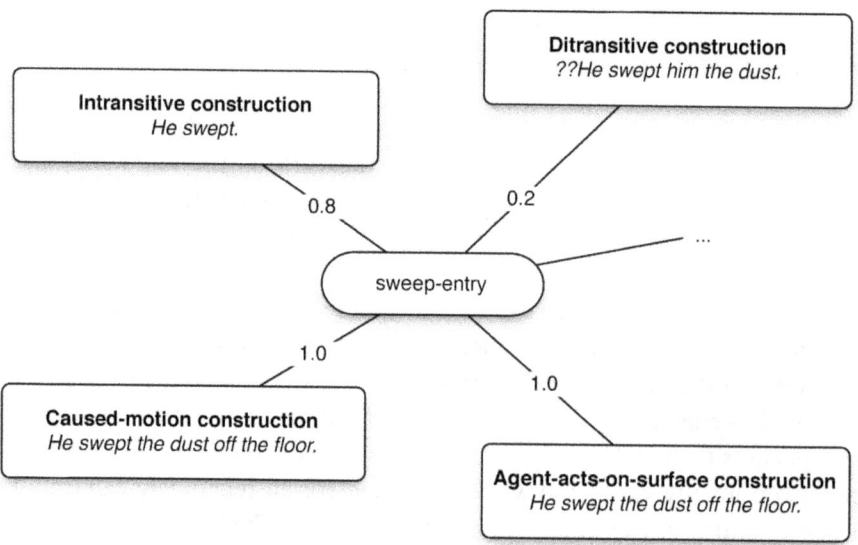

Figure 2.6: Lexical entries keep a link to all the constructions that they integrated with. Each link has a specific confidence score which reflects how confident the language user is that the lexical entry can be fused with the construction. The higher the score, the more conventionalized the link is. The lower the score, the more "strain" the speaker will have to use the entry and the construction together. This network thus captures conventionalised patterns in a language.

3 Baseline experiments

3.1 Introduction

The grammatical square (see Figure 1.4) illustrates the multifunctional and indirect nature of case marking. It can also be read as a "research roadmap" for experiments on the emergence of a grammar for case. More specifically, the experiments must investigate how a population of agents can evolve a grammar which takes care of (1) the mapping between event-specific participant roles and generalized semantic roles, (2) the mapping between semantic roles and grammatical cases, and (3) the mapping between cases and surface case markers. Constructing and aligning this kind of grammar in a multi-agent population is incredibly difficult because all mappings are agent-internal and are thus not directly observable by other agents. Moreover, these mappings vary depending on the communicative and linguistic context so the agents have to be capable of dealing with polysemy. Finally, linguistic conventions may constantly change so the agents have to be able to adapt to newly propagated constructions.

In this Chapter I will present three baseline experiments which first replicate simulations reported by Steels (2002b; 2004a) and then lift them towards a multi-agent simulation. I will specifically focus on which diagnostics, repairs and alignment strategies are needed for each step of increased complexity. In the next section, I will first give an overview of the experimental set-up that is shared by all experiments after which the simulations themselves are reported.

3.2 Experimental set-up

3.2.1 Overview

The simulations in this book investigate how a population of artificial agents can autonomously construct a shared grammatical system for marking event structure (in the form of a case grammar). As argued in §1.3.3, we need to hypothesize which cognitive mechanisms and external pressures are the minimal ingredients that enable the agents to do so, and we need to operationalize them into computational processes and a world environment. Since case marking is a complex

3 Baseline experiments

phenomenon, I will divide the topic into several subparts that follow the stages of development identified in §1.2.7.

Table 3.1: This table shows the key cognitive abilities which are given to the agents in the baseline experiments. In the first experiment, agents are "intelligent" enough to resolve variable equalities by using their world model but they cannot express these equalities in their language. In experiment 2, the agents can decide to invent new markers to indicate the linking of equal variables but they cannot generalize or abstract. In the third experiment, the agents can perform analogical reasoning over event structures to generalize existing markers.

	Detecting and resolving variable equalities	Invention and adoption of new markers	Reuse and generalisation of existing markers
Baseline experiment 1	+	−	−
Baseline experiment 2	+	+	−
Baseline experiment 3	+	+	+

3.2.2 Key abilities and self-assessment criteria

In the problem-solving approach adopted in this book, innovation and language change happens in three steps: (1) the speaker innovates and is therefore the main cause of potential language change, (2) the hearer tries to infer and learn the innovation through an "abductive process" (as opposed to uniquely relying on induction or genetically evolved innate knowledge), and (3) the innovation propagates in the population. Step (1) may be skipped when the hearer overgeneralizes or imposes more systematicity on the utterance than introduced by the speaker. Hearer-based innovation or "reanalysis" can be described in terms of the same cognitive processes as involved in speaker-based innovation so the two sources of innovation are complementary to each other (Hoefler & Smith 2008). Step (3) implies that an innovation only becomes a linguistic convention if it has been adopted by a sufficient number of language users. Propagation is made possible through the alignment strategies of the agents.

3.2 Experimental set-up

This approach requires a population of agents endowed with rich cognitive capabilities. As argued in §1.3.3, agents can only make use of local measures such as communicative success and cognitive effort for steering their linguistic behaviour. The cognitive mechanisms of the agents therefore have to enable the agents to move into a meta-level in which they can **self-assess** what problems they encounter during communication, whether there is opportunity for optimization, or what the reasons for success and failure are in a language game. They need to be able to couple this **diagnosis** to **repair strategies** in order to solve their communicative problems and to their **alignment strategies** in order to converge on a shared language. All the experiments in this book mainly focus on the effect of these three aspects: diagnostics, repairs, and alignment strategies.

The baseline experiments reported in this Chapter first of all replicate the two-agent simulations reported by Steels (2002b; 2004a). These experiments only focus on the first three stages of case marker development ranging from no marking to the formation and marking of semantic roles. Additionally, the experiments are pushed forward to multi-agent simulations in which language convergence becomes the main issue. All three baseline experiments share the same world environment, communicative task, and assumptions and scaffolds (see below). However, they differ in the **key cognitive abilities** that the agents are endowed with. I define "key cognitive abilities" as those mechanisms that are hypothesized to be crucial for the transition in the grammar from one stage to the next, and of which the simulations need to demonstrate or falsify whether this is indeed the case. Table 3.1 illustrates the difference between the baseline experiments in terms of key cognitive abilities and can be summarized as follows:

1. In baseline experiment 1 (corresponding to stage 1 – §1.2.3), agents are given the diagnostic to figure out how the meanings of lexical items are linked to each other by exploiting the situatedness of the interaction. However, the agents have no means of extending their language to explicitly mark the relations between words;

2. In baseline experiment 2 (corresponding to stage 2 – §1.2.4), agents are endowed with a repair strategy which enables them to invent a participant role-specific case marker for optimizing communication;

3. In baseline experiment 3 (corresponding to stage 3 – §1.2.5), agents are endowed with the capacity to perform analogical reasoning over event structures. They can exploit this capacity for generalizing existing markers to cover new participant roles. As I will show later, generalization is not a

goal in itself but rather a side-effect of the need for optimizing communication.

These key cognitive abilities will be explained in more detailed along with the experiments further down in this Chapter. The abilities are each time given and fixed by the experimenter and the simulations do not explain where they come from. However, the global vision underlying this work is that speakers and hearers can autonomously configure their language capacity by recruiting cognitive mechanisms that are also used for other tasks such as hierarchy building operators (Steels 2007). This process is driven by needs in communicative success, expressive power and the conventions adopted by other agents in the population. Here again, agents have to be capable of self-assessing when to recruit a mechanism, which ones are the best candidates, and to self-regulate the semantic complexity of their communication. For simulations that investigate self-regulation and reconfiguration of the language faculty on the longer run, see Steels & Wellens (2006; 2007). In the remainder of this section, I will describe those aspects of the simulations which are shared by all the experiments.

3.2.3 Description games

An obvious requirement for developing a grammar for marking event structure is **communication about events**. This is operationalized in the form of the **description game**, a routinized communicative interaction which involves the complete semiotic cycle as illustrated in Figure 3.1. Applied to the simulations in this book, the interaction pattern conforms to the following script:

1. Two agents are randomly selected from the population. One will act as speaker, the other as hearer. The speaker and hearer start a **local language game** so the other agents cannot observe it;

2. **Joint attention** (Tomasello 1995) between the agents is required and assumed. This is operationalized by giving the agents a shared context. The context contains one or more events (depending on the complexity of the game) which are observed by the agents;

3. Both the speaker and the hearer build a **world model** based on the observed events. The world model consists of a series of facts in the memory;

4. The speaker is given a communicative goal. In this book, the goal is always to **make an assertion** about a certain state of affairs in the context (i.e. the speaker has to describe an event);

3.2 Experimental set-up

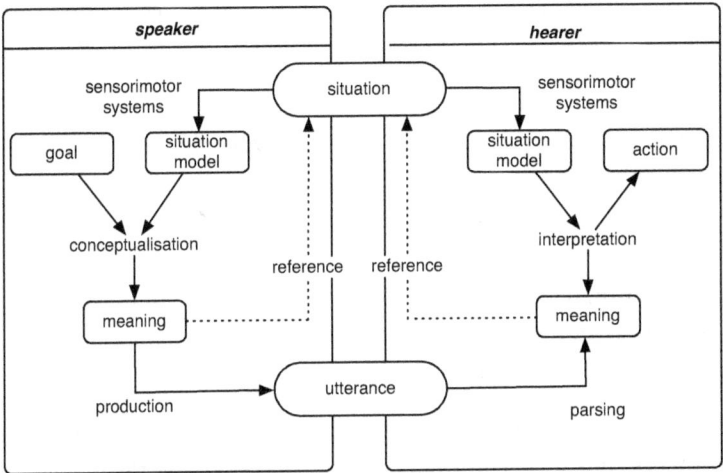

Figure 3.1: The semiotic cycle involved in language games. There are three systems working in tight interaction with each other: the sensory-motor system (perception and modeling), the conceptual/intentional system (conceptualization and interpretation), and the linguistic system (production and parsing). This book mainly focuses on the latter one and is complementary to other research efforts on grounded language use and conceptualization.

Figure 3.2: The world environment consists of dynamic scenes in which puppets perform various actions such as walking and pushing blocks to each other. Here, one puppet "gives" a block to another puppet by sliding it over a table. The scene contains four participants (two puppets, a block and a table), a "ground" and various micro- and macro-events.

5. The speaker chooses an event to describe and **conceptualizes** a meaning for it. Conceptualization involves profiling of the event and finding a discriminating meaning for the participants in the event (see further below);

6. The speaker then verbalizes the meaning by **producing** an utterance which is transmitted to the hearer;

7. The hearer observes the utterance and **parses** it;

8. The hearer then **interprets** the parsed meaning by comparing it to the facts in the world model. This leads to the **mental action** of agreeing or disagreeing with the description;

9. The hearer signals agreement with the description if the parsed meaning is unambiguously compatible with the hearer's world model, or signals disagreement if it is not. Agreement means **communicative success**, disagreement means **communicative failure**. No other kinds of feedback or requests for information are included;

10. Based on the outcome of the game, both agents **consolidate** their linguistic inventories.

3.2.4 The world, sensory-motor input and conceptualization

3.2.4.1 Overview

The semiotic cycle in Figure 3.1 clearly shows that linguistic processing is only one part of the general cognitive architecture which is involved in communication. Even though the experiments in this book mainly focus on the production and parsing of linguistic utterances, at least two other systems are directly relevant for communication: the sensory-motor system (in a broad sense responsible for dealing with the sensory experience and for building a world model) and the conceptual-intentional system (responsible for conceptualization and interpretation as well as concept formation). These three "systems" work together in tight interaction and without a clear-cut division between them.

In this section, I will describe what kind of world environment is used in the experiments, what kind of world model is built by the sensory-motor system, and what kind of meanings are conceptualized for communication. These three elements remain constant and are shared by all the experiments.

3.2.4.2 The environment

The environment in the experiments consists of dynamic real-world scenes from a small puppet theater. The puppets perform various actions such as moving, disappearing from a scene, walking towards each other, and carrying objects. The use of real-world scenes is part of earlier work on grounded language communication (Steels 2002b; Steels & Baillie 2003) and is not essential to the dynamics of the models reported in this book: a simulated world suffices for the scope of this book and can in fact be used for scaling up the experiments to larger worlds. The choice for using data from real-world scenes was made in order to demonstrate that the models *can* be incorporated into research on the grounding of communication.

For the baseline experiments, 20 different scenes were recorded comprising 207 event tokens belonging to 15 different event types. There are 103 event tokens which take one participant (e.g. a 'move-event'), 99 event tokens which potentially take two participants (e.g. a 'walk-to'-event) and 5 event tokens which potentially involve three participants (e.g. a 'give-event'). Given the conceptualization algorithm (see below), this leads to a frequency of about 64% of utterances involving one participant, about 34% of utterances involving two participants and only 2% of utterances involving three participants. In most experiments each event type was given the same frequency in order to balance this skewed frequency. As I will demonstrate later, equal frequency offers a much clearer picture of the propagation and convergence dynamics in the experiments.

3.2.4.3 Sensory-motor input

The real-world scenes were recorded using two SONY pan-tilt cameras (EVI-D31) which were hooked up to computers running the PERACT system (Baillie & Ganascia 2000; Steels & Baillie 2003), which was designed for the visual recognition of events and which is related to other attempts in visual-recognition such as Siskind (2000). Even though two cameras were used, this book uses only the data obtained through one of them. The simulations are thus not affected by differences in world models due to noisy recognition of the events or differences in visual perspective. These difficulties are very interesting for investigating the robustness of the model in grounded communication, but are not part of this book.

Since the vision system is quite complex (but fortunately well-documented in Baillie & Ganascia (2000)), I will restrict my discussion to its general architecture and to the design choices that are important for understanding what information

3 Baseline experiments

is delivered to the language system. The PERACT system first delineates objects based on colour histograms and then groups the pixels belonging to the same object together. These objects (two puppets, a table, two blocks, etc.) were learned in advance and PERACT can handle seven of them simultaneously in one scene. Starting from basic visual "primitives" or "micro-events" such as touching, movement and appearance, the system tracks the objects in real-time and assembles more complex descriptions (or "macro-events") when it recognizes a pattern in the scene. This recognition is often unreliable, but saliency, confidence and hierarchy are used to categorize the scene in terms of micro- and macro-events. This categorization of events is then supplied to the linguistic system.

For each agent, the filtered results of sensory processing is then represented as a series of facts in the memory. For example, an event in which one of the puppets 'moves inside a yellow house' is represented as follows:

(1)
```
(move-inside event-163190 true)
(move-inside-1 event-163190 jill)
(move-inside-2 event-163190 house-1)
(girl jill) (jill jill) (house house-1)
(yellow house-1) (boy jack) (jack jack)
```

As can be seen in example 1, there are three objects in the scene (two puppets called "Jack" and "Jill", and a house), but only two of them are participants in the move-inside-event ("Jill" and the house). For each object, the vision system delivers at least two facts which can be used during conceptualization for discriminating the objects from the other ones in the same scene (see below). These facts are very simple (for example 'house' and 'yellow' for the house-object), but can be interpreted in a more general sense as being the features describing an object (e.g. in a more detailed implementation, the feature-values of a R(ed)G(reen)B(lue)-channel could be used instead of the feature 'yellow').

The labels of these facts thus carry English names, **but should not be interpreted as such.** For example, 'move-inside' actually involves a puppet moving behind another object. The vision system, which is based on colour recognition, does not have any notion of a container or some kind of 'insideness'. Instead it sees one colour blob (the girl puppet) moving towards another one (the yellow 'house') until the colour regions "touch" each other after which the girl puppet disappears out of sight. So the label 'move-inside' does not reflect what actually happens in the scene (in terms of human conceptualization) but it is used for facilitating the analysis of the event recognition by the experimenter.

From the above it should also be clear that the PERACT system describes dynamic scenes in different levels of complexity. For example, the move-inside-event is itself a macro-event which can be decomposed into sub-events (which are macro-events themselves or micro-events, and which are also represented as facts in the memories of the agents). The micro-events for a move-inside-event are primitive relations such as 'visible', 'distance-decreasing', 'movement', 'touching' and 'disappearing'. The PERACT system offers a hierarchical description of events including time stamps for their beginnings and ends. As I will explain in §3.5, the simulations reported in this book disregard this temporal and hierarchical information and treat the event structure of an event as a flat list of micro-events. This choice was made in order to focus on the participant roles as a whole rather than on causal-aspectual parts of the event-structure. I will come back to this choice when discussing the experiments on Stage IV in the development of case markers.

One final remark regarding the sensory-motor input has to do with the status of the visual 'primitives'. I do not make any claims about whether they are innate or not, nor do I claim that they represent a realistic set for categorizing events in human cognition (neither in terms of size nor in terms of quality). The idea is rather that events can be decomposed into a much richer representation that allows analogical reasoning and the comparison of event structures.

3.2.4.4 Conceptualization

The categorization of the scenes in terms of event types and objects (and their features) is already taken care of by the sensory-motor system. Conceptualization in the simulations is therefore a very basic, but nonetheless crucial operation. First of all, during conceptualization the speaker agent decides on the **event profile** that it wants to express. "Event profile" should be interpreted in roughly the same way as commonly assumed in cognitive linguistics (see for instance Croft 1998). Since the agents do not take temporal-aspectual information of the events into account, profiling events essentially consists of deciding which participants have to be expressed explicitly. For the aforementioned move-inside-event, the speaker can thus conceptualize three different event profiles so the agents have to be able to deal with multiple argument realization:

- One in which only the puppet "Jill" is expressed (playing the participant role 'move-inside-1');

- One in which only the object 'house' is expressed (playing the participant role 'move-inside-2');

- One in which both participants are expressed.

3 Baseline experiments

The meaning of events is a simple copy of the facts in the memory of the agent, so the meaning of the move-inside-event would simply be conceptualized as:

(2)
```
(move-inside event-163190 true)
(move-inside-1 event-163190 jill)
(move-inside-2 event-163190 house-1)
```

For those objects that have to be expressed explicitly according to the event profile, the agent plays a simple discrimination game (Steels 1996c; 1997a). Suppose that the agents observe a scene in which there are two blocks represented as the following facts:

(3)
```
(ball object-1) (blue object-1)
(ball object-2) (green object-2)
```

If the agent wants to talk about the blue ball, it needs a feature or a feature set which discriminates this ball from the green one. Since both objects have the feature 'ball', this cannot be used for discriminating the blue ball from the green one. The colour-feature, however, is discriminating so the speaker would conceptualize the following meaning for the blue ball:

(4)
```
(blue object-1)
```

If there are more than one discriminating features (e.g. the features 'girl' and 'jill' in example 1 both discriminate the puppet "Jill" from the puppet "Jack"), the agent randomly chooses one. The objects are defined in such a way that there is always at least one feature discriminating them from other objects in the same scene.

Suppose that the speaker profiles the move-inside-event such that only the house-object has to be expressed explicitly – roughly meaning something like '(something) moved inside the house / the yellow thing'. Conceptualization could then possibly yield the following meanings:

(5)
```
(move-inside event-163190 true)
(move-inside-1 event-163190 jill)
(move-inside-2 event-163190 house-1)
(yellow house-1)
```

3.2.5 Additional assumptions and scaffolds

The agents in these simulations are endowed with strong (cognitive) capacities that enable them to communicate linguistically with each other. Listing all aspects of language that are assumed, scaffolded or ignored would take too much space, so I will restrict myself to the most important ones:

- The agents are assumed to be social and cooperative. All agents are equally involved in the formation of their language, so the simulations ignore the possible influence of differences in social status;

- All agents are "adult" language users. No growth of cognitive capabilities occurs and the models do not take specific child language acquisition restrictions into account. All agents are endowed with the same capacities;

- The agents are assumed to be able to communicate about compositional meanings (i.e. meanings which are related to each other in some way). In the simulations, Fluid Construction Grammar is used as a formalization of the capacity to combine and manipulate hierarchical symbolic form-meaning mappings. The models further ignore how these symbolic units should be coupled to neurological processing;

- The agents do not have real "speech". Instead, all utterances are perfectly transmitted from the speaker to the hearer in the form of strings of words. The influence of phonological changes on grammaticalization processes is well understood in theoretical linguistics, but computational models on the formation of phonological and syllabic conventions are scarce and not advanced enough to be used for example to model phonological reduction (although see Steels & Kaplan 1998b). The phonological development of case markers is therefore ignored in this book, but remains a topic of interest for the future;

- The agents also do not care about morphology. There is no meaningful word-internal structure and the capacity of segmentation is assumed. The language-specific segmentation process is scaffolded so the agents can perfectly cut up utterances into words and markers. The markers themselves can thus be seen as adpositions rather than as true markers found in case languages such as German.

Another very important scaffold is the fact that the agents start with a **predefined lexicon, but no grammar**. There are several reasons for giving the agents

3 Baseline experiments

a lexicon in advance. One reason is methodological: as in any other kind of controlled experiment, this book focuses only on the emergence of a case grammar and not on the formation of a lexicon. Other experiments have already extensively investigated how adaptive lexicons can be formed and shared by large populations of agents (see §1.4.2). All forces working on the lexicon are therefore completely scaffolded. This also means that the meanings of lexical entries are fixed and known by the agents, so they never have to perform word sense disambiguation either. One of the future steps of the research program would, however, involve the integration of lexical and grammatical development in order to verify whether the current results and conclusions remain valid.

A second reason has to do with a very important assumption that the mechanisms underlying the *very first* emergence of grammatical constructions are the same ones as those identified in attested cases of present-day grammaticalization processes. These cases (almost) always display a development from more lexical to more grammatical functions:

> Grammaticalization is the gradual drift in all parts of the grammar toward tighter structures, towards less freedom in the use of linguistic expressions at all levels. Specifically, lexical items develop into grammatical items in particular constructions [...]. In addition, constructions become subject to stronger constraints and come to show greater cohesion.
> Haspelmath (1998: 318)

So the agents start from a lexicon and build their grammar on top of that. This strategy is however not uncontroversial in the field artificial language evolution. For example, Wray (1998; 2002) argues that modern language evolved through the analysis of a holistic protolanguage. Similarly, many simulations (especially in Iterated Learning Models) feature the analysis of holistic utterances into smaller linguistic units. Apart from the many arguments against the realism of the "holistic utterances-first" hypothesis (see De Pauw (2002): 345–348; and Wellens, Loetzsch & Steels (2008)), the most compelling argument for starting from a lexical language is Ockham's razor: since there are no data available from the first language(s), we should first of all investigate what can be explained and learned from applying present and attested processes of grammaticalization rather than starting from a hypothetical holistic language (Hoefler & Smith 2008).

One important observation is that even though the agents start with a lexical language, case markers can be constructed in grammatical languages as well (see §1.2.7). Rather than thinking of the initial stage as a "lexical language" it is more fruitful to think of individual constructions that do not mark event structure

3.2 Experimental set-up

grammatically as the seedbed for grammatical markers. The existence of such constructions also shows that **grammaticalization is not a determined process**: speakers of a language can but do not have to decide to tighten their linguistic items towards more grammatical uses.

The lexical entries provide the agents with a language which conforms to what Gil (2008: 124) calls an "Isolated-Monocategorial-Associational Language" (IMA):

1. All the words are morphologically isolating (i.e. they have no internal morphological structure);

2. There are no formal grounds to distinguish syntactic categories such as nouns or verbs. The words are thus syntactically monocategorial. There is only a semantic distinction between words that refer to objects and those that predicate and refer to event types;

3. Utterances are semantically associational: no grammar exists for marking event structure so the hearer has to find out himself how meanings relate to each other.

The lexical entries thus look very much as those presented in §2.4.2 but this time no semantic or syntactic categories are assumed. The entry for words that refer to event types only contain their event-specific participant roles in their meaning but no potential semantic roles (yet). For example, the semantic pole of the entry of *give* lists a giver, a given and a givee (which have been assigned the more neutral and arbitrary labels give-1, give-2 and give-3). The form-feature in the syntactic pole simply looks for the string "give" and does not give any information yet about the word's potential valents. Both poles feature a J-operator which is used for pulling the form and meaning of *give* into a separate unit. The complete entry of *give* looks as follows:

(6)
```
<Lexical entry: give
((?top-unit
   (meaning (== (give ?event-x true)
                (give-1 ?event-x ?obj-x)
                (give-2 ?event-x ?obj-y)
                (give-2 ?event-x ?obj-z))))
 ((J ?new-unit ?top-unit)
  (referent ?event-x)))
<==>
((?top-unit
   (form (== (string ?new-unit "give"))))
 ((J ?new-unit ?top-unit)))>
```

3 Baseline experiments

The entry of the word *jack* looks as follows:
(7)
```
<Lexical entry: jack
 ((?top-unit
    (meaning (== (jack ?object-1))))
  ((J ?new-unit ?top-unit)
   (referent ?object-1)))
<==>
 ((?top-unit
    (form (== (string ?new-unit "jack"))))
  ((J ?new-unit ?top-unit)))>
```

In the baseline experiments 20 different scenes were recorded featuring 15 distinct event types including ten macro-events (move-inside, move-outside, hide, give, take, cause-move-on, touch, grasp, fall and walk-to) and five micro-events (borderscreen, visible, move, distance-decreasing and approach). Every micro-event type (except for "borderscreen") can take the value of true or false, which leads to word-pairs such as *visible* versus *invisible*. This makes up for 19 different words that can be used for referring to events. The total number of event-specific participant roles is 30 resulting from three one-place predicates (borderscreen, visible and move), nine two-place predicates (move-inside, move-outside, hide, touch, grasp, fall, walk-to, distance-decreasing and approach) and three three-place predicates (give, take and cause-move-on). The event types and the corresponding words are summarized in Table 3.2.

Besides the words for event types, the agents are given 11 unambiguous words for referring to objects. These words map in a one-to-one relationship to facts about objects in the memories of the agents. The words are: *blue, block, boy, girl, green, ground, house, jack, jill, table* and *yellow*. These words can be used for referring to the seven objects that occur in the twenty recorded scenes (a puppet called "Jill", a puppet called "Jack", a blue block, a green block, a table, a yellow house and the ground).

3.3 Baseline experiment 1: no marking

3.3.1 Overview

The aforementioned debate on holistic versus compositional languages implicitly assumes a dichotomy between languages that are either holistic or compositional in a grammatical way. However, "compositional" does not necessarily mean "grammatical". There is at least one additional possibility and that is a

Table 3.2: This table gives an overview of the different event types that occur in the baseline experiments. For each event type, it is specified what participant roles it takes, what truth-values are possible and which word is used for it.

Event-types	Participant roles	Truth values	Words
borderscreen	object-1	false	'disappear'
move	move-1	true false	'move' 'rest'
visible	visible-1	true false	'visible' 'invisible'
approach	approach-1 approach-2	true false	'approach' 'no-approach'
distance-decreasing	distance-decreasing-1 distance-decreasing-2	true false	'get-closer' 'separate'
fall	fall-1 fall-2	true	'fall'
grasp	grasp-1 grasp-2	true	'grasp'
hide	hide-1 hide-2	true	'hide'
move-inside	move-inside-1 move-inside-2	true	'move-inside'
move-outside	move-outside-1 move-outside-2	true	'move-outside'
touch	touch-1 touch-2	true	'touch'
walk-to	walk-to-1 walk-to-2	true	'walk-to'
cause-move-on	cause-move-on-1 cause-move-on-2 cause-move-on-3	true	'cause-move-on'
give	give-1 give-2 give-3	true	'give'
take	take-1 take-2 take-3	true	'take'

3 Baseline experiments

language that relies heavily on content words rather than on grammatical constructions. In the extreme case this is an entirely lexical language which also forms the first stage in the experiments reported in this book. The goal of this first baseline experiment is to **demonstrate that agents can infer the speaker's intended meaning without using grammar but by exploiting the situatedness of the language game.**

3.3.2 An inferential coding system

3.3.2.1 Inferential coding

Languages across the world vary a lot as to which aspects of meaning are expressed using grammatical constructions and which are left implicit in the message. Speakers are nevertheless capable of filling in the blanks and reaching communicative success. This is possible because language is an inferential coding system (Sperber & Wilson 1986) in which the interpreter is assumed to be intelligent enough to infer the correct meaning by using all the possible resources at hand such as the shared context and previous experience. This view is nicely put as follows by Langacker (2000: 9):

> It is not the linguistic system *per se* that constructs and understands novel expressions, but rather the language user, who marshals for this purpose the full panoply of available resources. In addition to linguistic units, these resources include such factors as memory, planning, problem-solving ability, general knowledge, short- and longer-term goals, as well as full apprehension of the physical, social, cultural, and linguistic context.

As a consequence the representation or categorization system (in this case language) can be much more compact and does not encode the entire meaning. This is different from "Shannon coding" which is typically used in computer programs where all the information is stored and fixed in the message. The capacity of inferring the intended meaning of the speaker on the basis of partial linguistic input is a **necessary prerequisite** for the emergence of grammar in a cognitive-functional framework: without it, innovation and learning would be impossible.

Applied to the topic of this book, the first key cognitive ability that the agents need is therefore the capacity to find out how the meanings of the individual words uttered by the speaker should be linked to each other. This is implemented using the same formalization of meanings as presented in §2.2 of the previous Chapter. I will illustrate this with an example. Suppose that the speaker and hearer both observe a scene in which the puppet "Jack" walks towards the puppet

3.3 Baseline experiment 1: no marking

"Jill" and that sensory-motor processing yields the following facts in the memory of the agents:

(8)
```
(boy object-1) (jack object-1)
(girl object-2) (jill object-2)
(walk-to event-1 true)
(walk-to-1 event-1 object-1)
(walk-to-2 event-1 object-2)
```

3.3.2.2 The speaker

The speaker first conceptualizes a meaning for communicating to the hearer. First the event is profiled and then a discriminating description is found for all the participants that have to be expressed explicitly according to this event profile. Let's assume that the speaker profiles the entire event so both participants need to be expressed. For both puppets, there are two distinctive features in the factbase so the speaker randomly chooses one for each. This yields the following meaning after conceptualization:

(9)
```
(jack object-1)
(girl object-2)
(walk-to event-1 true)
(walk-to-1 event-1 object-1)
(walk-to-2 event-1 object-2)
```

Next, the speaker starts a production task which runs entirely as explained in the previous Chapter. Since the speaker only has a lexical language, only the lexical information of the entries for *walk-to, jack* and *girl* is added. This results in the following node in the speaker's reaction network:

(10)
```
<Node-3: coupled-feature-structure
((top-unit
  (sem-subunits (jack-unit walk-to-unit girl-unit)))
 (jack-unit
  (meaning ((jack object-1)))
  (referent object-1))
 (walk-to-unit
  (referent event-1))
  (meaning ((walk-to event-1 true)
            (walk-to-1 event-1 object-1)
            (walk-to-2 event-1 object-2))))
 (girl-unit
```

3 Baseline experiments

```
        (meaning ((girl object-2)))
        (referent object-2)))
    <==>
    ((top-unit
        (syn-subunits (jack-unit walk-to-unit girl-unit)))
      (jack-unit
        (form ((string jack-unit "jack"))))
      (walk-to-unit
        (form ((string walk-to-unit "walk-to"))))
      (girl-unit
        (form ((string girl-unit "girl")))))>
```

In the original experiments, each unit also had a 'goal'-feature in the semantic pole with the values 'assert' for the top-unit, 'reference' for the units of the participants, and 'predicate' for the units of the event types. In the syntactic pole, there was also a 'scope'-feature (e.g. with the value 'utterance' for the top-unit). Since they play no role in the simulations, I left them out in the replicating experiments. Since the speaker has unified and merged all the possible linguistic items, we get the following utterance (word order is completely random because it was not specified in the coupled feature structure):

(11) "walk-to jack girl"

3.3.2.3 The hearer

The hearer observes the speaker's utterance and starts parsing it. This involves segmenting the utterance into words and then unifying and merging all possible linguistic items with the current node in the reaction network. The hearer, too, only knows lexical words so only lexical information is added to the coupled feature structure. This results in the following node:

(12)
```
        <Node-3: coupled-feature-structure
          ((top-unit
            (sem-subunits (jack-unit walk-to-unit girl-unit)))
          (jack-unit
            (meaning ((jack ?object-a)))
            (referent ?object-a))
          (walk-to-unit
            (referent ?event-x))
            (meaning ((walk-to ?event-x true)
                      (walk-to-1 ?event-x ?object-x)
                      (walk-to-2 ?event-x ?object-y))))
          (girl-unit
```

```
        (meaning ((girl ?object-b)))
        (referent ?object-b)))
    <==>
     ((top-unit
        (syn-subunits (jack-unit walk-to-unit girl-unit))
        (form ((meets jack-unit walk-to-unit)
              (meets walk-to-unit girl-unit))))
      (jack-unit
        (form ((string jack-unit "jack"))))
      (walk-to-unit
        (form ((string walk-to-unit "walk-to"))))
      (girl-unit
        (form ((string girl-unit "girl")))))>
```

The hearer can now extract the following meaning from the semantic pole of this coupled feature structure:

(13)
```
    ((jack ?object-a) (girl ?object-b) (walk-to ?event-x true)
     (walk-to-1 ?event-x ?object-x)
     (walk-to-2 ?event-x ?object-y))
```

Note that the hearer does not know from this meaning which participant played which role in the event. Both Jack and Jill could be the participant which is moving towards the other, or perhaps even another (implicit) participant plays a role. The hearer can **interpret** the parsed meaning by unifying it with the facts in the memory, which yields the following set of bindings:

(14)
```
    ((?event-x . event-1) (?object-x . object-1)
     (?object-y . object-2) (?object-a . object-1)
     (?object-b . object-2))
```

Since unification successfully returns a single hypothesis, the hearer can now infer that the variables '?object-x' and '?object-a' are equal because they both refer to the same object ('object-1'). The hearer also infers that the variables '?object-y' and '?object-b' are equal because they both refer to 'object-2'. The hearer thus successfully infers that the puppet Jack played the participant role 'walk-to-1' and that the puppet Jill played the participant role 'walk-to-2'.

3.3.2.4 Communicative success

In the above example, the parsed meaning is unambiguously compatible with the hearer's world model so the hearer signals agreement to the speaker. This

3 Baseline experiments

means that the language game was successful. The game fails if the parsed meaning would not match the hearer's world model or if the hearer still has multiple hypotheses left after interpretation (for example when the context consists of several similar events). In this case the hearer would signal disagreement.

In this first baseline experiment, success in the game does not influence the linguistic behaviour of the agents since the lexicon is given and assumed to be fixed. The point here is rather to demonstrate that the agents can reach success in communication even though they have no grammar yet.

3.3.3 Results and discussion

The above experimental set-up was tested in **a population of two and a population of ten agents** engaging in peer-to-peer description games without a cross-generational population turnover. In each game, the agents share a context of five events from the same scene. Two measures were used: **communicative success** and **cognitive effort** (see the Appendix for a description of all measures).

3.3.3.1 Results

The results of baseline experiment 1 are illustrated in Figure 3.3. The graph displays communicative success and cognitive effort for 10 series of 500 language games. Since the language of the agents is given and static, and since the task difficulty never changes, the results show a constant behaviour over time. Experiments using a population of ten agents yielded the same results for the same reasons.

The results indicate that the agents can indeed reach a fair amount of communicative success without using grammar: in about 70% of the games, the hearer is capable of unambiguously inferring the intended meaning from the context. For this, the hearer needs an average cognitive effort of 0,6 during interpretation. Cognitive effort is fairly high since all failed games are counted as requiring maximum cognitive effort of 1. If the results of the failed games are ignored, cognitive effort drops to 0,5 on average. The simulations were run using the skewed frequency of event types.

3.3.3.2 Discussion

The results of baseline experiment 1 demonstrate that the agents can still reach communicative success if they use their world model for inferring the intended meaning. The proposed machinery thus works but only under certain conditions.

3.3 Baseline experiment 1: no marking

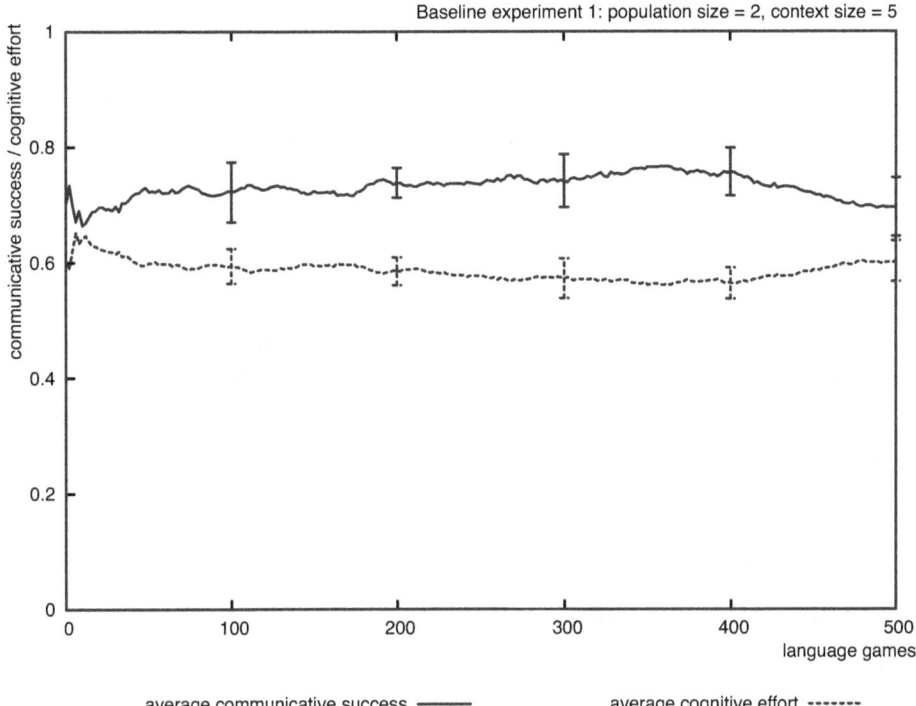

Figure 3.3: This graph shows the average cognitive effort and communicative success in baseline experiment 1 for 10 series of 500 language games in a population of two agents and a context size of five events. Success is reached in about 70% of the games. Cognitive effort during interpretation amounts to 0,6 on average.

For one thing, the hearer needs to have witnessed the scene in order to make the correct inferences. Second, the context cannot be too ambiguous otherwise interpretation can involve multiple hypotheses. As can be read from the average communicative success measure, this happens in 30% of the cases. Failed games typically occur when the scene contains at least two event tokens which have the same event type but which involve different participants.

Improving communicative success in the failed games could be achieved in many ways: agents can be given more complex dialogue strategies, the speaker can use pointing, the hearer can be more bold in making assumptions about the speaker's intention or ask for additional feedback, etc. These strategies would however involve more negotiation and do not reduce the cognitive load during interpretation for the hearer. Additional marking, however, would be a solution

3 Baseline experiments

which could resolve ambiguity and reduce cognitive effort during interpretation at the same time. This solution will be tested in the next baseline experiment.

3.4 Baseline experiment 2: specific marking

3.4.1 Overview

Baseline experiment 1 showed how agents can still reach communicative success without using grammar. In the second baseline experiment, agents can exploit this ability to autonomously detect whether it might be useful to make changes to their linguistic inventories in order to optimize communication. The hypothesis investigated here can be formulated as follows: **ambiguity or too much cognitive effort during parsing and interpretation can be a trigger for the invention of functional markers for optimizing communicative success.**

3.4.2 Speaker-based innovation

3.4.2.1 Innovation and expansion

In baseline experiment 1 the hearer is faced with the cognitive load of figuring out who's doing what in events during each interaction. Moreover, if the context is complex enough it may not be clear which event the speaker was referring to. In this experiment, the agents are therefore endowed with a second key cognitive ability which involves the **innovation and expansion** of their language through event-specific markers. This ability comprises three subparts:

1. Expanding the agents architecture with a "re-entrant" mapping for detecting opportunities for optimization and learning innovations;

2. Endowing the agents with the capacity of inventing a marker and the corresponding constructions;

3. Endowing the agents with a consolidation mechanism which allows them to converge on a shared set of markers.

3.4.2.2 Re-entrance

In baseline experiment 1, the agents could confidently use their lexical items to communicate with each other since the lexicon in this model is fixed, unambiguous, and shared by all the agents. However, should this scaffold be taken away, the agents would have to worry about whether the words they use are

3.4 Baseline experiment 2: specific marking

also known and understood by the other agents. They would thus somehow have to be capable of predicting the parsing and interpretation behaviour of the hearer in order to increase the chances of reaching communicative success. This can be achieved through "re-entrance" (Steels 2003b) – also called the "obverter" strategy by Smith (2003a).

Re-entrance can be thought of as self-monitoring in which the speaker does not directly transmit his utterance to the hearer, but first "re-enters" the utterance into his own linguistic system and parses and interprets the utterance himself as if he was the hearer. By taking himself as a model to simulate the linguistic behaviour of the hearer, the speaker can detect whether there might be problems or difficulties during parsing and interpretation. If so, the speaker will try to solve this problem. This strategy is illustrated in Figure 3.4. Similarly, the hearer can also use a re-entrant mapping for simulating the behaviour of the speaker. Technically speaking, achieving re-entrance is not so difficult since the agents in these experiments can act both as a speaker and as a hearer.

Re-entrance is thus a crucial strategy in inferential coding systems: if the

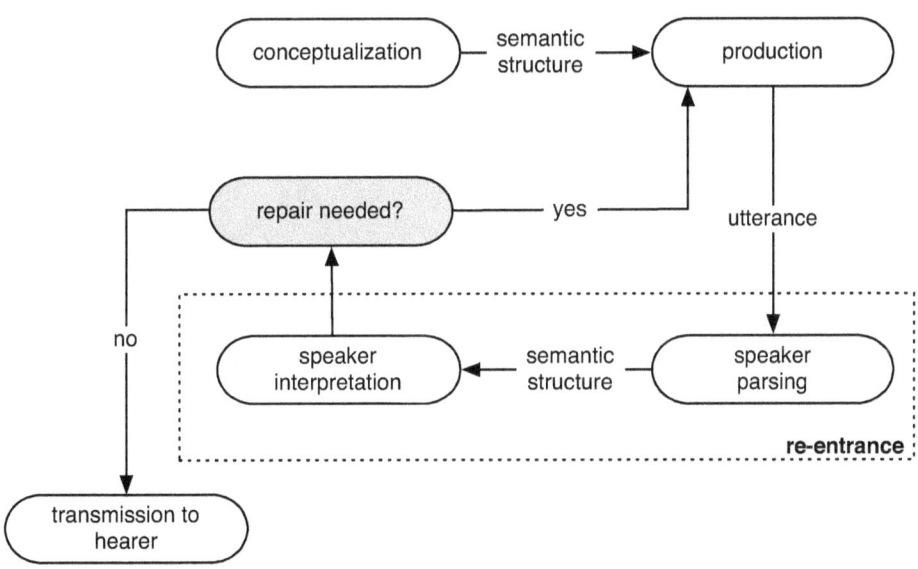

Figure 3.4: Before transmitting an utterance to the hearer, the speaker "re-enters" her own utterance in her language system and uses herself as a model of the hearer. In this way the speaker estimates whether there might be problems or too much complexity for the hearer during parsing. If so, the speaker tries to repair the problem.

3 Baseline experiments

speaker wants to solve a problem through innovation, he needs to have an educated guess about the hearer's knowledge and which aspects of the common ground can be exploited for getting the message across. The hearer has to perform the same kind of reasoning for guessing the speaker's intentions. Human language users obviously adapt their linguistic behaviours to their speech partners (e.g. when speaking to children or second language learners). Given the fact that all agents in the experiments are each other's peers, the best model they can have of other agents is themselves.

3.4.2.3 Innovation

It is unavoidable that language users come across situations in which the speaker does not know an adequate and well-entrenched convention for expressing a certain meaning, especially in the extreme case where there is no grammar at all. In this experiment, the speaker will invent a specific marker for explicitly expressing a particular participant role if there are possible ambiguities in the context or if the hearer needs to do more inference than is desirable. This is implemented through **diagnostics and repair strategies** which run in this experiment along the following algorithm:

1. **Diagnostic 1**: Re-enter the utterance into the linguistic system and start a parsing and interpretation task.
    a. If interpretation returns a failure or multiple hypotheses, report a problem;
    b. If there is one possible hypothesis which contains at least one unexpressed variable equality, report a problem;
    c. If there is no inference needed and if there is only one hypothesis, transmit the utterance to the hearer.

2. **Repair strategy 1**: If a problem of ambiguity or unresolved variable equalities has been reported, trigger repair strategy 1.
    a. If there is only one unexpressed variable equality, invent a new marker for it and start a new production task;
    b. If there are more than one unexpressed variable equalities left (i.e. the repair is too difficult), ignore the problem and transmit the utterance to the hearer.

3.4 Baseline experiment 2: specific marking

I will now illustrate this algorithm with a concrete example. Suppose that the speaker and hearer both observe the same scene as the one used in §3.3 in which Jack was walking to Jill; and that the sensory-motor processing delivers the same facts as in example 1. This time the speaker only profiles the part of the event involving Jack and conceptualizes the following meaning:

(15)
```
(jack object-1)
(walk-to event-1 true)
(walk-to-1 event-1 object-1)
(walk-to-2 event-1 object-2)
```

Since the speaker has no grammar yet, only the lexical entries of *Jack* and *walk-to* are unified and merged with the coupled feature structure which results in the following, randomly ordered utterance:

(16) "jack walk-to"

Instead of directly transmitting the utterance to the hearer, the speaker first re-enters the utterance into her own linguistic system and parses the following meaning:

(17)
```
(jack ?object-a)
(walk-to ?event-1 true)
(walk-to-1 ?event-x object-x)
(walk-to-2 ?event-x object-y)
```

Interpreting this meaning by unifying it with the speaker's world model yields the following set of bindings:

(18)
```
((?event-x . event-1) (?object-x . object-1)
 (?object-y . object-2) (?object-a . object-1))
```

Unification is successful and returns only one hypothesis so the speaker does not detect ambiguity. However, there is a variable equality left between the variable '?object-x' and '?object-a': both refer to 'object-1'. **Diagnostic 1 will therefore report a problem that triggers repair strategy 1.**

The repair strategy assesses the difficulty of the problem: if there are more than one unexpressed variable equalities left, the problem is classified as "too difficult to solve" and then the utterance is transmitted anyway. Here, however, there is only one variable equality so the speaker will invent a new marker for it. This

3 Baseline experiments

marker is specific to the walk-to-1 role and can thus almost be seen as a lexical item itself. The speaker then invents a **verb-specific construction** in which the new marker (let's say -*bo*) binds the referent of the walk-to-1-role to the referent of the argument that fills this role by using the same variable '?object-x'. The syntactic pole states that this argument plays 'syn-role-1' which is nothing more than a direct mapping of the walk-to-1-role.

(19)
```
<Construction: construction-1
 ((?unit-1
    (meaning (== (walk-to ?event-x ?truth)
                 (walk-to-1 ?event-x ?object-x)
                 (walk-to-2 ?event-x ?object-y))))
  (?unit-2
    (referent ?object-x)))
 <==>
 ((?unit-2
    (syn-role syn-role-1)))>
```

The morphological rule states that the marker immediately follows the argument which plays the walk-to-1-role. As explained in the previous Chapter, the morphological rule will create a new marker-unit and make it a sub-unit of the argument-unit. Both the verb-specific construction and the morph-rule look slightly different from the original proposals by Steels (2002b) due to changes in the grammar formalism, but they have the same performance.

(20)
```
<Morph-rule: -bo
 ((?top-unit
    (syn-subunits (== ?unit-1)))
  (?unit-1
    (syn-role syn-role-1)))
 <==>
 ((?top-unit
    (form (== (string ?marker-unit "-bo")
              (meets ?unit-1 ?marker-unit))))
  ((J ?marker-unit ?top-unit))
  ((J ?unit-1 ?top-unit (?marker-unit))))>
```

The speaker now starts a new production task for the same meaning. In the initial node in the reaction network, the whole meaning is still grouped together in one unit. The speaker then unifies and merges the lexical entries of *jack* and *walk-to* with the initial node which leads to a separate unit for each word. The new coupled feature structure looks as follows:

3.4 Baseline experiment 2: specific marking

(21)
```
<Node-2: coupled-feature-structure
((top-unit
  (sem-subunits (jack-unit walk-to-unit)))
 (jack-unit
  (meaning ((jack object-1)))
  (referent object-1))
 (walk-to-unit
  (referent event-1))
  (meaning ((walk-to event-1 true)
            (walk-to-1 event-1 object-1)
            (walk-to-2 event-1 object-2))))
<==>
((top-unit
  (syn-subunits (jack-unit walk-to-unit)))
 (jack-unit
  (form ((string jack-unit "jack"))))
 (walk-to-unit
  (form ((string walk-to-unit "walk-to")))))>
```

Before the repair, this would be the final node in the reaction network. This time, however, the speaker has the newly made construction at her disposal. Since this is a production task, the semantic pole of the construction needs to unify with the semantic pole of node-2. This is successful: the construction needs any unit containing the meaning of a walk-to-event and another unit of which the referent is the same one as the referent of the walk-to-1-role ('object-1'). The syntactic pole of the construction then simply merges the feature-value pair '(syn-role syn-role-1)' to the argument-unit. The construction thus licenses the following node in the reaction network:

(22)
```
<Node-3: coupled-feature-structure
((top-unit
  (sem-subunits (jack-unit walk-to-unit)))
 (jack-unit
  (meaning ((jack object-1)))
  (referent object-1))
 (walk-to-unit
  (referent event-1))
  (meaning ((walk-to event-1 true)
            (walk-to-1 event-1 object-1)
            (walk-to-2 event-1 object-2))))
<==>
((top-unit
  (syn-subunits (jack-unit walk-to-unit)))
 (jack-unit
```

3 Baseline experiments

```
        (syn-role syn-role-1)
        (form ((string jack-unit "jack"))))
       (walk-to-unit
        (form ((string walk-to-unit "walk-to")))))>
```

Next, the speaker can unify and merge the new morph-rule with node-3. The left-pole of the morph-rule (which is syntactic, see §2.4.3) looks for any unit containing the feature-value pair '(syn-role syn-role-1)' which is indeed present in the syntactic pole of node-3. Next, the right-pole of the morph-rule is merged with the right-pole of node-3:

(23)
```
       <Node-4: coupled-feature-structure
        ((top-unit
          (sem-subunits (jack-unit walk-to-unit)))
         (jack-unit
          (meaning ((jack object-1)))
          (referent object-1))
         (walk-to-unit
          (referent event-1))
          (meaning ((walk-to event-1 true)
                    (walk-to-1 event-1 object-1)
                    (walk-to-2 event-1 object-2))))
         <==>
         ((top-unit
          (syn-subunits (jack-unit walk-to-unit)))
         (jack-unit
          (syn-subunits (bo-unit))
          (syn-role syn-role-1)
          (form ((string jack-unit "jack"))))
         (bo-unit
          (form ((string bo-unit "-bo") (meets jack-unit bo-unit))))
         (walk-to-unit
          (form ((string walk-to-unit "walk-to")))))>
```

The speaker has no other items that can be unified and merged so node-4 is the final node in the reaction network. The speaker then renders the form-features of the syntactic pole into an utterance. The ordering between the words *jack* and *walk-to* are still random, but the coupled feature structure specifies that the marker *-bo* immediately follows *jack*. This results in the following utterance:

(24) "jack -bo walk-to"

The speaker now re-enters this utterance again into his linguistic system to check whether the innovation has the intended effect. I will not repeat the entire

3.4 Baseline experiment 2: specific marking

trace of parsing here since this is completely analogous to the example given in Chapter 2. Parsing the utterance yields the following meaning:

(25)
```
(jack ?object-x)
(walk-to ?event-x true)
(walk-to-1 ?event-x object-x)
(walk-to-2 ?event-x object-y)
```

Note that this time, the meaning-predicates 'jack' and 'walk-to-1' share the same variable '?object-x'. Interpretation then returns the following set of bindings:

(26) `((?event-x . event-1) (?object-x . object-1)`
     `(?object-y . object-2))`

As can be seen in the set of bindings, there are no unexpressed variable equalities left so no additional inferences are needed. The speaker is thus satisfied with the utterance and transmits it to the hearer.

3.4.2.4 Learning

Learning a new marker is very similar to inventing one and is achieved through the same cognitive mechanisms. The hearer first observes the utterance and then parses it. If there are unknown strings, such as the marker *-bo* which was just invented by the speaker, the hearer will ignore it and try to parse as much as possible. Then the hearer tries to interpret the parsed meaning. If there are unexpressed variable equalities left, the same diagnostic as was used by the speaker will report a problem. The repair strategy then tries to find out whether the utterance contains elements which could carry this particular meaning or function.

1. **Hearer diagnostic 1**: Parse the utterance and interpret its meaning.

    a. If interpretation returns a failure or multiple hypotheses, report a problem;

    b. If there is one possible hypothesis which contains at least one unexpressed variable equality, report a problem;

    c. If there is no inference needed and there is only one hypothesis, signal agreement to the speaker.

2. **Hearer repair strategy 1**: If a problem of ambiguity or unresolved variable equalities has been reported, trigger repair strategy 1.

a. If there is only one unexpressed variable equality, check whether there was one unknown string in the utterance. If so, add a new verb-specific construction to the inventory which records the unknown string as a marker for the variable equality. If not, ignore the problem and signal agreement or disagreement to the speaker depending on success of the game;
b. If there are more than one unexpressed variable equalities left or if there were multiple unknown strings, ignore the problem. Transmit success to the hearer if inference is nevertheless possible.
c. If interpretation fails or leads to multiple hypotheses, ignore the problem and signal disagreement.

3.4.2.5 Consolidation

In the original two-agent simulations variety never occurs since the agents only observe each other's inventions except for the extremely rare cases in which the learning task was too difficult and the learner later on invents a different solution for the same problem. So consolidation is fairly trivial and means just storing the newly created or learned items in the linguistic inventory.

However, as soon as we scale up the experiments to multi-agent populations involving at least three agents, a pool of synchronic variation naturally arises since the agents can independently come up with different innovations for the same problems. The agents therefore need to have an alignment strategy that enables them to deal with the variety and to converge on a shared set of preferred markers.

In §1.4.3 I argued that the experiments on grammar first of all try to move all the previous work on lexicon formation onto the domain of grammar, so this experiment starts with a similar alignment strategy as was suggested in prior work. This strategy goes as follows: each construction has its own **confidence score** between 0 and 1. The higher the score, the more confident the agent is that the item is a conventionalized unit in the population. Based on the game's success and based on the speaker's behaviour, the hearer will update the scores in the inventory as follows:

- In case of success, increase the score of the applied construction(s) by 0.1 and decrease the scores of all its competitors through **lateral inhibition** by 0.1. Competitors of a construction are constructions which either have the same semantic pole but a different form (competing synonyms), or the same form but different semantics (competing homonyms);

- If the game was a failure, do nothing.

The fact that only the hearer performs score updating captures the intuition that agents first of all want to **conform to** the behaviours of other agents in the population rather than imposing their own preferences. A mathematical model by De Vylder (2007) also shows that this strategy results in smoother convergence dynamics. In case of game failure, neither the speaker nor the hearer updates any scores. The reason for this is that the description game does not offer enough explicit feedback for the agents to find out whether there might be parts in the processing chain which were harmful for communication.

3.4.3 Results and discussion

The above diagnostics and repair strategies have been implemented and tested in three different simulations. The first series (set-up 2a) features a population of two agents and replicates the results obtained by Steels (2002b; 2004a). The second experiment (set-up 2b) involves a population of ten agents in which the consolidation strategies become necessary for convergence. Both experiments feature the skewed frequency of event types mentioned in §3.2.4. A third set-up (set-up 2c) also features 10 agents, but this time the skewed frequency was replaced by an equal frequency of event types in order to study the convergence and competition dynamics more easily. All the results were obtained after ten series of language games for each simulation.

3.4.3.1 Results of set-up 2a

The results obtained from the replication experiment confirm the results of the original case experiment. The top graph in Figure 3.5 shows that the average cognitive effort needed by the speaker rapidly drops to zero if the agents start inventing and using specific markers to indicate relations between events and their participants. With the markers the agents are also capable of overcoming ambiguity in the context since communicative success rises to 100%. However, there is a price to pay for this optimization, which is shown in the bottom graph: for each participant role, the agents have to learn and store a specific marker in the inventory. In this two-agent simulation, no variation occurs so agreeing on a set of 30 markers is fairly trivial.

3 Baseline experiments

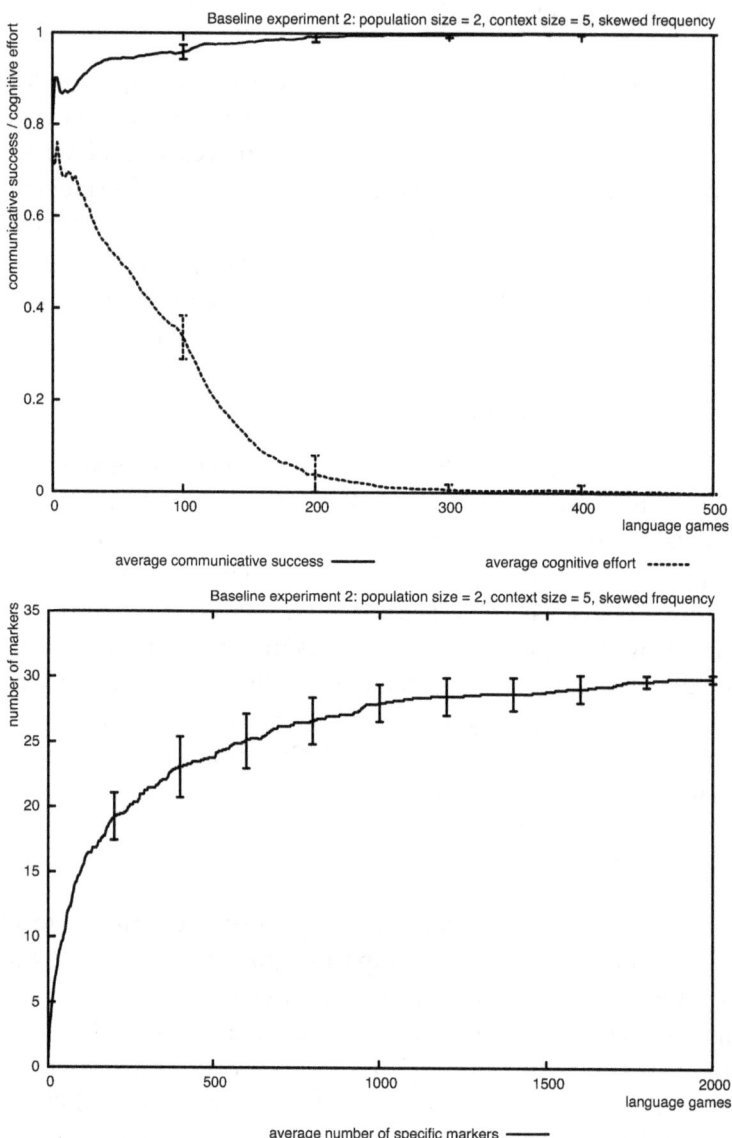

Figure 3.5: The top graph shows that the agents rapidly reach 100% communicative success in the two-agent set-up. The agents also succeed in reducing the cognitive effort to zero. The bottom graph shows that they need to learn and store 30 specific markers in their inventory to do so.

3.4 Baseline experiment 2: specific marking

3.4.3.2 Results of set-up 2b

If the population size is increased, the agents need much more time to learn all the variations floating in the population and to converge on a shared set of 30 markers. As Figure 3.6 shows, the agents need 80.000 language games in order to agree on this set. This is still fairly rapid: it means that each agent needs to play an average of 8.000 games in order to conform to the language of its peers.

The graph first shows a steep rise to an average of 40 markers in the beginning after which an alignment phase seems to start. However, the number of markers starts to climb up again after 7.000 games and reaches a height of about 45 markers by the time 20.000 games have been played. Then there is a long and gradual slope towards convergence at 80.000 games. The two peaks in the graph are the result of the skewed frequency of event type occurrences: markers for three-participant events are very rare and are therefore constructed, learned and propagated later than the frequent markers. Even so, the agents still reach agreement and communicative success while reducing the cognitive effort needed if they are given enough time.

3.4.3.3 Results of set-up 2c

In the third set-up all the event types occur with the same frequency so we can better study the convergence dynamics without other influences. Figure 3.7 shows that the agents indeed need significantly less time than in the second set-up: between six and seven thousand language games. On average this means about 600–700 games per agent, which comes close to the 500 games needed by the agents in two-agent simulations. The convergence task here is comparable in difficulty to a multiple word naming game involving 30 objects (see Van Looveren 2005). The graph shows that the agents keep innovating and learning new markers during the first 1.500 language games after which they rapidly converge on a shared set of 30 markers. The peak of 70 markers – as opposed to the peak of 45 with the skewed frequency – is normal since there are more competing markers floating in the population at the same time.

Figure 3.8 gives a snapshot of one agent's knowledge of markers for the participant role 'walk-to-1'. The agent learns three markers at about the same time: *-pev*, *-duin*, and *-hesae*. The marker *-duin* seems to be the winning marker and reaches a confidence score of 0.9 by the time the agents have played 2.000 language games. However, the agent then learns a new marker *-zuix* which seems to be quite successful in the population: its confidence score rapidly increases to the maximum while *-duin* goes downhill very fast because of lateral inhibition. In the end, *-zuix* wins the competition.

3 Baseline experiments

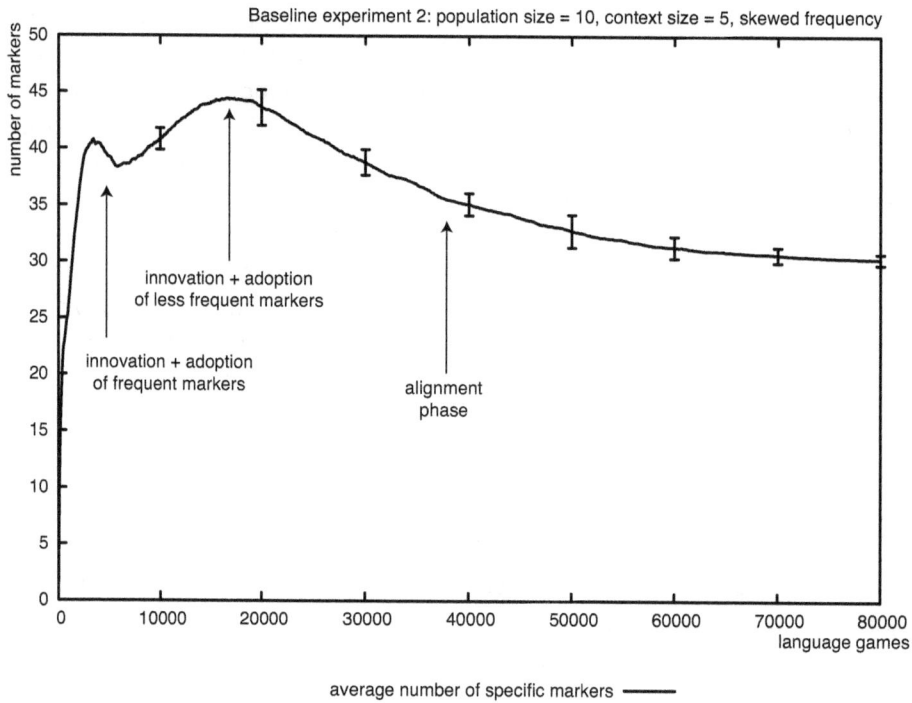

Figure 3.6: This graph shows the number of specific markers in baseline experiment 2b for 10 series of 80.000 language games in a population of 10 agents and a context size of five events. The agents start innovating and learning markers rapidly during the first 3.000 games after which a short period of alignment seems to kick in. The number of markers then rises again between game 7.000 and game 20.000. This is due to the skewed frequency of the event-tyes: events that potentially take three participants are very rare in the data and markers for them are only now being acquired by all agents. Finally, a long alignment period starts which also takes much more time for the less-frequent event types.

3.4 Baseline experiment 2: specific marking

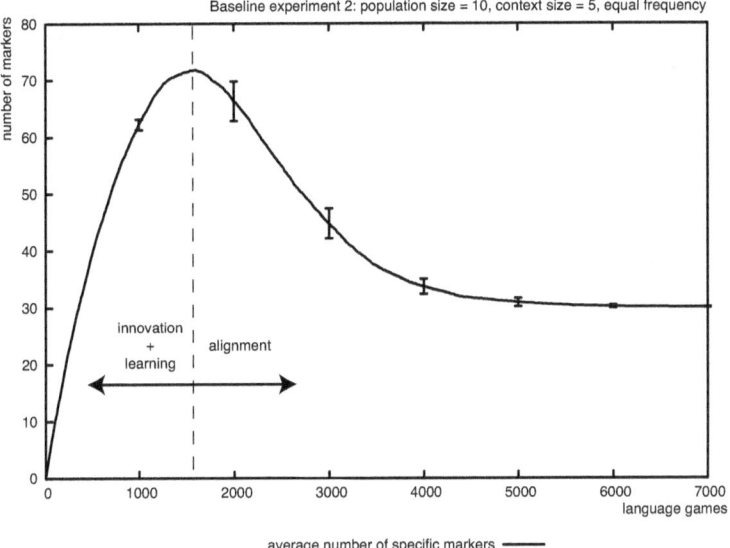

Figure 3.7: This graph shows the number of specific markers in baseline experiment 2c for 10 series of 7.000 language games in a population of 10 agents and a context size of five events. This case, all event types occur with the same frequency so we can see the convergence dynamics in the population more clearly: agents invent and learn new markers during the first 1.500 language games. The agents then need another 4.500 language games in order to align their linguistic inventories with each other.

3 Baseline experiments

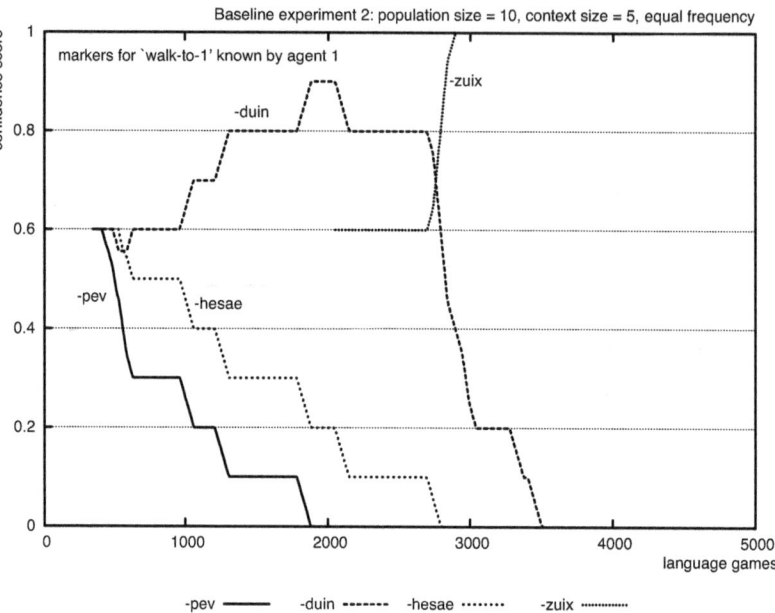

Figure 3.8: This graph shows a snapshot of the competition between forms for marking the participant role 'walk-to-1' within agent 1. Agent 1 learns the marker *-pev* at first, but soon also observes *-duin* and *-hesae*. The marker *-duin* seems to win the competition and even reaches a confidence score of 0.9 after 2.000 language games. However, the agent then learns another marker *-zuix* which is apparently shared by a lot of other agents in the population: at game 3.000 it has already pushed *-duin* down and it reaches 1.0 confidence score.

Finally, Figure 3.9 shows the average communicative success and cognitive effort again. The results show that the agents in the multi-agent simulations also rapidly reach 100% communicative success by using markers. Cognitive effort also goes down until no inferences need to be made anymore.

3.4.3.4 Discussion

The results of baseline experiment 2 clearly illustrate how agents can use locally available information to assess their own linguistic interactions and couple this assessment to repair and consolidation strategies in order to improve communication. In this case, the agents mainly acted to reduce the semantic complexity

3.4 Baseline experiment 2: specific marking

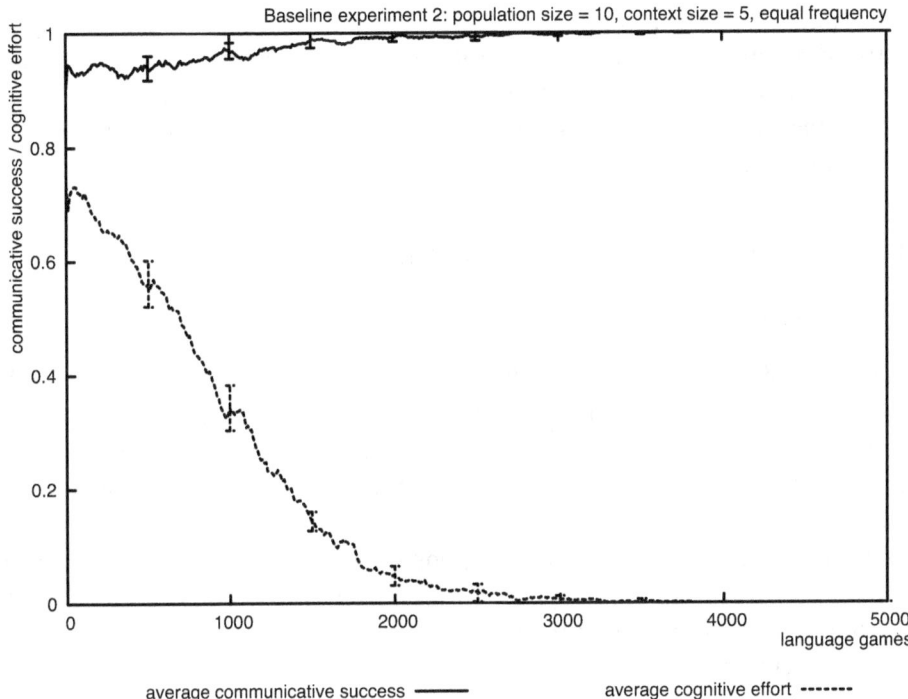

Figure 3.9: In the multi-agent populations too the agents succeed in reaching communicative success as well as reducing the cognitive effort needed for interpretation.

of interpretation for the hearer: if additional markers are introduced for explicitly indicating the relations between events and their participants, parsing leads the agents immediately to the desired bindings in interpretation. Without the markers, additional inferences would still be needed.

However, a price has to be paid for reducing the effort of interpretation and that is an increased inventory size. During the language games, the agents learn 70 markers on average and retain 30 of them, each one specific to a particular participant role. The inventory size is in fact not the main problem here but a side-effect of a bigger issue: since the markers are restricted to one function only, the agents (given their present capabilities) cannot use them to go beyond the data of known events. Hence there is no generalization. Inventing new markers for each participant role may be an efficient strategy in a small and fixed world, but becomes problematic once agents have to adapt to new meanings and communicative challenges.

85

3 Baseline experiments

Coupling these results back to natural languages, there are thus two clear qualitative differences: (a) markers in natural languages *do* generalize and become polysemous; and (b) they are not randomly invented but recruited from existing lexical items (see sections 1.2.4 and 1.2.5). Both issues will have to be addressed in other experiments.

3.5 Baseline experiment 3: semantic roles

3.5.1 Overview

The results of baseline experiment 2 indicate that the agents can reduce the problem of ambiguity and cognitive effort if they make use of additional marking. However, the proposed innovation strategy requires new markers to be invented all the time so (a) there is no generalization beyond the known data, and (b) this may lead to an explosion of the inventory size in the long run. Baseline 3 investigates how the same principles of diagnosis and repair in order to reach communicative success can lead to generalization. The hypothesis is that **analogical reasoning over event structures can account for an increased generalization and productivity of case markers.**

3.5.2 Generalization as a side-effect

3.5.2.1 Analogical reasoning

When repairing a problem of unexpressed variable equalties in the previous baseline experiment, the speaker assessed the repair to be too difficult to learn if the context was too ambiguous. In a more complex simulation, however, one can imagine that ambiguity is rather the rule than the exception so the speaker needs to innovate in a more clever way to give the hearer additional clues about what he meant. One such strategy is to reuse existing items as much as possible in semantically related or analogous situations. In baseline experiment 3, the speaker can reuse the existing markers in new situations by performing analogical reasoning over event structures. The analogy algorithm comprises the following steps:

1. Given a target participant $role_i$, find a source $role_j$ for which a case marker already exists;

3.5 Baseline experiment 3: semantic roles

2. Elaborate the mapping between the two:
   a. Take the target event structure in which participant role$_i$ occurs (provided by sensory-motor processing);
   b. Take the source event structure of the event that was used to create source role$_j$;
   c. Select from the source event structure all the facts and micro-events involving the filler of source role$_j$ and retrieve the corresponding facts and micro-events of the target event structure.

3. Keep the mapping if it is good. A good mapping means that:
   a. the filler of source role$_j$ always maps onto the same object in the corresponding facts and micro-events;
   b. the corresponding object fills the target role$_i$ in in the target structure.

4. If there are multiple analogies possible, choose the best one (based on entrenchment and category size);

5. Build the necessary constructions and make the necessary changes to existing items.

Step 3b in the algorithm ensures that an analogical role is also discriminating enough to distinguish the target role from other possible participant roles in the same or other events. By reusing existing items in novel but similar situations, the speaker reduces the hypothesis space for the hearer and facilitates the abduction process. The hearer can retrieve the analogy using the same algorithm if he also knows the other marker. In this strategy, the generalization of existing linguistic items is not a goal in itself but rather a side-effect of optimizing communicative success.

3.5.2.2 The target and the source

I will illustrate the analogy algorithm of this experiment through an example. Suppose that the speaker wants to construct a marker for the participant role 'walk-to-2' of the following walk-to-event:

(27)
```
(walk-to event-100 true) (walk-to-1 event-100 jack)
(walk-to-2 event-100 jill)
```

3 Baseline experiments

I will from now on refer to 'walk-to-2' as the *target role* and to 'jill' as the *target filler*. Instead of inventing a new marker immediately, the speaker will first check whether he already knows a marker which is analogous and hence could be reused. Suppose that the speaker already knows the marker *-mi* for the participant role 'move-inside-1'. I will from now on refer to this participant role as the *source role* and its filler as the *source filler*. The speaker has stored the original event which he used for creating the marker and retrieves it from his memory:

(28)
```
(move-inside event-163190 true)
(move-inside-1 event-163190 jill)
(move-inside-2 event-163190 house-1)
```

3.5.2.3 Elaborate the mapping between the two

In order to elaborate the mapping between the two events, the complete event structure is taken. The target event (walk-to) consists of four micro-events: one participant is moving and approaching another participant, which stands still until the two participants touch each other:

- ```
  (move event-165641 true) (move-1 event-165641 jack)
  ```
  ```
  (move event-165419 false) (move-1 event-165419 jill)
  ```
- ```
  (approach event-165486 true) (approach-1 event-165486 jack)
  (approach-2 event-165486 jill)
  ```
  ```
  (touch event-165633 true) (touch-1 event-165633 jill)
  (touch-2 event-165633 jack)
  ```

The source event (move-inside) is made up of eight micro-events. The event starts with two visible participants, of which one is standing still. The distance between both objects becomes smaller as one participant moves to the other. This continues until they "touch" each other after which the moving participant disappears out of sight.

- ```
  (visible event-161997 true) (visible-1 event-161997 jill)
  ```
  ```

3.5 Baseline experiment 3: semantic roles

- (visible event-161791 true) (visible-1 event-161791 house-1)

- (move event-161794 false) (move-1 event-161794 house-1)

- (distance-decreasing event-162441 true)
  (distance-decreasing-1 event-162441 jill)
  (distance-decreasing-2 event-162441 house-1)

- (touch event-161801 false) (touch-1 event-161801 jill)
  (touch-2 event-161801 house-1)

- (touch event-162493 true) (touch-1 event-162493 jill)
  (touch-2 event-162493 house-1)

- (borderscreen event-162377 false) (object-1 event-162377 jill)

- (visible event-162665 false) (visible-1 event-161997 jill)

Analogy is commonly defined as a mapping from a source domain to a new target domain. The next step in the algorithm is therefore to check how the existing role maps onto the target event structure. This can be achieved by selecting all the micro-events of the source event that involve the source filler and map them onto the corresponding micro-events of the target. If the micro-events do not exist in the target event, they are ignored. Other information such as time-stamps and hierarchical structure is also ignored. This yields the mapping in Figure 3.10.

source event	==>	target event
(touch-1 event-162493 jill)	==>	(touch-1 event-165633 jill)
(touch-1 event-161801 jill)	==>	(touch-1 event-165633 jill)

Figure 3.10: Mapping source event and target event

3.5.2.4 A good mapping

There are two requirements for a mapping to be good. The first is that the source filler must always map onto the same object in the target structure. This is indeed the case in the above example: 'jill' always maps onto 'jill' in the target event. The algorithm thus found an analogy between the source role and a role in the target

3 Baseline experiments

event. The second requirement for a good mapping is that this corresponding role is the same one as the target role. Again, this is the case in the example: 'jill' was indeed the target filler of the target role 'walk-to-2'. The speaker can thus decide that the existing marker -*ma* can be reused.

In this example, the speaker does not have any other markers yet to check for analogy. If there would be competing analogies, **type frequency** decides which analogy will be chosen (i.e. the semantic role which covers the most participant roles, ranging from one to many). I follow the same definition of type frequency as Bybee & Thompson (2000: 77):

> [T]ype frequency determines productivity: type frequency refers to the number of distinct lexical items that can be substituted in a given slot in a construction, whether it is a word-level construction for inflection or syntactic construction specifying the relation among words. The more lexical items that are heard in a certain position in a construction, the less likely it is that the construction will be associated with a particular lexical item and the more likely it is that a general category will be formed over the items that occur in that position. The more items the category must cover, the more general will be its critical features and the more likely it will be to extend to new items. Furthermore, high type frequency ensures that a construction will be used frequently, which will strengthen its representational schema, making it more accessible for further use, possibly with new items.

> As type frequency can range from one to a very large number, so there are varying degrees of productivity associated with ranges of type frequency.

3.5.2.5 Adapting the inventory

If no analogy can be found, the agent will invent a new marker as in baseline experiment 2. In this example, however, the agent already knows a suitable marker and it will have to incorporate this new use in its inventory. There are basically two options: either a new verb-specific construction is created for 'walk-to-2' featuring the same case marker as the construction for 'move-inside-1'; or the use of the existing construction is extended. In this experiment, the latter solution is tested.

The changes to the inventory are schematized in Figure 3.11 and can be summarized as follows: the specific meaning in the semantic pole of the construction is removed and replaced by a semantic frame which contains the generalized semantic role. This semantic role shares the same variable as the referent of the

3.5 Baseline experiment 3: semantic roles

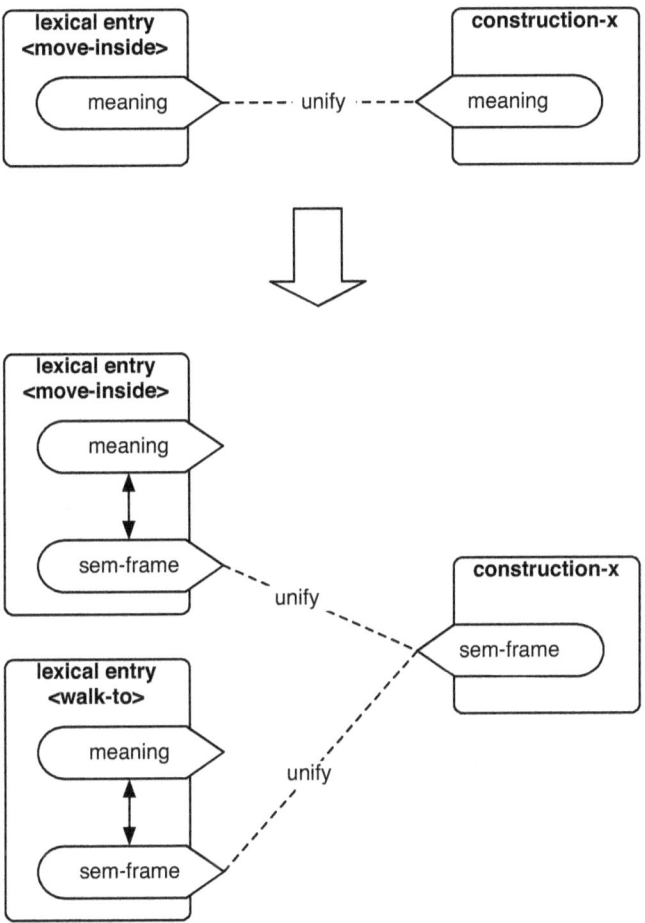

Figure 3.11: This diagram shows how the semantics of lexical entries and constructions integrate with each other. At first, constructions are verb-specific and unify with the meaning of a lexical entry. If the agent however decides to reuse this construction in a new situation, a generalized semantic role is constructed. The relevant lexical entries are extended with a potential semantic frame which unifies with the semantic frame of the construction. The links between the meaning and the semantic frames are taken care of by variable equalities.

other argument unit which was already present in the construction. The two lexical entries which have to be compatible with the new construction (*move-inside* and *walk-to*) are extended with a semantic frame as well. As explained in Chapter 2, this is not a frame in the traditional sense but rather a list of the potential valents of the verb. Since that Chapter also gives a full trace of parsing and production, I will not repeat the same operation here.

3.5.2.6 Learning

The hearer learns the marker by following the same strategy as before. If he didn't know the marker yet, he will create a new verb-specific construction if the context is clear enough. If he already knew the marker, he will get into trouble during parsing because its present use does not correspond to its previous function. The hearer will ignore the problem for the time being and parse the utterance as good as possible. Using the parsed meaning, inferred variable equalities and re-entrance, the agent can then (possibly) retrieve the analogy introduced by the speaker. If the hearer cannot retrieve any analogy, he will nevertheless accept it as imposed by the speaker.

The agents in this experiment can thus be characterized as (incremental) instance-based learners (and innovators) (Mitchell 1997: Chapter 8): the agents are "lazy" learners in the sense that they postpone generalization until new instances have to be classified as opposed to "eager" learners that try to make abstractions over the data immediately. Each innovation or novel classification is not based on abstract rules but by examining its relation to previously stored instances. This kind of learning (and innovation) fits usage-based models of language which presuppose "a bottom-up, maximalist, redundant approach in which patterns (schemas, generalizations) and instantiations are supposed to coexist, and the former are acquired from the latter" (Daelemans & Van den Bosch 2005: 20).

3.5.2.7 Consolidation

The original two-agent simulations did not need to care about alignment strategies or consolidation too much since the two agents always share the same communicative history. So the replicating experiment should pose no problems in both the alignment of case markers and the alignment of the internal structure of semantic roles. The same prediction cannot be made for multi-agent simulations in which alignment strategies are needed for convergence. Three additional set-ups have therefore been implemented: one which uses the same mechanism for updating the confidence scores of linguistic items as in baseline experiment 2

3.5 Baseline experiment 3: semantic roles

(set-up 3b), one in which a more fine-grained scoring mechanism has been implemented (set-up 3c), and finally one in which (token) frequency decides on the speaker's behaviour (set-up 3d). In this section I will not go into the reasons for experimenting with these different set-ups: they have been inspired by the experimental results and are therefore discussed later on. Instead, I will restrict myself to explaining the two new consolidation strategies. The four different set-ups (and their effects on the results) are summarized in Table 3.3.

Set-up 3c. The more fine-grained scoring mechanism implemented in set-up 3c is based on the idea that linguistic items are not "good or bad", but that they may be more suitable in some particular contexts and less suitable in others. A single confidence score for every linguistic item cannot go beyond its black-or-white updating scheme and thus cannot handle a more nuanced way of processing. Instead, agents need more clever self-assessment criteria: next to communicative success, they can use **co-occurrences** of linguistic items as a source for aligning their inventories.

Co-occurring items are locally observable to the agents since they form one chain in the reaction network during processing. The general idea is reminiscent of Hebbian learning ("what fires together, wires together"): a link is kept between co-occurring items and a confidence score is kept for this link based on the successful co-occurrence of both items. Suppose that the agent has the case marker *-ma* (see the example earlier in this section) which may cover either the participant role walk-to-2 or the role move-inside-1. The idea is now that the agents keep a link between co-occurring linguistic items, so the agent would now have a link between construction-x one the one hand and the two lexical entries *walk-to* and *move-inside* on the other. Instead of positing a score on the complete construction, each co-occurrence link has its own confidence score:

(29)

$$\text{<Construction-x>} \leftarrow \begin{array}{l} 0.5 \to \text{<move-inside> (for move-inside-1)} \\ 0.5 \to \text{<walk-to> (for walk-to-2)} \end{array}$$

Suppose that the speaker also has the marker *-bo* which can be used for marking 'move-1' and 'move-inside-2':

(30)

$$\text{<Construction-y>} \leftarrow \begin{array}{l} 0.5 \to \text{<move-inside> (for move-inside-1)} \\ 0.5 \to \text{<move> (for move-1)} \end{array}$$

3 Baseline experiments

If the agent then observes the co-occurrence of construction-x and *move-inside* (i.e. the agent analyzes an utterance in which *-ma* was used for marking move-inside-1), the score of the link is increased with 0.1 and the score of competing links (here the link between *move-inside* and construction-y) is decreased by 0.1. The other confidence scores based on co-occurrence remain untouched:

(31)

$$\text{<Construction-x>} \leftarrow \begin{array}{l} 0.6 \rightarrow \text{<move-inside> (for move-inside-1)} \\ 0.5 \rightarrow \text{<walk-to> (for walk-to-2)} \end{array}$$

$$\text{<Construction-y>} \leftarrow \begin{array}{l} 0.4 \rightarrow \text{<move-inside> (for move-inside-1)} \\ 0.5 \rightarrow \text{<move> (for move-1)} \end{array}$$

Note that this score is not the actual co-occurrence frequency, but a confidence score between 0 and 1 which only indirectly reflects co-occurrence and which is updated based on communicative success.

Set-up 3d. The fourth set-up in baseline experiment 3 removes the explicit lateral inhibition consolidation of the previous set-ups and replaces it with a combination of **token frequency and memory decay**. Frequency is implemented as a simple counter which can be updated after each interaction. This set-up has the following features:

- During production, the speaker will use the linguistic items which have the highest frequency score;

- After each *successful* interaction, the hearer will increase the counter of all the constructions that were applied during parsing by one;

- When an agent has engaged in 50 interactions, all the frequency scores are decreased by one (= memory decay).

This kind of (token) frequency favours more general constructions: the larger the type frequency of a certain class or category, the more chances it has to increase its token frequency. The memory decay implemented here is unaffected by population size since it is based on each agent's individual history. It is, however, sensitive to inventory size and frequency: linguistic items can only survive if they occur at least once before the next decay is performed. In the present set-up, each participant role occurs one time out of thirty interactions on average.

3.5 Baseline experiment 3: semantic roles

3.5.3 Results and discussion of set-up 3a

3.5.3.1 Results

The replicating experiment featuring a population of two agents confirms the results obtained by Steels (2002b; 2004a). The agents succeed in reusing existing markers and generalizing them to semantic roles as is shown in Figure 3.12 . During ten series of 500 language games, the agents constructed on average 6 to 8 markers which could be used for covering at least two participant roles. In total, up to 24 participant roles out of 30 were grouped together in more general roles. In each simulation, also 6 to 9 markers survived which cover specific participant roles.

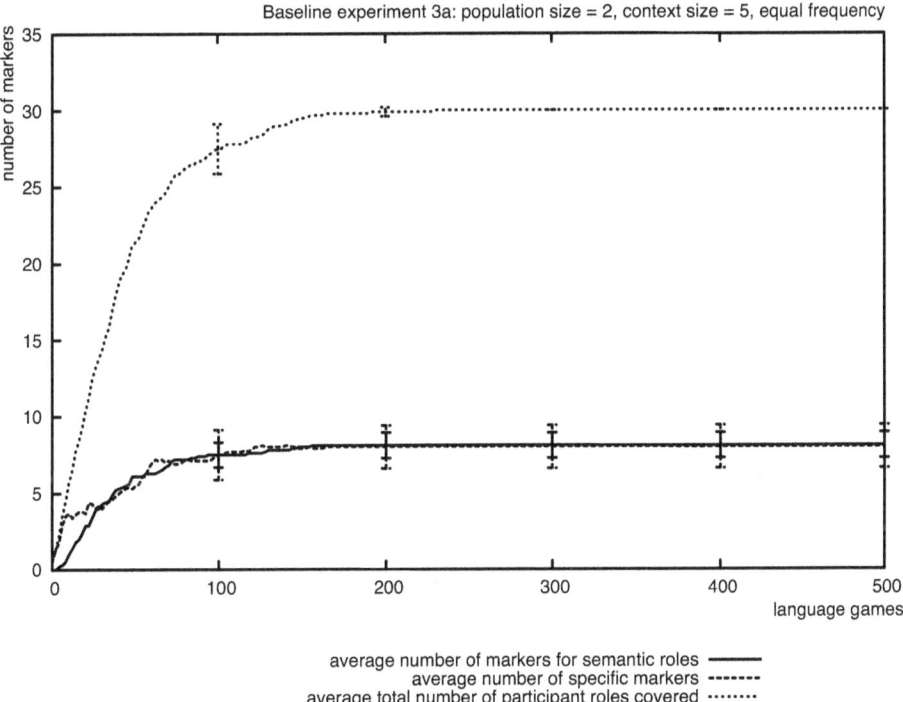

Figure 3.12: In the two-agent simulations, the agents have no problems aligning their inventories since there is no variation in the population. In ten series of 500 language games, the agents came up with an average of 6–8 markers for semantic roles and an average of 6-9 markers for specific participant roles. The semantic roles gather together up to 24 participant roles out of 30.

95

3 Baseline experiments

A closer examination of the semantic roles learns us that they tend to be small generalizations mostly covering two participant roles. Some roles exceptionally gather four or even six participant roles. Here are some example sentences from one of the simulations and their glosses:

(32) jack -cui   walk-to jill -ge
jack sem-role-6 walk-to jill sem-role-26
'Jack walks to Jill.'

(33) touch jill -cui   house -shae
touch jill sem-role-6 house-1 sem-role-29
'Jill touches house-1.'

(34) house -lu   move-inside boy -cui
house-1 sem-role-10 move-inside boy sem-role-6
'The boy moves inside house-1.'

In the same simulation, the following markers and their corresponding participant roles were constructed (ranging from 7 specific markers to 8 more general ones):

- -vuh: cause-move-on-1
- -yaem: cause-move-on-2
- -jibui: cause-move-on-3
- -shuip: give-3
- -vot: take-3
- -me: visible-1
- -naez: move-outside-2
- -zo: fall-1, approach-1
- -tui: fall-2, approach-2
- -shae: touch-2, give-2
- -fe: distance-decreasing-1, grasp-1
- -lu: move-inside-2, distance-decreasing-2

3.5 Baseline experiment 3: semantic roles

- -we: move-1, give-1, take-1
- -cui: walk-to-1, object-1, grasp-2, hide-2
- -ge: touch-1, move-inside-1, move-outside-1, hide-1, walk-to-2, take-2

3.5.3.2 Discussion

The results show that the construction of generalized semantic roles allows the agents to reduce the number of markers by 65–70%. However, the most important observation is that by endowing the agents with the capacity of analogical reasoning, they are capable of generalization beyond previous linguistic experience as is shown in the increasing productivity of some markers.

In the results there is still a fairly large residue of verb-specific markers which is partly due to the analogy algorithm and partly due to the fact that only two agents were involved in the simulation. First, the analogy algorithm is very strict in the sense that two roles are either analogous or not: there is no in-between value that allows for some flexibility. Second, since there are no variations in the population, the construction of semantic roles is entirely dependent on the linguistic history of both agents: once an analogy is constructed and successfully applied in communication, the agents will not try to come up with better or more general analogies later on. In other words, the solutions that the two agents come up with may not be optimal given their search space so they end up in a local maximum. A larger population may give this search an additional boost.

3.5.4 Results and discussion of set-up 3b

3.5.4.1 Results

In set-up 3b the population size is increased to 10 agents so there will be more variation among the agents. This is indeed confirmed in Figure 3.13 which shows that there are a total of 140 variations floating in the population for marking 30 participant roles. This is an average of 4,7 possible ways for marking each participant role. This number of possibilities does not drop to 30, which is a first indication that the agents do not converge on a shared set of grammatical markers. As for the nature of the markers, the results indicate that there are about 20 markers that can be used for covering at least two participant roles whereas there are about 50 specific participant role markers as well. The average inventory size of the agents is thus far from optimal.

Figure 3.14 confirms that the agents do not reach convergence: the meaning-form coherence indicates the degree to which the agents prefer the same case

3 Baseline experiments

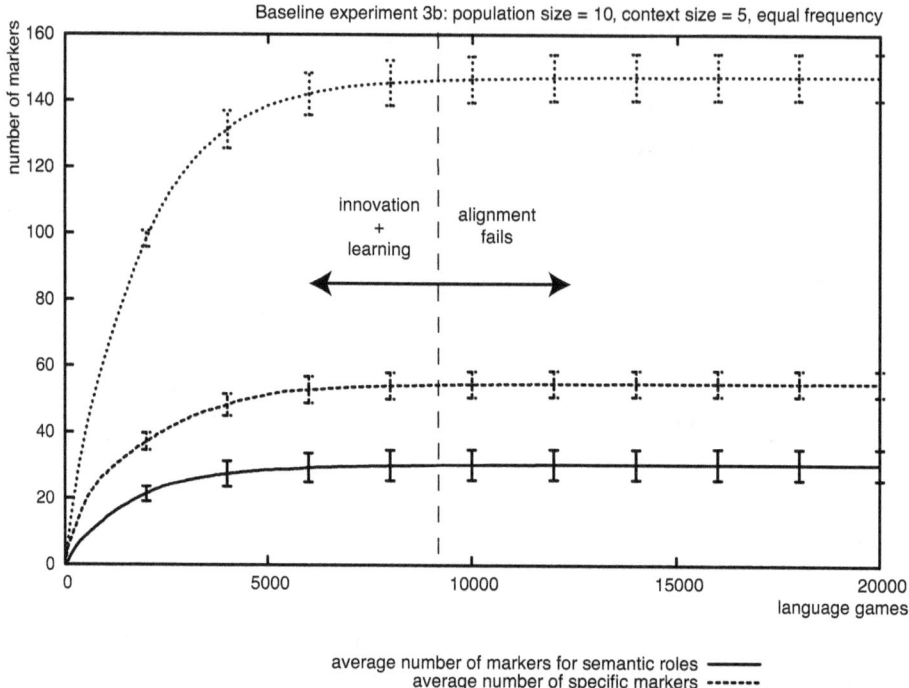

Figure 3.13: When scaling the experiments up to multi-agent simulations, the traditional alignment strategies used in prior experiments on lexicon formation are not sufficient for the population to reach convergence. For thirty participant roles, the agents have to remember 140 variations to communicate successfully, which is an average of 4,7 possible ways for marking each participant role.

marker for a particular participant role. As the graph shows, coherence only reaches 40% which means that the agents use a different marker for the same participant role in more than half of the language games. Yet, as the graph also shows, the agents are capable of reaching 100% communicative success and reducing the cognitive effort to zero.

3.5.4.2 Discussion

The results of baseline experiment 3b seem to be contradictory at first sight: even though the agents do not agree an a shared preferred set of markers, they nevertheless reach communicative success. This is possible because success in com-

98

3.5 Baseline experiment 3: semantic roles

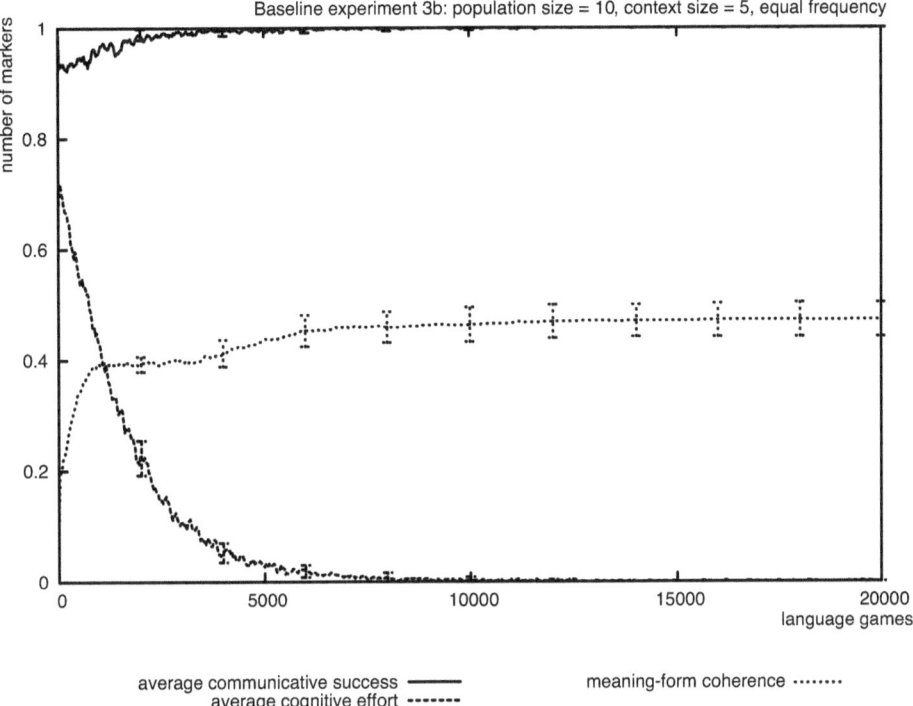

Figure 3.14: This graph shows that the agents reach 100% communicative success and reduce the cognitive effort needed for interpretation. However, the meaning-form coherence only reaches about 40% which indicates that the agents did not converge on a shared set of markers but keep using divergent preferences in more than half of the language games.

munication does not require meaning-form coherence: if the agents learn all the variations floating around in the population, they can still parse all utterances correctly. This happens indeed in this experiment.

The lack of convergence on a preferred set of markers clearly indicates that the proposed alignment strategy is insufficient. The reason is that the alignment strategy in which each item has its own single confidence score is best suited for simulations in which there is always a *one-to-one* mapping between form and meaning (as was the case in baseline experiment 2). However, when markers get generalized to cover more than one participant role, they become polysemous *one-to-more* mappings.

I will go through an example to explain why the single confidence score cannot be sufficient for polysemous form-meaning mappings. Suppose that an agent

3 Baseline experiments

knows three markers: *-ma*, *-bo* and *-li* and that the first two are generalized to cover two roles each whereas *-li* is still a verb-specific marker. For convenience's sake, I will not include all the linguistic items involved but treat the markers as if they were lexical items:

(35)

$$\begin{matrix}\text{<move-inside-1>} \\ \text{<walk-to-2>}\end{matrix} \leftleftarrows (0.5) \rightarrow \text{-ma}$$

(36)

$$\begin{matrix}\text{<move-inside-1>} \\ \text{<move-1>}\end{matrix} \leftleftarrows (0.5) \rightarrow \text{-bo}$$

(37)

$$\text{<move-1>} \leftarrow (0.5) \rightarrow \text{-li}$$

Suppose now that the agent observes the utterance *boy -ma move-inside* in which the marker *-ma* was successfully used for marking 'move-inside-1'. The score for *-ma* is thus increased and the score for its competitor *-bo* is decreased. The consequences for *-bo* are far-reaching, because it is now not only less successful than *-ma* for covering 'move-inside-1', but also than *-li* for marking 'move-1':

(38)

$$\begin{matrix}\text{<move-inside-1>} \\ \text{<walk-to-2>}\end{matrix} \leftleftarrows (0.6) \rightarrow \text{-ma}$$

(39)

$$\begin{matrix}\text{<move-inside-1>} \\ \text{<move-1>}\end{matrix} \leftleftarrows (0.4) \rightarrow \text{-bo}$$

(40)

$$\text{<move-1>} \leftarrow (0.5) \rightarrow \text{-li}$$

3.5 Baseline experiment 3: semantic roles

In another game, the same damage can be done for the marker *-ma* so *-bo* can recover from its score decrease. Generalization thus tends to be harmful for the markers if only one score is used: the more general a role marker gets, the more competitors it has and thus the more chances that its score will be decreased. Specific markers can escape punishment through lateral inhibition much more easily. On the other hand, if it has competing markers which are generalized, they can get punished too even if a different participant role was involved. Suppose that *-bo* was observed for marking 'move-inside-1' this time, then not only *-ma* is seen as a competitor, but also *-li* because it overlaps with *-bo* for marking 'move-1'.

There is thus a constant push-and-pull effect in which markers may get cornered by others but then all of a sudden get more successful again. This is the reason why the agents can never converge on a preferred set: the single confidence score does not allow markers to be successful in one particular context but unsuccessful in another.

3.5.5 Results and discussion of set-up 3c

3.5.5.1 Results

The results of baseline experiment 3c indicate that the alignment strategy of reinforcement and lateral inhibition can lead to convergence if it is applied in a more fine-grained way. This time, the agents not only use communicative success as a guidance but also co-occurrence links: instead of positing one score on the linguistic item as a whole, they now keep a link between co-occurring items and assign a confidence score to that link. In case of success, the score of the link is increased and only scores of competing *links* are decreased. In this model, a marker disappears from the linguistic inventory once it has no links to other linguistic items anymore with a confidencescore higher than zero.

Figure 3.15 shows that the number of variations peaks at 70 possible markings for 30 participant roles. This means that the agents only have to deal with an average of 2,3 competing markers for each participant role. Innovation and adoption of markers stops at about 1.500 language games after which the agents rapidly converge on a shared set of markers. The graph also shows that the agents converge on a set of 5 generalized semantic role markers and about 20 verb-specific markers. This means that the verb-specific markers managed to win the competition more often than generalized markers and that semantic roles on average only cover two participant roles.

3 Baseline experiments

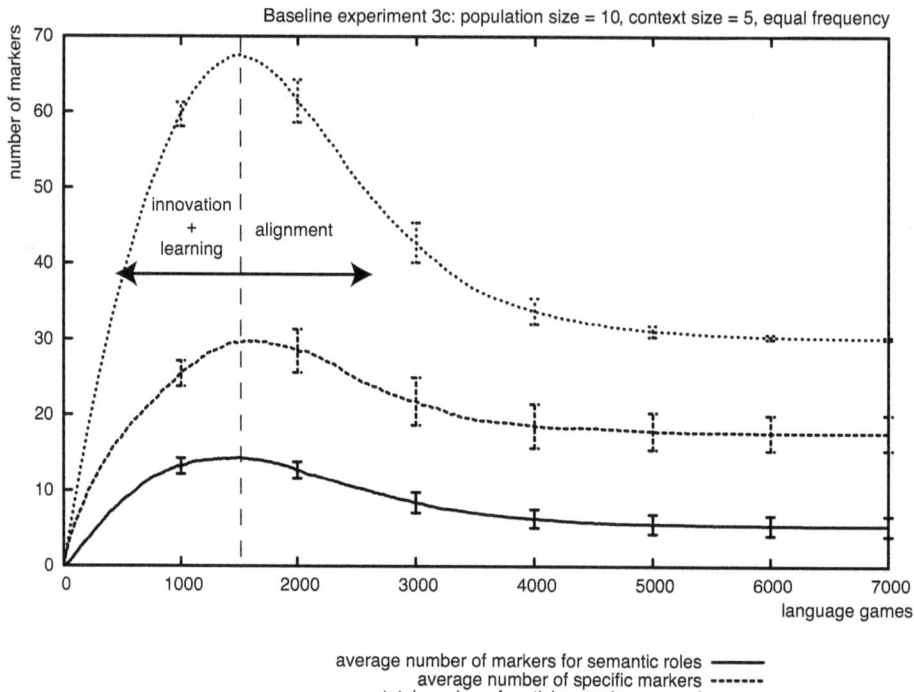

Figure 3.15: The more fine-grained alignment strategy allows the agents to converge on one possible marking for each of the thirty participant roles. There are 5 semantic roles on average which each cover about two participant roles. The remaining 20 roles are covered by specific markers.

Figure 3.16 shows that fine-grained alignment allows the agents to converge on a shared set of preferences: meaning-form coherence reaches 100% after 5.000 language games which corresponds to the moment where the agents have pruned all the variations down to 30 in Figure 3.15. The agents also reach communicative success and manage to reduce the cognitive effort needed during parsing.

3.5.5.2 Discussion

The results show that the fine-grained scoring mechanism suffices to solve the problem of convergence among the agents. However, the gain in inventory optimization is minimal: the agents end up with an average of 25 markers for 30

3.5 Baseline experiment 3: semantic roles

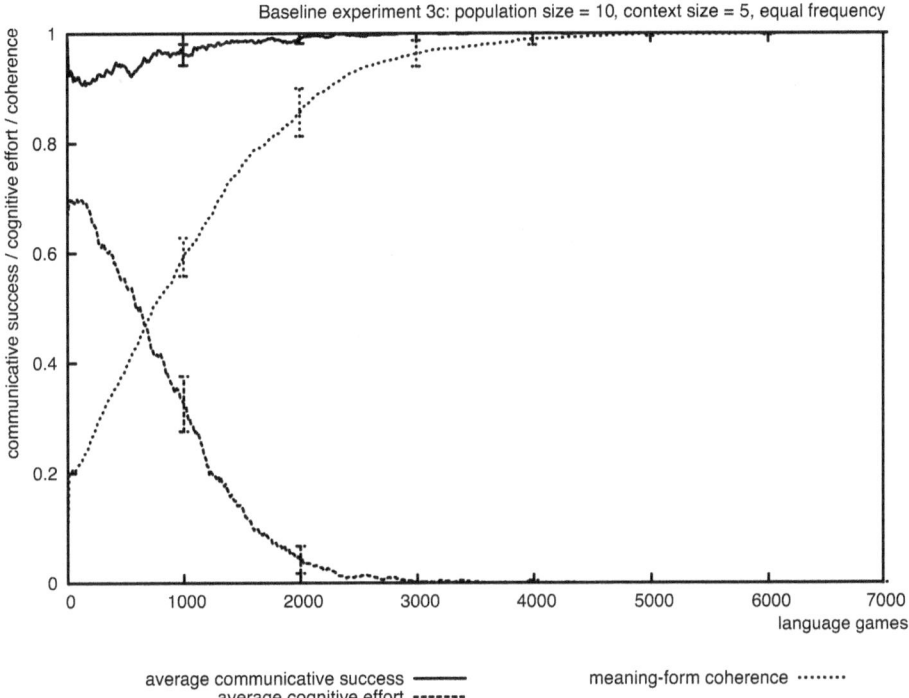

Figure 3.16: Using the more fine-grained alignment strategy, the agents not only succeed in reaching communicative success and reducing cognitive effort, they also converge on a shared set of meaning-form conventions.

participant roles. Also the benefits of generalization are on the low side with an average of two participant roles covered by a semantic role.

By solving the problem of the single confidence scores, the fine-grained scoring mechanism created a new one: since only competing links are taken into account during consolidation, the influence of the frequency of the entire category is neglected. This means that a verb-specific marker has the same chances of surviving the competition as generalized semantic role markers do, even though the latter ones are as a whole more frequent and productive. If a semantic role loses the competition from a specific marker, its type frequency is reduced and hence its productivity.

To overcome this problem, the agents need another alignment strategy which both recognizes the impact of generalized roles and is capable of dealing with

3 Baseline experiments

the context-sensitive nature of polysemous markers. Experiment 3d implements such a strategy.

3.5.6 Results and discussion of set-up 3d

3.5.6.1 Results

The final set-up in baseline experiment 3 does not use confidence scores or lateral inhibition. Instead, agents rely on token frequency of successful interactions for producing utterances. Figure 3.17 shows that the agents spend roughly the same time as in set-up 3c innovating and learning new markers. The average amount of variation reaches a total of 35–40 possibilities for 30 markers, which is an average of less than two variations for each participant role. The innovation rate is in fact

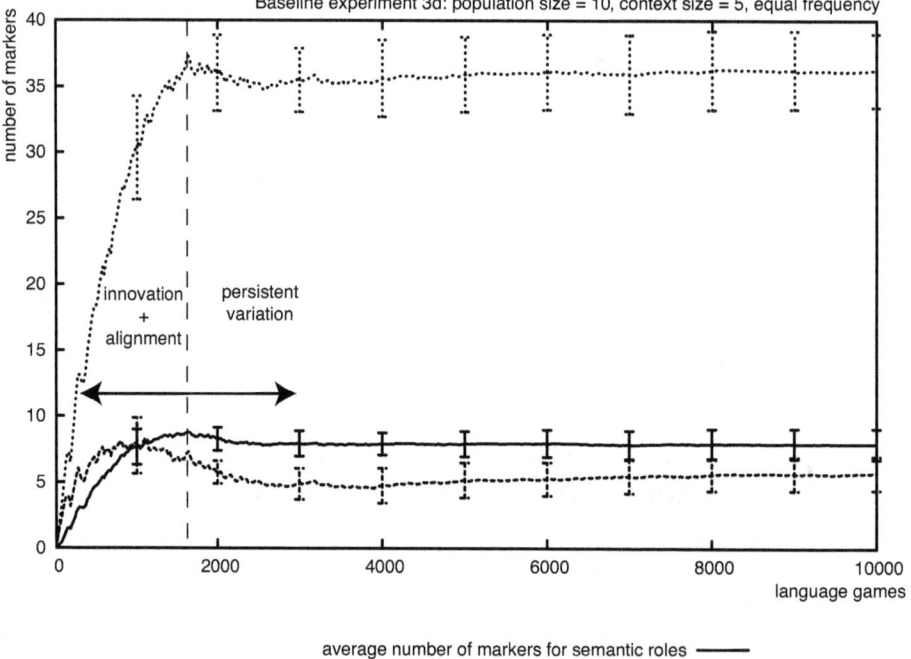

Figure 3.17: When adapting their linguistic behaviours to frequency, the agents tend to use more generalized semantic role markers rather than specific ones. Here, about seven semantic roles cover 25 of the 30 participant roles. The top line indicates that some amount of variation persists over time.

104

3.5 Baseline experiment 3: semantic roles

as high as in the previous set-up, but many innovations are excluded very early on by memory decay. Innovations that do survive the memory decay during the first 2.000 interactions are quite frequent so they persist in memory for a very long time afterwards. Getting rid of them is therefore very slow and may take thousands of additional language games before they are "forgotten" or in some cases they persist over time. A closer look at the markers themselves learns us that there are on average eight semantic roles and six markers for specific participant roles. This means that the semantic role markers can cover up to 24 participant roles.

Figure 3.18 indicates that even though the agents do not reduce their grammars to a single variation for all 30 participants, they nevertheless converge on a shared set of preferred markings: coherence rises to 100% in 6.000 language games. Communicative success reaches 100% and the agents rapidly succeed in reducing the cognitive effort needed for interpretation.

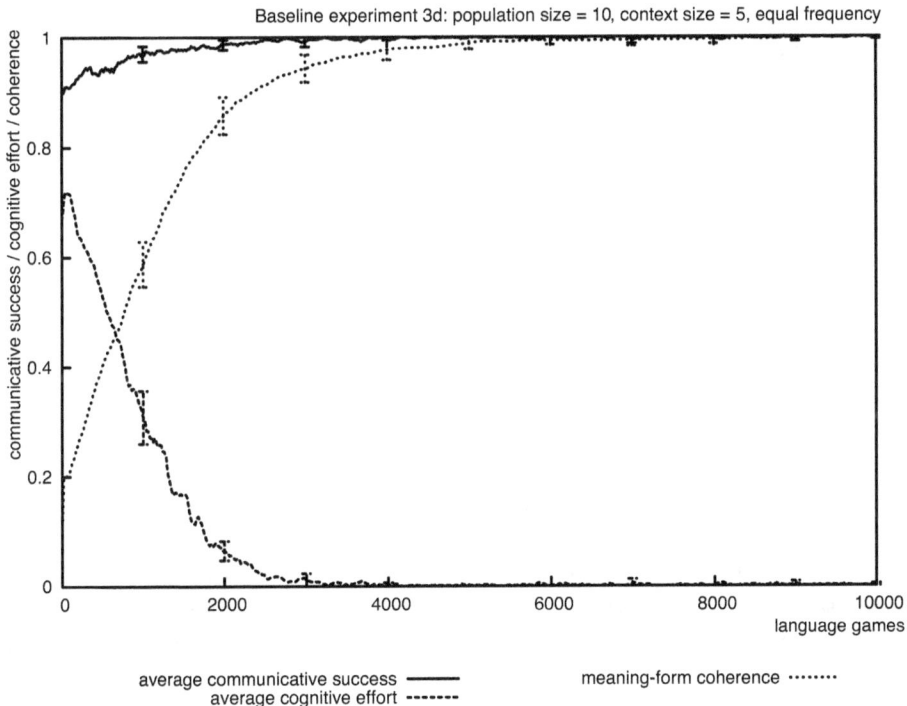

Figure 3.18: This graph shows that the agents reach communicative success, reduce the cognitive effort needed for interpretation and converge on a shared set of case markers.

105

3 Baseline experiments

3.5.6.2 Discussion

In order to interpret the results of set-up 3d correctly, a closer examination of the artificial languages of the agents is needed. In one of the simulations, a population of ten agents all preferred the following 14 markers and their corresponding participant roles:

- *-zoti*: cause-move-on-1
- *-ruko*: cause-move-on-2
- *-jaexi*: grasp-2
- *-mad*: approach-1
- *-zima*: give-1
- *-wobae*: give-2
- *-ha*: take-3
- *-qui*: cause-move-on-3, visible-1
- *-fechui*: touch-2, take-1
- *-kuwae*: touch-1, take-2
- *-yuis*: fall-2, approach-2
- *-pae*: give-3, walk-to-2, move-outside-1
- *-ru*: walk-to-1, distance-decreasing-2, move-1, move-inside-2, hide-2, move-outside-2
- *-gahu*: object-1, move-inside-1, fall-1, distance-decreasing-1, hide-1, grasp-1

The above markers suggest that there were seven specific markers left and seven semantic role markers. However, the marker *-jaexi* can in fact be counted as a semantic role because it can also cover the participant roles 'hide-2' and 'distance-decreasing-2'. In both cases, however, the marker is in competition with *-ru* which has both a higher type and token frequency. Similarly, *-pae* can also cover 'hide-1' but this participant role is dominated by the frequent role marker *-gahu*. This explains why in this simulation there remain 33 possibilities for 30 participant roles instead of only 30: the markers *-jaexi* and *-pae* have found their own 'semantic niche' in which they occur frequently enough to avoid memory decay. Synchronic variation like this is in fact more realistic than the competition dynamics in the previous set-ups since it causes a pool of variation which may trigger future changes in the language: both markers may disappear after a while or they may extend their usage and become stronger rivals for the now more successful markers *-ru* and *-gahu*.

When comparing the results to the two-agent simulations, set-up 3d improves in terms of generalization: more participant roles are covered by the same marker. The improvement is however not that big so the simulations do not demonstrate that the collective solution found by larger populations can avoid the local maxima that two agents encountered in their communicative interactions. In order to fully test this hypothesis, experiments are needed involving a larger and more controlled search space.

The alignment strategy however does succeed in favouring the more general roles through function and frequency: markers which have a higher type frequency and therefore a wider usage tend to have a higher token frequency as well. This creates the same rich-get-richer dynamics of the strategy involving one score and lateral inhibition in baseline experiment 2: the more frequent a marker is, the more likely it will win the competition in the future and the more likely it will increase its type frequency as well. At the same time, the alignment strategy allows for the same context-sensitivity as the fine-grained scoring mechanism because it does not feature explicit lateral inhibition so no categories are unrightfully harmed by it. This allows more lexical markers to still survive in their (sometimes verb-specific) semantic 'niche' if they are frequent enough to survive memory decay.

3.5.7 Conclusions and future work

In this section I discussed the various set-ups of baseline experiment 3 and reported on its results. Common to all simulations was the additional cognitive ability of analogical reasoning over event structures. This cognitive mechanism allowed the agents to reuse (and generalize) existing markers in new situations and contexts. By exploiting analogy, the agents are thus capable of generalizing their grammars beyond the input of previous experiences. generalization is thereby not a goal in itself, but rather a side-effect of the need for optimizing communication in an inferential coding system.

Four set-ups were implemented and compared to each other. The first set-up successfully replicated the original case experiment and set the baseline for the other three multi-agent simulations. Set-up 3b indicated that a single confidence

3 Baseline experiments

score is not a sufficient alignment strategy for converging on a shared set of preferred markings: this strategy is optimized for one-to-one mappings but cannot deal with the context-sensitiveness of polysemous one-to-many mappings. An alternative was therefore implemented in set-up 3c in which the agents also exploited the co-occurrences of linguistic items: this time, a specific link was kept between all co-occurring items with a confidence score for each link. The strategy proved itself sufficient for reaching coherence in the population but at the cost of generalization. Finally, an alignment strategy was proposed based on token frequency and memory decay. This strategy led the agents to convergence on a set of preferred markings and improved slightly over the results of the two-agent simulations. The various set-ups are summarized in Table 3.3.

In the simulations, analogy is the source of generalization and increased productivity of existing markers. This suggests that (at least for innovation and learning), analogy can be used as a unified account for both the more "regular" forms in the language and the more "irregular" forms as opposed to rule-based accounts which posit abstract rules and a list of exceptions. In order to exploit the power of analogy, however, the agents need the right kind of alignment strategy that favours the more general categories.

Evidence from natural languages suggests that analogy is also responsible for the first innovation by recruiting an existing lexical entry for a more grammatical use instead of inventing a new marker (see §1.2.4). Additional experiments are thus needed in which the innovation strategies of baseline experiments 2 and 3 are combined into one. The recruitment of existing and well-entrenched lexical entries would naturally follow from the same assumptions that language is an inferential coding system and that speakers and hearers will exploit whatever resources that are available for solving communicative problems: using a conventionalized linguistic unit has the major advantage that it offers the hearer a strong grounding point for inferring the meaning or function of the innovation. In the present experiments, the new markers do not contain any clues about what their source events were, so this may differ strongly from agent to agent which explains why the hearer can't retrieve the analogy in all cases. In the abstractions and scaffolds of the present set-up, however, this poses no problems.

Implementing a more realistic model of stage 2 in the development of case markers, however, is not a trivial matter and requires more study on how this happens in natural languages. From the evidence gathered so far (see §1.2.4), it seems that the present algorithm for analogy cannot handle this. The first reason is that the recruited lexical item in serial verb language constructions, which are typical sources of case markers, seems to "fit" naturally in the utterance by for

3.5 Baseline experiment 3: semantic roles

Table 3.3: This table compares the four alignment strategies implemented in baseline experiment 3. In set-up 3a, no additional alignment strategies were needed since there were only two agents and hence no variation was observed in the population. Set-up 3b showed that direct competition did not yield successful alignment because a confidence score on each linguistic item cannot deal with polysemous usage of the items. Set-up 3c solved the problem of alignment through a confidence score on each co-occurrence link. This strategy however led to equal opportunities for each marker in the population so unproductive markers survived as easily as general ones. The final strategy involved the frequency of construction tokens which favoured more general markers because they have wider application and are thus more frequent.

Exp.	Pop.	Consolidation	Effect
3a	2	store innovations	–
3b	10	store innovations + confidence score on all items + lateral inhibition	alignment fails
3c	10	store innovations + confidence score on links + lateral inhibition	alignment succeeds (arbitrary winners)
3d	10	store innovations + frequency of constructions + memory decay	alignment succeeds (general roles favoured)

example presupposing the same subject as was demonstrated in example 5 which I repeat here:

(41) thân cà bin maa krungthêep
    he will fly come Bangkok
    'He will fly to Bangkok.'
    (Blake 1994: 163)

The present analogy algorithm already expects a marker and would not know how to deal with the other participant roles of the recruited verb. The task can involve even three participants in cases where for example *give* evolves into a dative or recipient marker. The data thus show that next to a more general-purpose algorithm for analogy, we also need to find solutions for coordination and ellipsis so that the recruited lexical entry can naturally blend in the utterance. Before we can do this, however, we first need to investigate how the syntactic categories can be formed that have to be coordinated.

A second problem has to do with morphology and phonological reduction. In the attested examples, the second verb in a serial verb language construction is implicitly marked for its more grammatical function because it typically occurs in a non-finite or a non-conjugated form. In the experiments, there is no morphology or syntax that could distinguish two verbs from each other so the hearer would have a very hard time at figuring out which verb was meant as the "main verb" and which one was meant as the "marker". Moreover, the hearer would have no reasons to assume that one of the verbs has been recruited for a new use in the first place. The problem with phonological reduction is that there is no phonological component in the experiments so recruited lexical items cannot evolve towards a new form which distinguishes them more clearly from their original uses.

Next to work on syntax, coordination and morphology, a dynamic representation of categories and word meanings is needed. First steps have already been taken by Wellens (2008) who investigates how word meanings can become more flexible and therefore change over time. This work however only deals with words for objects so more effort is needed to integrate it with the architecture of the experiments in this book. Another particular issue with the model of Wellens is that it does not allow true polysemy: the agents continuously shape the meaning of a lexical entry but they cannot use the same word in multiple ways. The meanings are therefore still one-to-one mappings between form and meaning, but what the exact content of the "one" meaning is may change over time. Grammaticalization of case markers, however, requires one-to-many mappings or even many-to-many mappings, so the agents have to be capable of distinguishing between different uses of the same form. I believe that coordination and pattern formation could be a key in solving this issue, as I will explain in more detail in the following Chapter.

4 Multi-level selection and language systematicity

4.1 Introduction

The baseline experiments of the previous chapter looked at how analogy could be exploited for the generalization of case markers for covering semantic roles. The experiments focused on the development of these semantic roles in isolation of each other in order to identify the diagnostics, repairs and alignment strategies that make the emergence of such roles possible. However, the behaviour and functionality of case markers can only be fully understood when they are studied in relation to the other elements in their linguistic context. In other words: case markers have to be investigated in relation to the patterns in which they occur. This chapter therefore presents experiments in which case markers can be combined in larger patterns.

The next section first gives a brief overview of pattern formation in language and operationalizes one strategy of pattern formation in the form of diagnostics, repairs and alignment strategies. §4.3 implements this operationalization and shows that the "systematicity" of the artificial languages gets lost once smaller linguistic units are starting to combine into larger patterns. In this section I will also briefly discuss other experiments in the field in which the problem of systematicity occurs but is either overlooked or misinterpreted by the experimenter. The next section then presents the results of another experiment that uses the more complex alignment strategy of multi-level selection to overcome this problem. Three variations of multi-level selection are implemented and compared to each other in terms of systematicity and coherence. The insights of these experiments are ported to experiments involving analogy and the formation of semantic roles in §4.5. §4.6 finally offers a first step towards simulations involving the formation of syntactic cases (corresponding to stage 3 in §1.2.5). Even though stage 3 is not fully accomplished yet, this section offers a clear idea of the work that needs to be undertaken in order to form syntactic cases.

4.2 Pattern formation

4.2.1 Overview

One crucial aspect of grammaticalization (see Martin Haspelmath's definition in §3.2.5) is the evolution towards tighter structures and a lesser degree of freedom. For example, lexical items develop into more grammatical items and become part of (larger) constructions. Within these constructions or patterns, the freedom of the individual parts is restricted and depends on the pattern as a whole. This would explain why for example an allative case marker only makes sense in a motion-pattern. However, linguistic items that become part of a larger construction may still have a life on their own in their original sense, a phenomenon traditionally known as "layering" (Hopper & Traugott 1993: 124–126). For example the preposition *like* can still be used for indicating similarity while at the same time it can be used as a marker for introducing reported speech:

(1) She looks nothing *like* her father.

(2) And he was *like* "Oh that is so not true!"

In the following subsection I will briefly touch upon some phenomena of grammaticalization involving pattern formation and offer an analysis which is somewhat different from the traditional linguistic approach. I will support my analysis through other examples of patterns and idioms in language. In the next subsection, I will then offer an operationalization of my analysis in terms of diagnostics and repair strategies for the artificial agents that will be used in the experiments in this chapter.

4.2.2 Pattern formation in language

4.2.2.1 Negation in French

A very good example of the development of a lexical item into a part of a grammatical structure can be found in French negation. Traditionally, the development of negation particles (also known as "Jespersen's cycle") is defined in terms of a cycle of reanalysis – analogy (generalization) – reanalysis Hopper & Traugott (1993: 65–66):

1. Negation in French originally only involved *ne* before the verb:

(3) Il ne va.
   he NEG go.3SG.PRS
   'He doesn't go.'

2. In the context of motion verbs, *ne* could optionally be reinforced by the noun *pas* 'step':

(4) Il ne va   (pas).
   he NEG go.3SG.PRS (step)
   'He doesn't go (a step).'

3. The word *pas* is reanalyzed as a negator particle in the construction [*ne* Vmotion *pas*];

4. The particle *pas* is extended analogically to non-motion verbs as well:

(5) Il ne sait   pas.
   he NEG know.3SG.PRS NEG
   'He doesn't know.'

5. The particle *pas* is then reanalyzed as an obligatory part of the construction [*ne* V *pas*];

6. In spoken French, *ne* is reanalyzed to become optional and is eventually lost:

(6) Il sait   pas.
   he know.3SG.PRS NEG
   'He doesn't know.'

4.2.2.2 Reanalysis versus pattern formation

Reanalysis is essentially a hearer-based analysis of this developmental cycle in which the hearer interprets the underlying structure of an utterance in another way than was intended by the speaker. Reanalysis is traditionally understood as "change in the structure of an expression or class of expressions that does not involve any immediate or intrinsic modification of its surface manifestation" (Langacker 1977: 58). Even though reanalysis is a plausible mechanism for step

4 Multi-level selection and language systematicity

3, its main problem is that it is invisible from the outside. Hopper & Traugott (1993) write that for "the French negator *pas*, we would not know that reanalysis had taken place at stage [3] without the evidence of the working generalization at stage [4]" (p. 66). As Haspelmath (1998) points out, however, this means that reanalysis cannot explain how the new use of *pas* got propagated and accepted in the speech community unless all speakers are assumed to make the same reanalysis at roughly the same time, which is very implausible. As I will explain more thoroughly in §5.5.4, reanalysis needs to be accompanied by other mechanisms in order to account for the empirical data.

I propose a different and simpler mechanism for step 3 that is in line with the general approach of usage-based models of language: pattern formation. If a certain group of words occur frequently enough together, they are stored as a new unit in the linguistic inventory. This means that the language user now knows two **competing** constructions in the case of motion verbs: [*ne* V] and [*ne* Vmotion *pas*]. This approach of pattern formation may seem redundant from the point of view of inventory size, but it may optimize linguistic processing because a pattern is a "pre-compiled" chunk that is readily available for use, whereas otherwise the language user needs to compose the structure over and over again. Since pattern formation is a relatively "simple" operation for optimizing processing, we can assume within a usage-based model that most language users will do this spontaneously for all recurrent patterns in the language as opposed to a collective operation of reanalysis. Once a pattern is stored in memory, it can start a life on its own and diverge from its original usage. Steps 1–5 in the negation cycle can thus be reinterpreted as follows in a more speaker-based analysis:

1. Negation in French originally only involved *ne* before the verb:

    (7) Il ne va.
        he NEG go.3SG.PRS
        'He doesn't go.'

2. The speakers of French start to reinforce the negation particle *ne* in some situations to put more emphasis on the negation or to solve communicative problems. In the context of motion verbs, the reinforcement is achieved through the noun *pas* 'step', whereas in other contexts such as verbs of visual perception, negation is reinforced through *point* 'point':

4.2 Pattern formation

(8) Il ne va (pas).
    he NEG go.3SG.PRS (step)
    'He doesn't go (a step).'

(9) Il ne voit (point).
    he NEG see.3SG.PRS (point)
    'He doesn't see (a point).'

3. The frequent use of these reinforcement nouns leads to the creation of readily available patterns which co-exist (and compete with) the standard negation construction;

4. The new patterns are extended analogically to non-motion verbs as well and start to compete with each other and with the old negation construction for becoming the new default negation;

5. The construction [*ne* V *pas*] wins the competition and becomes the new default construction for negation. Other competitors using different particles either disappear or take up their own semantic niche (*ne ... point* 'nothing' (old-fashioned), *ne ... plus* 'no more', *ne ... rien* 'nothing', *ne ... jamais* 'never', *ne ... guère* 'almost nothing', etc.). The old negation construction gets lost except for some archaic uses in writing.

4.2.2.3 Idioms

Evidence for pattern formation as opposed to reanalysis can be found in idioms. Idiomatic expressions have always been problematic for traditional linguistic theories that take a modular approach to language and assume a sharp distinction between conventional-lexical items and systematic-syntactic rules. Faced with such problematic issues, usage-based models and particularly construction grammars "grew out of a concern to find a place for idiomatic expressions in the speaker's knowledge of a grammar of their language" (Croft & Cruse 2004: 225). Idioms range from highly idiomatic expressions to more schematic constructions (Croft & Cruse 2004: chapter 9):

(10) by and large; no can do; be that as it may; make believe; so far so good
(11) kick the bucket; pull a fast one; spill the beans
(12) to answer the door; wide awake; bright red; to blow one's nose
(13) the bigger the better; the louder you shout, the sooner they will serve you

4 Multi-level selection and language systematicity

No theory of grammaticalization that I am aware of explains idioms such as *so far so good* or *by and large* in terms of reanalysis of the words that make up the idiom. Similarly, compound nouns are given their own lexical entry rather than introducing a notion of 'synchronic layering' (Hopper & Traugott 1993: 124–126) over the original words caused by reanalysis. Also pattern formation on other levels of language (e.g. reoccurring syllables, morphemes, etc.) are never treated as synchronic layers on top of one entry in the linguistic inventory. Reanalysis is therefore used in an ad-hoc way, or as Haspelmath (1998) writes, "as one pleases" (p. 341).

By taking pattern formation seriously, meaning that many redundant copies exist in memory, a simpler alternative exists for the ad-hoc mechanism of reanalysis. Just as there is no reason for differentiating 'core case markers' from 'peripheral semantic case markers' (see §1.2.6), the language user makes no difference between fully idiomatic expressions such as *by and large* and more grammatical constructions such as [*ne ... pas*]. The only difference between them is that the more schematic constructions were extended and generalized to new uses whereas the more idiomatic expressions remained unchanged depending on communicative needs in language use and frequency effects. This usage-based approach naturally leads to the continuum of linguistic items as observed in natural languages.

One problem with the alternative hypothesis is that it is invisible from the outside just like reanalysis is. This is where computational models can prove their worth: they can **demonstrate** the consequences of each alternative hypothesis and show what kind of cognitive apparatus is needed for both. Additional evidence can then be gathered from other disciplines such as psycholinguistics to determine which cognitive architecture is most plausible. So even though computational modeling cannot predict actual language change, they can demonstrate the effects of proposed mechanisms and help to fill in the blanks when there is a lack of empirical data.

4.2.3 Operationalizing pattern formation

The above idea of pattern formation needs to be implemented in terms of diagnostics and repair strategies that make use of information that is locally available to the agents. Consider the reaction network of Figure 4.1 in which an agent used two constructions which subsequently licensed node-2 and node-3 in the network and which licenses the utterance *jack -bo push block -ka*:

Suppose that the agent is in production mode. In this case node-1 is the coupled feature structure which was licensed after unifying and merging the lexical

4.2 Pattern formation

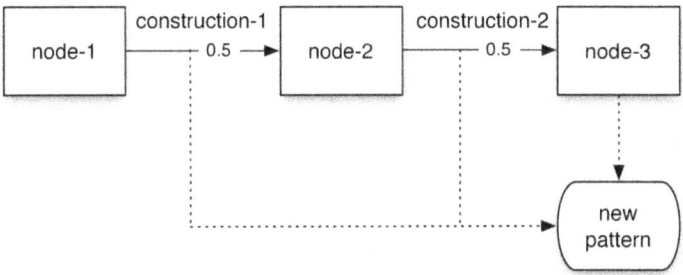

Figure 4.1: An agent's reaction network is the source for pattern formation. If the agents have to apply two constructions to license an utterance (production) or a meaning (parsing), they will create a pattern based on the applied constructions. This pattern has the same functionality as the constructions but only requires one step.

entries for *jack, push* and *block*. Next, the speaker has to unify and merge two constructions for marking the two participants of the push-event which licenses node-3. In a next step, which is not shown in the figure, the agent will unify and merge the morphological rules. As indicated in the figure, this reaction network forms the basis for a new pattern (which will be construction-3). In principle this pattern should combine the entire reaction network including the lexical entries, but for convenience's sake the agents will only make a pattern which combines the functionality of constructions 1 and 2, as shown in Figure 4.2.

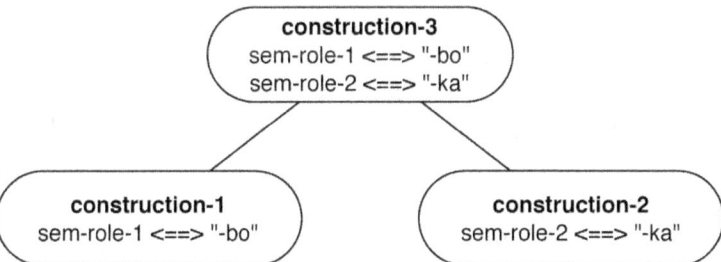

Figure 4.2: The two constructions that were used during processing are combined into a new construction. The agents keep a link between the new construction and the constructions that were used for creating it.

117

4 Multi-level selection and language systematicity

The new construction is stored in the linguistic inventory with information about its origins: the agents keep a link between the new pattern and the constructions that were used for creating it. If the speaker has to produce the same meaning again, the new construction now forms an alternative path in the reaction network. The speaker will prefer this new path because it is faster in processing (one step can be skipped) and the links between the constructions can be used for giving priority to larger constructions if they unify and merge. This new reaction network is illustrated in Figure 4.3.

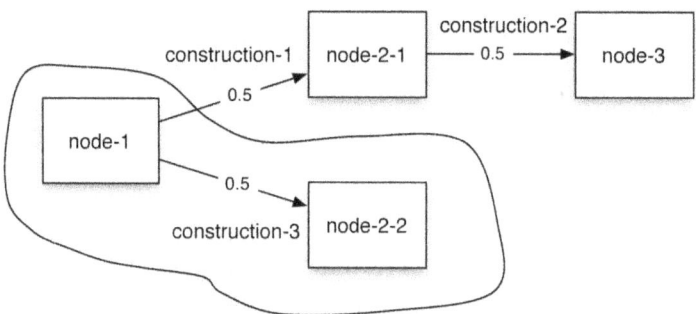

Figure 4.3: The new construction now offers the agent an alternative path in the reaction network. Since the new pattern yields the same coupled feature structure as node-3 in only one step, it is faster and therefore preferred. The links between the three constructions are used to give larger patterns priority if they unify and merge.

Apart from creating the new pattern, not much needs to be changed in the linguistic inventory apart from the fact that the agents have to link the new construction to the lexical entries that are compatible with it. The agents will not do this in one sweep but postpone this task until processing: lexical entries are only linked to the new construction instance by instance if this is required during a language game. The mechanism works entirely the same: the agent wants to unify and merge two constructions and wants to optimize processing by creating a pattern. This time, however, no new pattern needs to be created because there is already one. The pattern thus extends its use to a new verb as well. The newly-made construction looks as follows:

```
<Construction: construction-3
((?top-unit
    (sem-subunits (== ?unit-a ?unit-b ?unit-c)))
```

4.2 Pattern formation

```
(?unit-a
   (sem-frame (== (sem-role-1 ?unit-b ?obj-x)
                  (sem-role-2 ?unit-c ?obj-y))))
(?unit-b
   (referent ?obj-x))
(?unit-c
   (referent ?obj-y))
((J ?unit-b NIL)
   (sem-role sem-role-1))
((J ?unit-c NIL)
   (sem-role sem-role-2)))
<==>
((?top-unit
   (syn-subunits (== ?unit-a ?unit-b ?unit-c)))
(?unit-a
   (syn-frame (== (syn-role-1 ?unit-b)
                  (syn-role-2 ?unit-c))))
(?unit-b
   (syn-role syn-role-1))
(?unit-c
   (syn-role syn-role-2)))>
```

To summarize, the agents are equipped with the following diagnostic and repair strategy in all the experiments in this chapter:

1. **Diagnostic**: If two constructions are used together for licensing a node in the network, report an opportunity for optimizing processing (both for production and parsing);

2. **Repair strategy**: If there is a problem of processing effort:
   a) If a larger construction already exists for the same mapping, create a link between the lexical entry and the construction;
   b) Else combine the two constructions into a new construction and keep a link between them.

During processing, the link between constructions is used for giving priority to larger constructions. They can also be used for consolidation as I will show in sections 4.4 and 4.5. There are, however, no inheritance links: all relevant information is stored in the constructions themselves and no additional aspects are inherited from other constructions.

4.3 Experiment 1: individual selection without analogy

4.3.1 Overview

Before immediately picking up the experiments where the previous chapter left off, the influence of the diagnostic and repair strategy for pattern formation is first tested for stage 2 in the development of case markers: the invention and adoption of specific markers.

4.3.2 Experimental set-up

The experimental set-up for experiment 1 is entirely the same as the one in baseline experiment 2c but this time the new diagnostic and repair strategy for pattern formation are added to the agents. The set-up can be briefly summarized as follows:

- The population consists of 10 agents that engage in description games;

- The meaning space is the same one as detailed in Table 3.2 and all event types occur with the same frequency;

- The agents have two diagnostics: detecting unexpressed variable equalities and the new diagnostic detecting whether two constructions were applied during processing;

- The agents have two repair strategies: one for inventing and learning verb-specific markers and one for combining them into a larger construction;

- The agents use an alignment strategy of direct competition which I will further call 'individual selection'. This means that the hearer increases the confidence scores of successfully applied constructions by 0.1 and decreases the scores of their direct competitors by 0.1. The speaker does not perform score updating.

From the above follows that the agents will have to create and converge on one construction for each possible combination of meanings. There are thirty individual participant roles that need a single-participant construction, eighteen combinations of two participant roles and three combinations of three participant roles. Since the agents have no analogy, the target number of constructions should be 51 (the sum of all these possibilities). All the combinations can be verified in the Appendix.

4.3 Experiment 1: individual selection without analogy

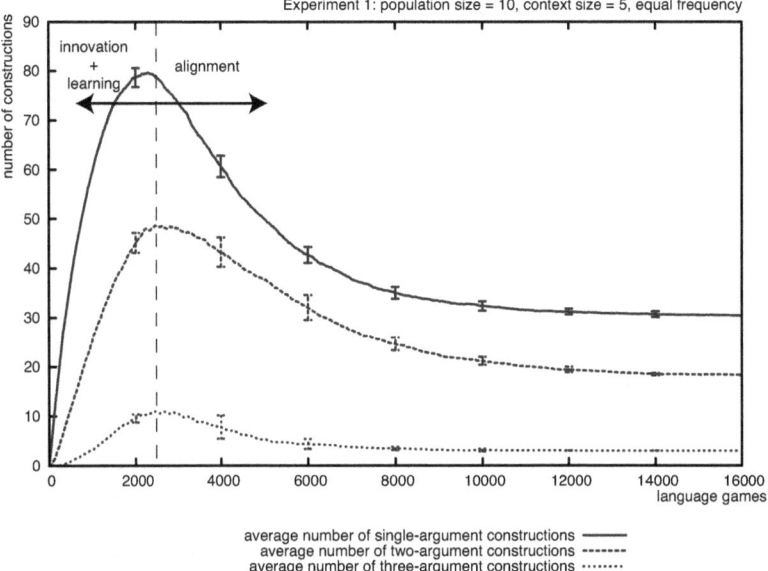

Figure 4.4: This graph shows the average number of constructions in a population of ten agents in experiment 1. In this set-up the agents succeed in converging on an optimal inventory size – given their cognitive abilities – of 30 single-argument constructions, 18 two-argument constructions and 3 three-argument constructions. The graph here indicates that there is still an average of 19 two-argument constructions but this competition also gets resolved if more language games are played.

4.3.3 Results and discussion

4.3.3.1 Results

The experimental set-up was tested in ten series of 16.000 language games. By looking at the same measures as in the baseline experiments, the simulations seem to yield successful results at first sight. Figure 4.4 plots the average number of constructions in the population. Here, the agents have almost reached the optimal state in terms of linguistic inventory. Only in the case of two-argument constructions there are additional language games needed for deciding on the competition between one or two surviving constructions. Acquiring the constructions happens quite fast (in less than 3.000 games), but alignment takes much more time than was needed in the baseline experiments. This is due to

4 Multi-level selection and language systematicity

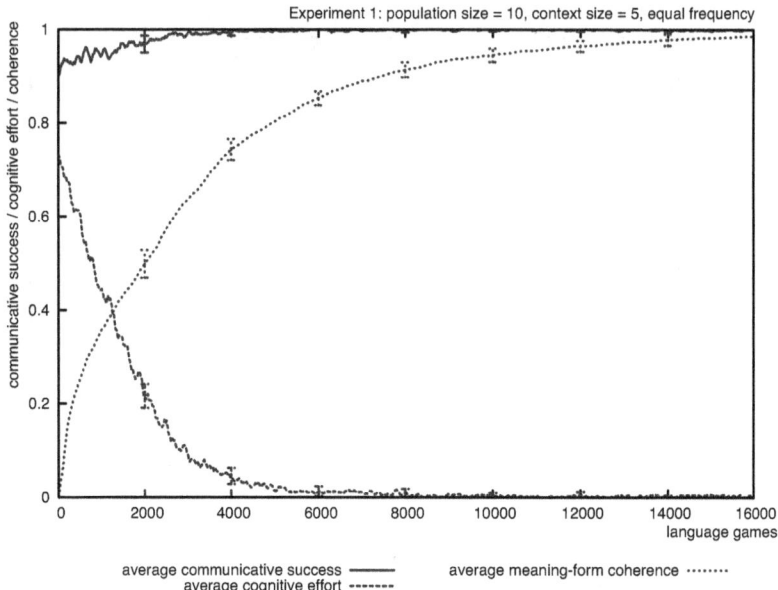

Figure 4.5: This graph shows average communicative success, cognitive effort and meaning-form coherence in a population of ten agents in experiment 1. The results show that the agents succeed in reaching 100% communicative success and reducing the cognitive effort needed for communication. Meaning-form coherence reaches almost 100% with only competition between one or two forms that is still undecided.

the individual selection alignment strategy: if a pattern was used, only competing patterns are punished through lateral inhibition. The individual markers or rather the single-argument constructions they occur in are not considered during consolidation.

The long alignment period is also illustrated in Figure 4.5, which displays average communicative success, cognitive effort and meaning-form coherence. The fact that communicative success rapidly rises to 100% within 4.000 language games and that cognitive effort drops to zero between 6.000 and 8.000 language games suggests that the agents have learned all the variations floating around in their population. However, meaning-form coherence takes much longer to rise to its maximum which is again due to the alignment strategy. Coherence reaches almost 100% after 16.000 games with only competition going on for one or two cases of two-argument constructions. This competition will in the end also be resolved after additional language games.

4.3 Experiment 1: individual selection without analogy

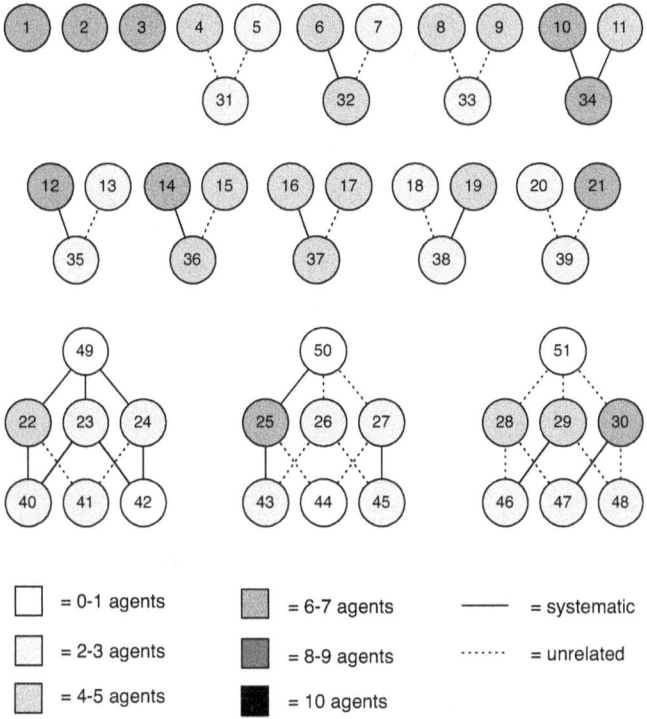

Experiment 1: snapshot after 1.000 language games - individual selection

Figure 4.6: This diagram gives a snapshot of the average coherence in a population of 10 agents after 1.000 language games using the direct selection alignment strategy. Each circle stands for a particular meaning (see the Appendix), for example circles 4 and 5 stand for 'appear-1' and 'appear-2'. The lines between circles means that the meanings combine into compositional meanings, for example circle 31 means the combination 'appear-1 appear-2'. The darker the circle is coloured, the more agents prefer the same case marker(s) for covering this meaning. A full line between circles means that both meanings are covered using the same markers (= systematic), a dotted line means that a different form is preferred for the same meaning (= unrelated). The diagram shows that for most meanings only half of the population prefer the same form and that in many cases there is no systematic choice for a certain case marker.

123

4 Multi-level selection and language systematicity

The longer alignment period is however not the most fundamental problem with the artificial languages that are formed by the agents. A closer examination of them shows that all meaning-form mappings that they agree on are totally arbitrary. The problem is illustrated in Figures 4.6 and 4.7 which give a snapshot of convergence and coherence in one simulation after 1.000 and 7.000 language games respectively. Each meaning or combination of meanings (see the Appendix) is represented as a circle. For example, the meaning 'approach-1' is represented as circle 4 and meaning 'approach-2' is represented as circle 5. Lines between circles indicate that the meaning of one circle is a combination of the meanings of the other circles. For example, circle 31 combines 'approach-1' and 'approach-2'. The colour of the circles represents the number of agents that prefer the most frequent form in the population for that particular word. A white circle means that there is either no form yet for this meaning or that there is no form which is preferred by more than one agent. A black circle means that all ten agents prefer the same form for this meaning. If all the circles are black, the agents have reached 100% convergence. If the lines between the circles are full lines, the same participant role is expressed by the same marker across constructions. If however the line is dotted, there is a different form for the same meaning.

This can best be illustrated through an example. The circle for meaning 4 (approach-1) indicates that there are 4 or 5 agents in the population which prefer the same form for marking this participant role at this stage of the simulation. For circles 5 (approach-2) and 31 (approach-1 approach-2), there are two or three agents that prefer the same form. The dotted lines between the circles, however, indicate that the most frequent pattern for circle 31 uses different markers than the single-argument constructions for circles 4 and 5:

(14) jack -lich   approach
 jack approach-1 approach
 'Jack approaches (someone)'.

(15) jill -sut   approach
 jill approach-2 approach
 '(Someone) approaches Jill'.

(16) jill -xa   jack -zuih   approach
 jill approach-2 jack approach-1 approach
 'Jack approaches Jill'.

4.3 Experiment 1: individual selection without analogy

Figure 4.7 shows that after 7.000 language games, the agents have almost converged on a form for every meaning, but the problem of systematicity remains: in half of the cases, a different case marker is winning the competition on the level of single-argument constructions than the one(s) winning on the other levels. The figure also shows that in most of the cases where there is no systematic use of a form for the same meaning, convergence is also still not complete. This is in contrast to the meanings which (accidentally) arrived at the same form across constructions. Here we see mostly black circles meaning that all agents prefer the same convention.

4.3.3.2 Discussion

The results clearly indicate that the agents are not capable of constructing a systematic language. The reason for this is that all constructions are basically treated as independent linguistic items. This means that once a larger pattern is created, it starts living its own life without influencing or being influenced by the constructions that were used to create it. This results in some case markers losing the competition for marking a certain participant role on the level of single-argument constructions but still becoming the most successful one as part of a larger pattern. In all the simulations, this happened in 40 to 60% of the cases (see Figure 4.10).

The fact that in more than half of the cases the same marker wins the competition on all levels is due to the small meaning space of the experiment and the fact that patterns are always created by combining the most successful constructions at a given point in the simulation. In fact, the agents can continue to create new patterns for a certain combination of participant roles even if they already know other patterns for it. For example, it may happen that on a lower level the average confidence scores of a new combination becomes more successful than the confidence score of the patterns. In this case the agents will still innovate which gives a slight advantage to those patterns that are in line with the most successful constructions of a lower level. As the results show, however, this is not enough.

Since natural languages are also not fully regular, it is important to see whether the lack of systematicity in the experiments is relevant for the many exceptions and sub-regularities found in natural languages. The answer is no: for most if not all irregular forms and sub-regularities in natural language, either a systematic origin can be found through diachronic changes or through external pressures such as language contact. For example, the -ed-participle in English did not manage to extend its use to all past tenses as can be observed in irregular verbs such

4 *Multi-level selection and language systematicity*

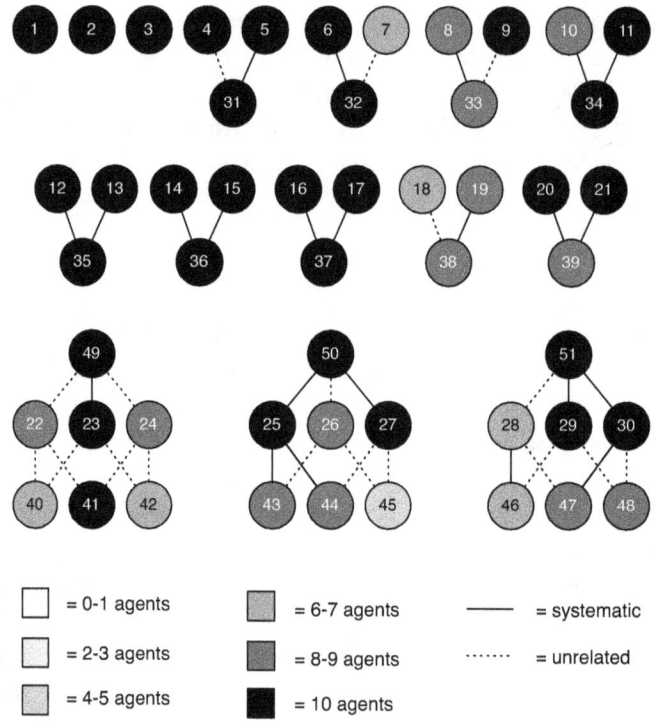

Experiment 1: snapshot after 7.000 language games - individual selection

Figure 4.7: This diagram gives a snapshot of the average coherence in a population of 10 agents after 7.000 language games using the direct selection alignment strategy. The agents have reached convergence for most meanings by now, but these form-meaning mappings are not always systematically related to each other. For example, the meanings related to 49 were pretty consistent in their meaning-form mappings after 1.000 games, but have now become totally unrelated to each other: for each possible combination a new form is introduced to cover the same meaning. In all the cases where there is no systematicity, the convergence is not complete yet.

as *to sing* and *to give*. These strong verbs are however remnants of completely regular classes of verbs in Proto-Indo-European that were able to survive thanks to their high token frequency. Despite all sociological factors, historical incidents, language contact, and other kinds of exceptions, natural languages succeed remarkably well in developing systematicity spanning over many constructions, as for example word order in English. Given the abstractions and scaffolds of the present experiments, the agents should thus be capable of developing a fully systematic language without any problems.

This leaves us the question of how systematicity can be achieved. As said before, all systematic form-meaning mappings have been formed by accident due to the small world and the nature of the innovation mechanism. For true systematicity, however, the agents need to be able to recognize relations between constructions rather than treating them as a list of independent units. This would mean that if a particular construction is successful, its systematically related constructions should also (perhaps indirectly) benefit from its success. In §4.4 I will introduce a biologically inspired mechanism that can be exploited to achieve this effect: multi-level selection.

4.3.4 The problem of systematicity in other work

As to my knowledge, the problem of systematicity has never been reported before in the field of the origins and evolution of language. This does not mean, however, that the problem never existed. In this section, I will give a brief overview of some prior work in the field in which the problem was either overlooked or in which it could not occur due to experimental assumptions.

4.3.4.1 Exemplar-based simulations

One computational simulation which is closely related to the work in this book is presented by Batali (2002). Batali investigates how a multi-agent population can form a recursive communication system by using exemplars stored in memory. This work can be categorized as a 'problem-solving model' because these exemplars have to be agreed upon in locally situated interactions. Each exemplar has a confidence score which is increased and decreased according to similar lateral inhibition dynamics as in the simulations of the previous section. The type of learner is thus the same one as the agents in this book: they build their language instance by instance in a bottom-up and redundant fashion. Batali's agents only keep exemplars and all generalization in the model is captured by directly ma-

4 Multi-level selection and language systematicity

nipulating these exemplars during processing. Figure 4.8 gives an example of an exemplar composed of two smaller ones (Batali 2002: exemplar 5.1.2.a).

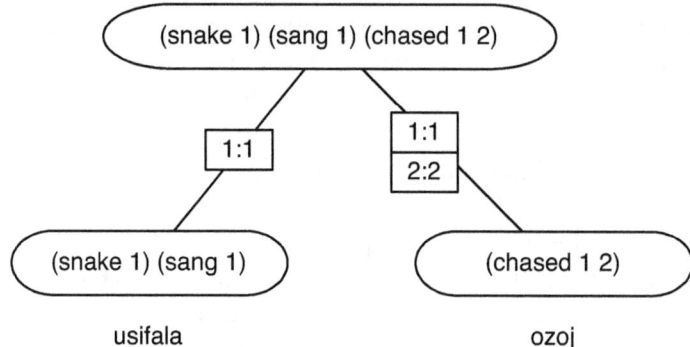

Figure 4.8: A complex exemplar from Batali (2002). The exemplar features a compositional meaning with 'argument maps' to the smaller exemplars that take care of variable equalities in the meaning.

Batali does not use event-specific variables as I do in this book but assumes a simple three-way contrast between arguments 1, 2 and 3. For example the meaning ((snake 1) (sang 1)) translates to something like 'the snake sang', whereas ((snake 1) (sang 2)) would mean something like 'there was a snake and something sang.' Event structure is stored immediately in the exemplar but can be overridden by argument maps between complex exemplars and their subcomponents. For example, the argument map '1:2' translates a meaning like (rat 1) to (rat 2). These argument maps are also stored as part of the complex exemplar. Apart from these argument maps between complex exemplars and their components, all exemplars are unrelated and listed in the memory.

The agents then engage in a series of description games. They are able to invent new words for new meanings and they are capable of combining existing words into larger patterns or breaking up a pattern again into smaller parts. The ultimate goal of the agents is two-fold: (a) agree on a shared lexicon for all the single meanings (e.g. cat, fox, chase, etc.) and (b) agree on a way to mark event structure through the argument maps (i.e. marking the difference between arguments 1, 2 and 3). The simulations make use of a single generation of agents.

The results indicate that the agents gradually reach communicative success and that they agree on the same exemplars. Goal (a) is therefore definitely reached. However, the results show that event structure is not always marked in the same way: all the simulations end up using specific ordering for each exemplar (even

4.3 Experiment 1: individual selection without analogy

though they may involve the same meanings) and using 'empty' words that accidentally evolved into markers for argument mappings. The agents thus do not succeed in agreeing on a systematic way of distinguishing participant '1' from participants '2' and '3'. The agents thus cannot generalize argument mapping to new predicates such as (give 1 2 3) and have to negotiate event structure for each word separately. This lack of systematicity is not noted by Batali as a problem and the use of the empty words is wrongly interpreted as corresponding to argument markers in natural languages.

4.3.4.2 Probabilistic grammars

Another experiment in which the systematicity problem is overlooked is reported by De Pauw (2002: chapter 10). De Pauw investigates how rudimentary principles of syntax can emerge from distributional aspects of communication rather than from the interface between syntax and semantics. This exclusive focus on syntax is different from the work in this book (even though some semantics is smuggled into De Pauw's simulations in the disctinction between animate and non-animate objects which results in different distributional patterns). Similar assumptions to this book are the heavy use of memory (even more so by De Pauw), a bottom-up and redundant formation of the language and a predefined lexicon in order to focus exclusively on the topic of interest. The population in De Pauw's simulations is dynamic in the sense that there is a generational turn-over, but no linguistic information is transmitted genetically from one generation to the next.

The agents engage in a series of language games in which they communicate about objects or events. If there are several objects, the agents can choose between six word orders: SVO, SOV, VSO, VOS, OSV or OVS. De Pauw therefore does not distinguish between verb-specific participant roles, but only assumes a two-way contrast between the subject (S) and the object (O). The agents start without any preference for a particular word order so variation naturally occurs in the population. The alignment strategy of the agents is simply storing bigrams or frequencies of co-occurrences and performing statistical induction on top of those bigrams (De Pauw 2002: 362):

During the simulations, the agents rapidly converge on fixed word order on simple relations. However, as De Pauw notes, there are no general tendencies in terms of a general word order. Each 'verb' rather has its own preferred ordering. For more complex relations, the agents do not always reach coherence. De Pauw concludes that the agents therefore reside in a local maximum and that they evolve from one local maximum of convergence to the next. De Pauw argues

4 Multi-level selection and language systematicity

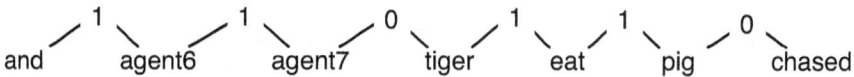

Figure 4.9: The agents in De Pauw (2002) store co-occurrence frequencies and use these bigram-probabilities to decide on a preferred ordering.

that this is not a shortcoming of the model but rather its greatest asset: whereas other models in the field are looking for the state of convergence, "language itself never converges and constantly adapts to a changing environment and seems to be driven by chaotic elements, introducing a large degree of randomness in language both from a synchronic, as well as a diachronic point of view" (p. 378).

There are however no such chaotic elements present in De Pauw's model which should prevent the agents from reaching complete coherence. The degree of randomness in his simulations seems to stem from the systematicity problem: by only looking at bigram probabilities, it is to be expected that there is an arbitrary word order which is verb-specific. In the case of more complex predicates, the preferred order depends on a combination of various bigrams which increases the randomness because the probabilities of these bigrams are constantly changing so it becomes much harder to agree on a fixed order for these complex meanings. De Pauw dismisses the possibility that the degree of convergence is the maximum that can be expected from the population, but this is in fact the only correct conclusion. Given the cognitive capabilities of the agents, convergence could only increase if the input would be more structured. In certain machine learning tasks, there is already a lot of structure present in the learning data so bigrams can be successfully used for making some predictions. In the case of language formation, however, agents have to start from scratch so there is no structure spanning multiple levels yet that can be induced.

De Pauw's concluding remark is that it is empirically impossible to know whether the agents succeed in "expressing the proper (agent, patient) relationship, or if it is just a side-effect of beneficial bigram probability distributions" (p. 376). I would argue, however, that since the agents are not endowed with the capacity of relating bigrams to each other but solely rely on these probabilities, all tendencies in word order are in fact a side-effect of the bigrams. The conclusion is that De Pauw (2002), just like Batali (2002), misinterpreted experimental results because the problem of systematicity was not noticed.

4.3.4.3 Iterated Learning Models

So far I only discussed models that featured lazy learners: agents which postpone generalization until processing time and which shape their language in a step-by-step fashion. As opposed to lazy learners there are 'eager learners'. Eager learners try to look for generalizations (and abstractions) before it is actually needed in processing and work on the complete inventory. Eager learners typically discard the examples that can be derived from a rule and thus try to optimize the inventory size. If the problem of systematicity also occurs with eager learners, then we know that the problem is not exclusive to the usage-based approach proposed in this book.

In the field of artificial language evolution, especially Iterated Learning Models feature agents that loop through their inventory after each interaction in order to make abstractions. In §5.2 I will draw a thorough comparison between my experimental results and those of Moy (2006), who investigated the same topic using the Iterated Learning Model so I will not go into details here. As a quick preview, I can already give away one of the conclusions which is that the problem of systematicity also occurs in Iterated Learning Models. This does not only happen in Moy's experiments, but also in the simulations reported by Kirby (2000) and Smith, Kirby & Brighton (2003) even though these models feature complete meaning transfer and a population of only two agents.

The conclusion is the same as for the other simulations reported in this section: the problem of systematicity goes by unnoticed in most Iterated Learning Models, but becomes very apparent in Moy (2006). The problem occurs for the same reasons as in all the other experiments: the agents only behave 'systematic' during innovation and learning, but then treat all linguistic items as an unstructured list of unrelated elements. So either there is no adequate model yet that avoids the problem of systematicity or the problem is **not restricted to the type of learner**. In the latter case, the problem seems to be caused by the fact that the linguistic inventory is unstructured.

4.3.4.4 Other models

Finally, there are many models that investigate certain aspects of grammar in which the problem of systematicity does not occur such as De Beule (2007); De Beule & Bergen (2006); Nowak & Krakauer (1999); Steels & Wellens (2006); etc. I will take the simulations by De Beule & Bergen (2006) as an example of why these models don't have the problem. The conclusions of this brief discussion extend to all the other models on grammar as well.

4 Multi-level selection and language systematicity

De Beule & Bergen investigate the competition between holistic and compositional utterances. In case of compositional utterances, one could expect the problem of systematicity to pop up, but it doesn't. The reason is that De Beule & Bergen designed their experiment in such a way that the agents had prior knowledge about what kind of categories and constructions to expect: individual words are immediately tagged with a certain syntactic category and grammatical constructions are fully schematic from the start. One construction can hence be used for all possible combinations of competing individual words that are tagged with the same category and remains agnostic as to which words should win the competition. The experiment thus made a clear separation between the lexicon on the one hand and grammatical constructions on the other; and it did not offer the agents the possibility of in-between patterns or idioms.

This is not a criticism of the model per se: given the fact that De Beule & Bergen only intended to focus on competition between holistic and compositional utterances, the design choice is justified in which the competition dynamics can be clearly investigated on each level. As such the experiment can be interpreted as investigating a prerequisite of grammar rather than the emergence of *actual* grammar. For the scope of this book, this experimental design is thus not warranted: the barrier between fully idiomatic items and fully schematic items needs to be broken down.

4.4 Experiment 2: multi-level selection without analogy

4.4.1 Overview

In the previous section I demonstrated the problem of systematicity that occurs during the emergence of a language if the agents treat all entries in their linguistic inventory as unrelated individuals and if their language comprises multiple layers of organization. An alignment strategy involving the individual selection of constructions leads to completely arbitrary form-meaning pairs whereas natural languages show greater cohesion and a higher degree of systematically related constructions. Even in idioms such as *he kicked the bucket*, some degree of schematicity is present such as the conjugation of the verb. The agents therefore need a new alignment strategy in which the success of one construction may have an impact on the success of other related constructions.

In this section I will present an experiment which features new alignment strategies that are inspired by the notion of 'multi-level selection' in evolutionary biology (Wilson & Sober 1994). Multi-level selection (formerly known as 'group

4.4 Experiment 2: multi-level selection without analogy

selection') acknowledges the fact that groups or other higher-level entities can act as 'vehicles' for selection. In this view, not all aspects of groups are reduced to by-products of individual (and usually selfish) interactions. In other words, being part of a group can increase the selectionist advantage of individuals.

Natural languages are clear instances of organisms with a hierarchical functional organization which can be conceived as 'groups within groups'. Competition is going on at multiple levels of this organization: between synonyms for becoming dominant in expressing a particular meaning, between idiomatic patterns that group a number of words, between different syntactic and semantic categories competing for a role in the grammar, between ways in which a syntactic category is marked, etc. Multi-level selections therefore seems to be readily applicable to language as well.

4.4.2 Experimental set-up

The most important requirement for implementing multi-level selection is that the agents have to be capable themselves of recognizing relations between linguistic items. This is in fact not so difficult to achieve: in §4.2.3 I explained that the agents keep a link between larger constructions and the constructions that were used for creating them. These links can now be used for implementing multi-level selection. Three different alignment strategies have been implemented for comparison:

- **Top-down selection**: if the game was a success, the hearer will not only reward the constructions that were applied during processing, but also all the related constructions on a lower level. The confidence scores of all the competitors of these constructions are decreased through lateral inhibition.

- **Bottom-up selection**: If the game was a success, the hearer will not only increase the score of the applied constructions, but also the scores of all the related constructions on a higher level. All the competing constructions are punished.

- **Multi-level selection**: If the game was a success, the hearer will not only increase the score of the applied constructions, but also the scores of all related constructions. All the competing constructions are punished through lateral inhibition.

4 Multi-level selection and language systematicity

Retrieving related constructions is performed recursively. For example, if a three-argument construction was applied using the top-down selection alignment strategy, its two sub-components are retrieved (a two-argument and a single-argument construction) as well as the two sub-components of the two-argument construction. The hearer thus increases the scores of five constructions. The competitors are all the direct competitors of these five constructions.

During processing, only the scores of the applied constructions are taken into account and not of the whole group of related constructions. The group selection dynamics therefore only matter during consolidation. The rest of the set-up is the same as for experiment 1.

4.4.3 Results and discussion

The three alignment strategies were compared to each other and to experiment 1 in ten series of 10.000 language games.

4.4.3.1 Results

Figure 4.10 illustrates the amount of systematicity in all four alignment strategies. The graph shows that the three alignment strategies involving multiple levels all improve on the baseline of individual selection of experiment 1. With the alignment strategy of individual selection, systematicity fluctuates between 40 and 60% depending on how 'lucky' the agents were. The behaviour of the other three strategies is much more consistent over the ten series. The graph shows that bottom-up selection allows the agents to improve systematicity to 80% but there they are faced with 'frozen accidents' as well. The top-down selection improves systematicity even further and allows the agents to reach full systematicity in some of the runs. However, in most cases, there were still two or three unsystematic patterns left. Only the multi-level selection strategy led to full systematicity in all the simulations.

Since the measure of systematicity only looks at the most frequent forms floating in a population, it needs to be complemented with meaning-form coherence to verify whether *all* the agents converge on the same preferences. Figure 4.11 therefore compares the performance of the four alignment strategies in terms of coherence. From the results of experiment 1 we already knew that in the case of individual selection, alignment takes longer than 10.000 language games. The coherence line for bottom-up selection runs almost parallel with it and does not improve on it in terms of convergence speed. The only two strategies that reach convergence within 10.000 games are top-down and multi-level selection. Full

4.4 Experiment 2: multi-level selection without analogy

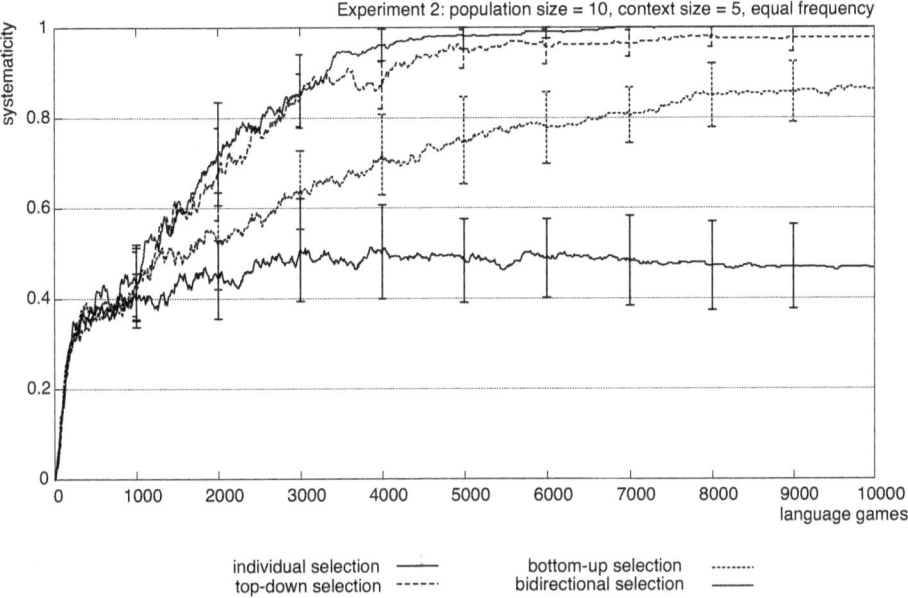

Figure 4.10: This graph compares the performance in terms of systematicity of four experimental set-ups. systematicity fluctuates around 50% in the baseline case where there is only individual selection (experiment 1). With the bottom-up selection strategy the agents improve the systematicity rate to 80% but then get stuck. Top-down selection leads to full systematicity in some of the runs, but most of the simulations feature some 'frozen accidents' as well. Only the multi-level selection strategy leads to full systematicity in all the series after about 7.000 language games.

coherence in the case of top-down selection however does not mean full systematicity, as was shown in Figure 4.10.

Figure 4.12 shows the average number of constructions in the ten series involving the alignment strategy of multi-level selection. The graph confirms the fact that the agents converge significantly faster on an optimal number of constructions than in experiment 1. At the peak of competing constructions, there are about 60 single-argument constructions, 30 two-argument constructions and 6 three-argument constructions or an average of two competing constructions for each possible meaning. This is much less than in experiment 1 (see Figure 4.4) which featured peaks of 80 single-argument, 50 two-argument and 10

4 Multi-level selection and language systematicity

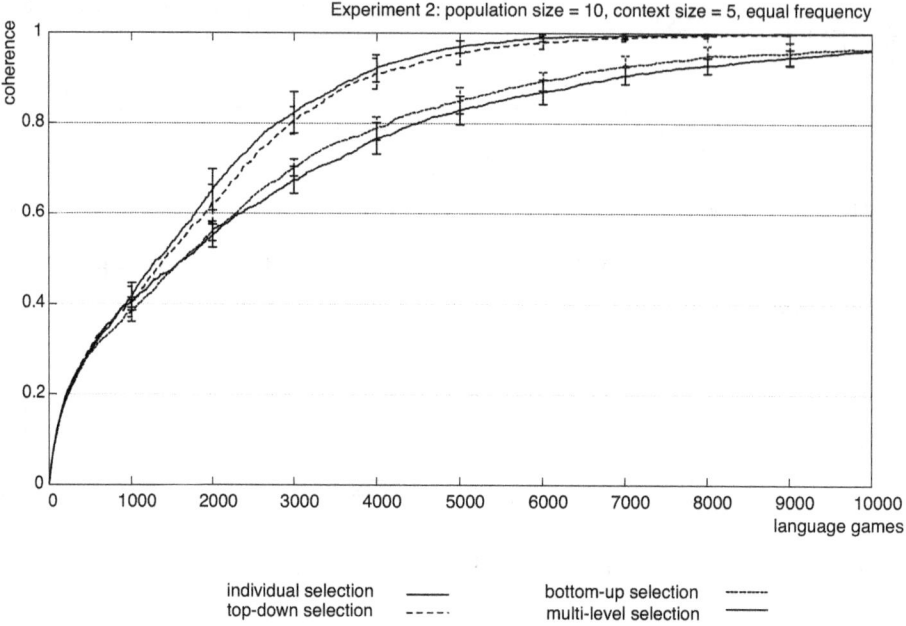

Figure 4.11: Since the systematicity graph only takes the most frequent forms into account, meaning-form coherence has to be checked in order to verify whether all the agents have converged on the same form-meaning pairs. We see that after 10.000 language games, only the top-down and the multi-level selection alignment strategies have already reached complete coherence. Multi-level selection slightly outperforms top-down selection but not significantly so. In the case of bottom-up and individual selection, the agents need additional language games for reaching coherence.

three-argument constructions. Also alignment happens much faster: with multi-level selection, the agents align after 6.000 games as opposed to 14.000 language games or more if the agents use individual selection.

Figures 4.13 and 4.14 offer a snapshot of the most frequent forms in a population using the multi-level selection alignment strategy. Both snapshots confirm the results indicated by the coherence and systematicity graphs. Figure 4.13 shows already much more dark grey circles than Figure 4.6 featuring individual

4.4 Experiment 2: multi-level selection without analogy

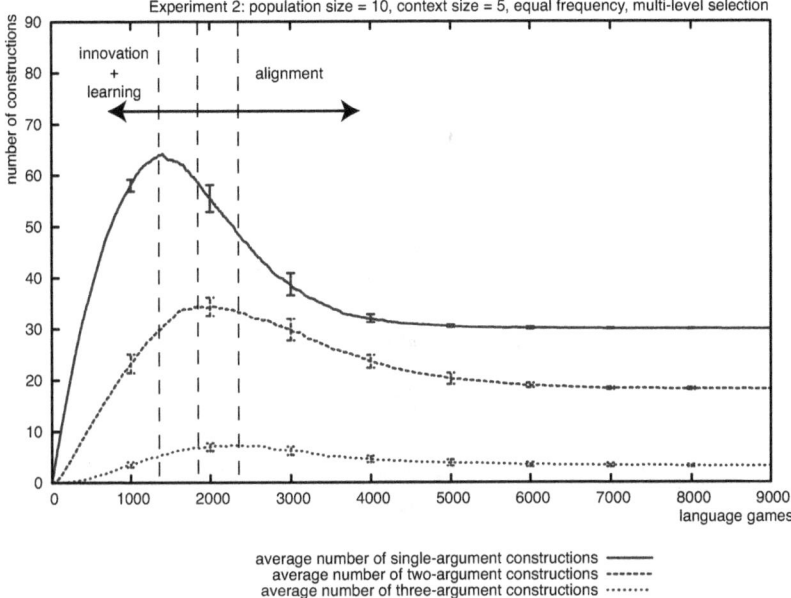

Figure 4.12: This graph shows the average number of constructions known by an agent using the multi-level selection alignment strategy. Compared to individual selection, multi-level selection allows the agents to discard competitors much more rapidly: there are significantly less variations floating around in the population. For example, the peak of single-argument constructions is about 60 instead of 80 in experiment 1. Also the alignment phase happens much faster.

selection, indicating that for most meanings there is already a majority of agents preferring the same form. The preferred forms are also to a higher degree systematically related to each other than in experiment 1, even for the more complex patterns. All black circles in the Figure feature meanings which are related to other meanings, which suggests that multi-level selection indeed favours groups of related items. The snapshot in Figure 4.14 only shows black circles, which means that all agents in the population prefer the same form for that particular meaning. There are also only full lines between the circles indicating that the same case markers are consistently used across patterns. This result significantly improves over the earlier results with individual selection.

4 Multi-level selection and language systematicity

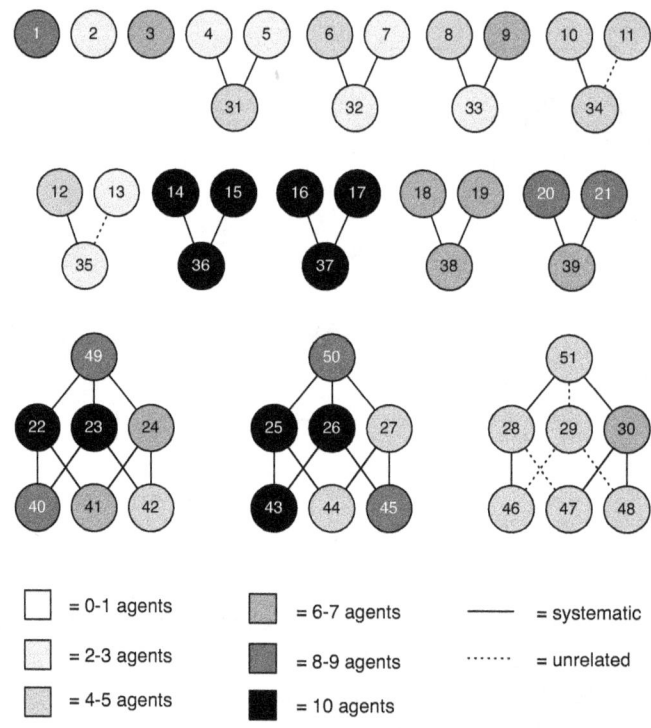

Experiment 2d: snapshot after 1.000 language games - multi-level selection

Figure 4.13: This diagram gives a snapshot of the average coherence in a population of 10 agents after 1.000 language games using the multi-level selection alignment strategy. Compared to the simulations using direct selection, the agents seem to be converging more rapidly on meaning-form mappings and have already settled on 11 of them. Whereas there was no convergence at all yet for the more complex meanings 49–51 in the simulations using the direct selection alignment strategy, here they are already shared by a majority of the population. This suggests that multi-level selection speeds up the convergence dynamics significantly especially for related meanings. For the meanings in the bottom right, there is less systematicity and hence convergence takes longer time.

4.4 Experiment 2: multi-level selection without analogy

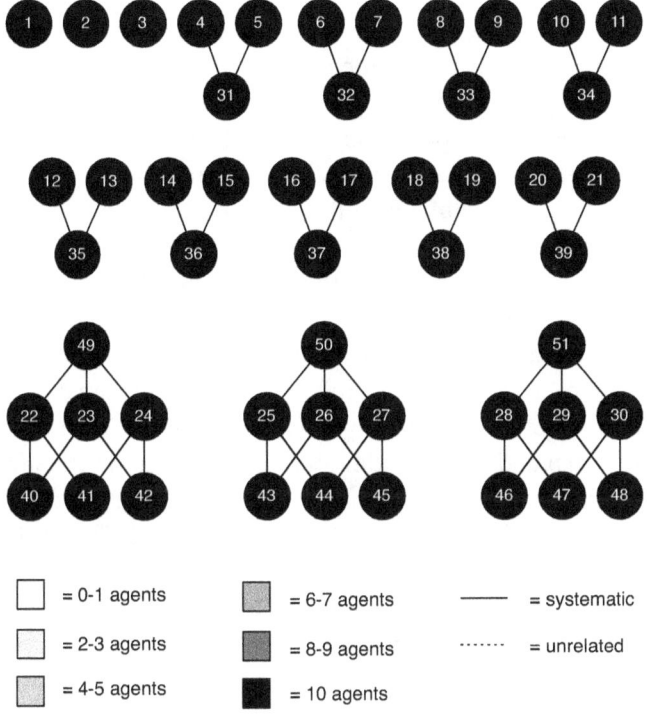

Experiment 2d: snapshot after 7.000 language games - multi-level selection

Figure 4.14: This diagram gives a snapshot of the average coherence in a population of 10 agents after 7.000 language games using the multi-level selection alignment strategy. All the circles are black which means that the entire population prefers the same meaning-form mappings. The language is also fully systematic so the agents have converged on 30 case markers which can be combined into 51 different constructions. The results indicate that even for instance-based learners/innovators systematicity can be reached by keeping a link between newly acquired constructions and the constructions that were used for learning or creating them.

4 Multi-level selection and language systematicity

4.4.3.2 Discussion

The results show that the agents reach full systematicity if each level in the linguistic inventory can have an influence on the competition in other levels. It is now important to understand why this is the case and why the other alignment strategies did not yield full systematicity.

First of all, bottom-up selection doesn't improve on the results of experiment 1 in terms of convergence speed and it doesn't lead to a systematic mapping of meaning to form across patterns. A closer examination of the the alignment strategy reveals that the relatively high systematicity of 80% is due to the higher frequency of single-argument constructions. The frequent use of these constructions each time has repercussions for the competition between larger constructions whereas this is not the case in the other direction. If there would be more patterns than single-argument constructions, the improvement would therefore be less high. The patterns that resist the bottom-up selection can do so because the competition is not fully decided yet on a lower level (each time reinforcing competing patterns) and there is additional competition on the level of the patterns themselves which may have different winners than those on lower levels. In the end, though, the bottom-up strategy should lead to full systematicity but only very slowly and because the smaller constructions are more frequent.

The top-down strategy is affected by frequency as well: competition between the larger constructions has significant impact on lower levels because it can increase the scores of up to six constructions while at the same time punishing all competitors. However, since the smaller constructions are actually more frequent than the larger ones, some divergent competition pathways may resist this influence from the patterns and survive nevertheless. As the results indicate, this in fact happens in most of the simulations. Top-down selection thus improves systematicity significantly, but it is affected by the frequency of the various levels of linguistic items and it is therefore no guarantee of full systematicity.

Finally, the agents can achieve full systematicity through multi-level selection. This strategy allows the competition of each level to influence the competition on others and given its n-directionality, it is not (or less) dependent on differences in frequency. Moreover, the agents do not need to differentiate between a 'higher' and a 'lower' level but can treat all links between constructions on equal footing. The results of experiment 2 confirm earlier results on multi-level selection and systematicity reported by Steels, van Trijp & Wellens (2007). In these experiments, which involved a scale-up in convergence space, multi-level selection outperforms the other strategies even more significantly.

4.5 Experiment 3: multi-level selection with analogy

4.5.1 Overview

Similarly to the previous experiments, experiment 3 investigates how baseline experiment 3 can be extended with a diagnostic and repair for pattern formation. Since the previous experiments identified the problem of systematicity, experiment 3 first of all needs to verify whether the conclusions of the second experiment also hold for the new set-up in which the agents are capable of performing analogical reasoning over events. I will then report an experiment that adapts the algorithm for multi-level selection to the token-frequency alignment strategy of baseline experiment 3d (see §3.5).

4.5.2 Experimental set-up

Experiment 3 features the same experimental set-up as baseline experiment 3 with the addition of a diagnostic and repair strategy for pattern formation. To summarize:

- The population consists of 10 agents that engage in description games;
- The meaning space is the same one as detailed in Table 3.2 and all event types occur with the same frequency;
- The agents have two diagnostics: detecting unexpressed variable equalities and the new diagnostic detecting whether two constructions were applied during processing;
- The agents have two repair strategies: one for inventing and learning new verb-specific markers and one for combining these markers into a larger construction. The invention and learning strategy also includes the possibility of extending and reusing existing markers through analogical reasoning. The algorithm for analogy is the same as in baseline experiment 3 and only looks at individual markers.

The experiment has been tested using five different alignment strategies. The first four strategies are individual selection, top-down selection, bottom-up selection and multi-level selection using the same fine-grained lateral inhibition mechanism as used in baseline experiment 3c. This means that competition is only held at the level of the co-occurrence links between a construction and a lexical entry rather than at the level of the constructions themselves. The algorithms can be summarized as follows:

4 Multi-level selection and language systematicity

- **Individual selection**: This is the exact same set-up as baseline experiment 3c. If a game was successful, the hearer will increase the score of the co-occurrence link between the applied lexical entry and the applied construction(s) by 0.1. He will also decrease the scores of the competing links by 0.1. The score of a link is always between 0 (high uncertainty) and 1 (high confidence).

- **Top-down selection**: In this strategy, the hearer will not only increase the score of the relevant co-occurrence link, but also the score of all the co-occurrence links that link the lexical entry to the smaller constructions which are related to the applied construction. The scores of the competitors of these links are decreased.

- **Bottom-up selection**: In this strategy, the hearer increases the score of the relevant link and of all the co-occurrence links that link the lexical entry to the larger constructions which are related to the applied constructions. All competitors of these links are punished.

- **Multi-level selection**: In this strategy, the hearer increases the scores of the relevant co-occurrence links and of all the links which link the lexical entry to constructions that are related to the applied constructions.

The fifth experimental set-up does not involve lateral inhibition but implements **multi-level selection and memory decay**. In this set-up, the hearer will not only increase the frequency score of the applied constructions, but also that of all the related constructions by 1. The frequency scores have no upper limit, so the higher the score, the more entrenched the construction is. After an agent has individually engaged in 200 language games, the frequency scores of all the items in the inventory are decreased.

In all five set-ups, the speaker will use the co-occurrence links to speed up processing. This means that not the entire inventory of constructions is considered, but only those constructions which are linked to the lexical entry. Links can be added through co-occurrence. When the speaker is faced with multiple hypotheses, he will choose the construction which either has the strongest co-occurrence link with the lexical entry (in the first four set-ups) or the one with the highest token frequency (in the fifth set-up). During processing, only the scores of individual competitors are taken into account. All simulations have been run in 10 series of 12.000 language games.

4.5 Experiment 3: multi-level selection with analogy

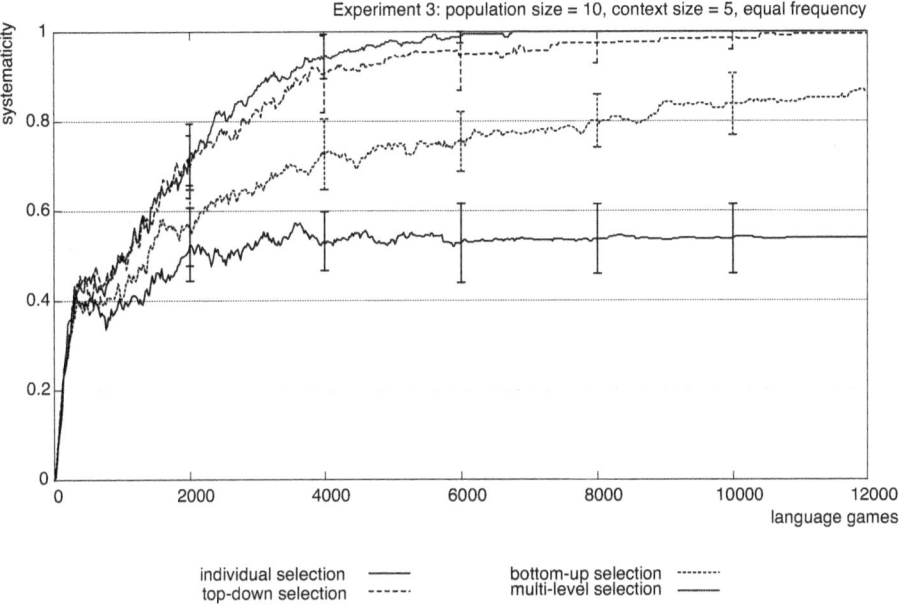

Figure 4.15: This graph compares systematicity in the first four experimental set-ups of experiment 3. The results confirm those of experiment 2. Even though there is potentially less variation because of the reuse of existing markers, individual selection stagnates at 50% systematicity. Bottom-up selection increases systematicity beyond 80% but also gets stuck. Top-down selection manages to reach full systematicity in more simulations than in experiment 2 because of the smaller variation space, but does not guarantee full systematicity. Only multi-level selection reaches systematicity in all the simulations and does so significantly faster than the other alignment strategies.

4.5.3 Results and discussion

In this section, the first four set-ups are again compared to each other to demonstrate the reoccurrence of the problem of systematicity. The fourth set-up (multi-level selection with lateral inhibition) is then compared more thoroughly to the fifth set-up using multi-level selection and memory decay. Finally, this section offers a closer look at one language evolved using the fifth set-up.

4 Multi-level selection and language systematicity

4.5.3.1 Results

Figure 4.15 compares the first four experimental set-ups to each other in terms of systematicity. The lines indicating systematicity for each set-up show the same behaviour as those in experiment 2 (Figure 4.10). The first set-up using the alignment strategy of individual selection fluctuates between 45 and 60% systematicity and stops evolving after 6.000 language games. The bottom-up strategy reaches more than 80% systematicity after 8.000 language games. In some simulations, this strategy leads up to 90% but never to maximum systematicity. Top-down selection performs a bit better than in experiment 2 due to the fact that the agent's capacity of reusing existing markers leads to a smaller variation space so 'frozen accidents' are less likely. Yet, as the results show, some simulations still involve an unsystematic convention and reaching systematicity takes a longer time than the multi-level selection strategy. The latter strategy is again the only one which leads to full systematicity in all the simulations.

The four set-ups also confirm the results of experiment 2 in terms of coherence. Figure 4.16 shows that bottom-up selection and individual selection again run almost parallel in terms of convergence. This time the agents reach coherence faster because of the smaller variation space. Multi-level and top-down selection also perform equally well and reach coherence between 6.000 and 8.000 language games.

Figure 4.17 gives an indication of the kinds of languages that are formed in the population if the agents use the fourth set-up (multi-level selection with lateral inhibition). The graph shows that the generalization rate of the agents is not really impressive: only three to five generalized roles survive the competition. Moreover, these roles only cover two or maximally three participant roles. This is clear from the fact that there are still 18 to 25 specific markers floating around in the population.

These results can be compared to the performance of the fifth set-up (multi-level selection with decay) which is illustrated in Figure 4.18. The top graph shows the results for communicative success, cognitive effort, meaning-form coherence and systematicity. As the graph indicates, the agents succeed in reaching full systematicity somewhere between 8.000 and 12.000 language games, which is a bit slower than the alignment strategy using lateral inhibition. The bottom graph shows the average number of markers floating around in the population. Here, we see that the average number of specific markers has made a significant drop from 18–25 markers to only 9. The number of semantic roles shifts from simulation to simulation between 4 and 6. The semantic roles also tend to be more general categories than in the simulations using lateral inhibition.

4.5 Experiment 3: multi-level selection with analogy

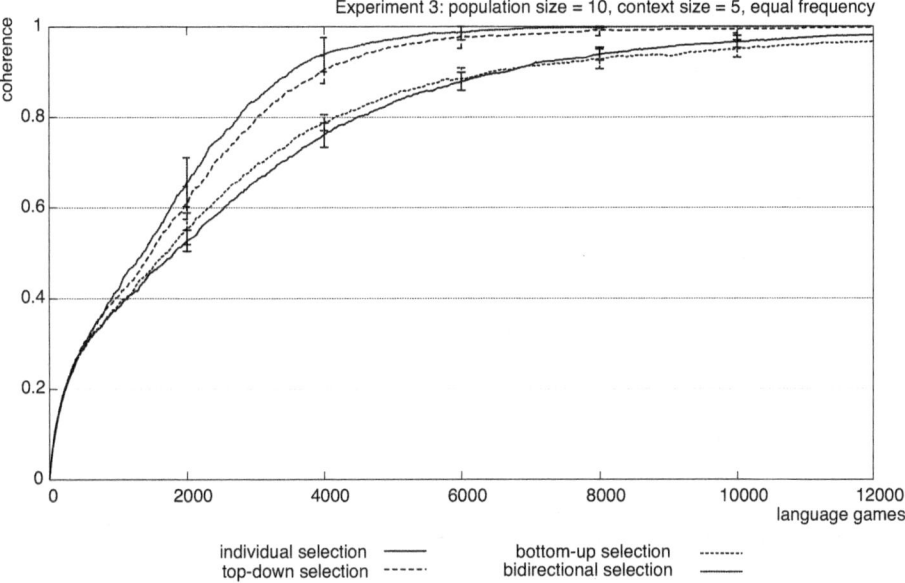

Figure 4.16: This graph compares the first four set-ups of experiment 3 in terms of meaning-form coherence. The graph shows that multi-level and top-down selection perform equally well and reach 100% between 6.000 and 8.000 language games. Bottom-up and individual selection again run almost parallel and reach coherence faster than in experiment 2 because of the smaller variation space.

Here is a list of markers and the participant roles they cover in one of the simulations (from more general to more specific):

- *-kad:* object-1, approach-1, fall-1, touch-1, move-outside-1
- *-fuir:* grasp-2, hide-2, move-inside-2, touch-2, walk-to-1
- *-kazo:* approach-2, fall-2, grasp-1, hide-1, walk-to-2
- *-hesa:* move-1, take-3
- *-ti:* visible-1, take-1
- *-qiwo:* move-inside-1, give-3
- *-fen:* distance-decreasing-1

145

4 Multi-level selection and language systematicity

- *-rem:* distance-decreasing-2
- *-gaeh:* move-outside-2
- *-wupu:* cause-move-on-1
- *-chuiw:* cause-move-on-2
- *-nuip:* cause-move-on-3
- *-tu:* give-1
- *-hozae:* give-2
- *-fut:* take-2

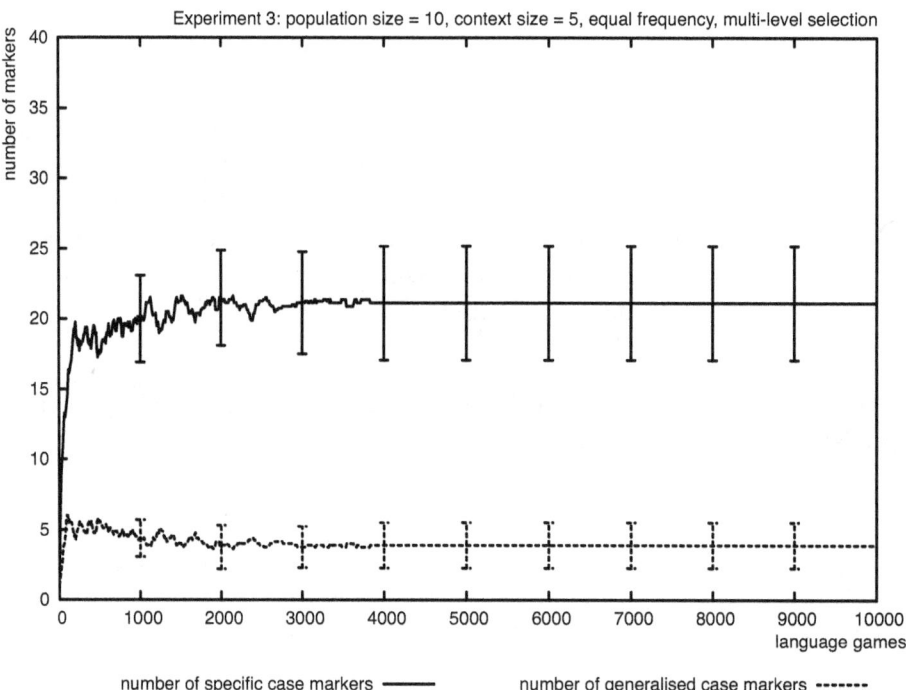

Figure 4.17: This graph shows the average number of markers known by each agent using the strategy of multi-level selection with lateral inhibition (the fourth set-up of experiment 3). The results show that the generalization rate of the agents is not impressive: only 3–5 semantic roles survive the competition as opposed to 18–25 specific markers.

4.5 Experiment 3: multi-level selection with analogy

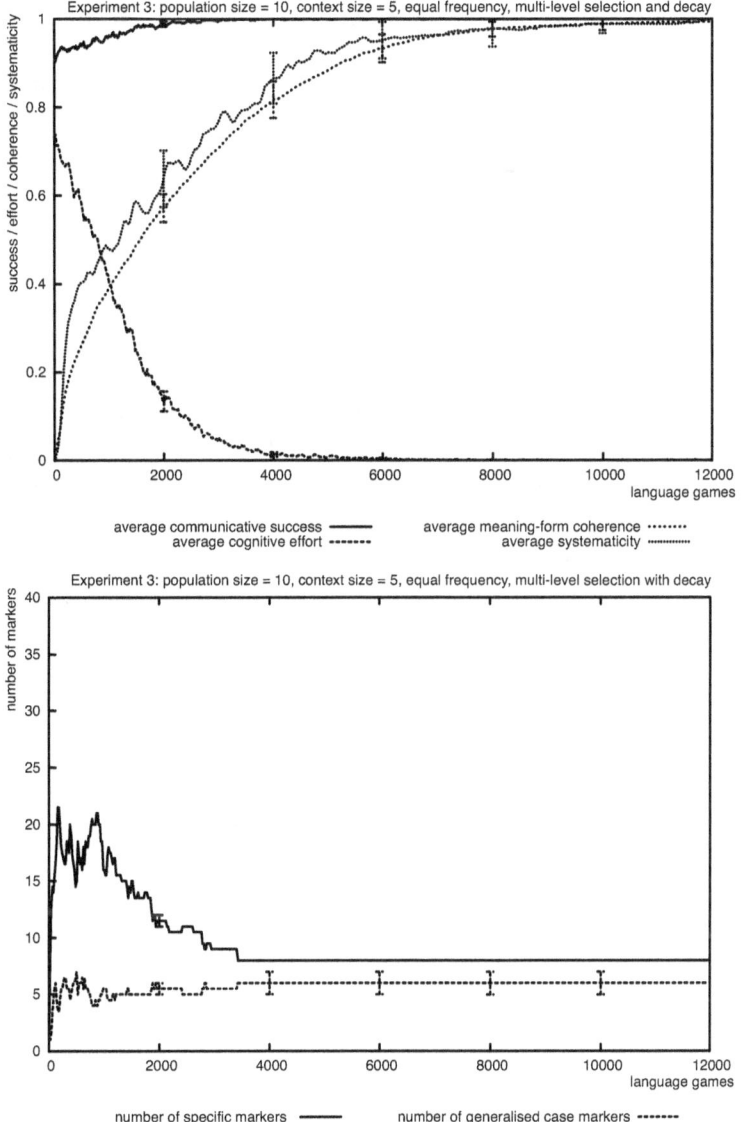

Figure 4.18: The top graph shows communicative success, cognitive effort, systematicity and meaning-form coherence in the set-up using multi-level selection and decay. The bottom graph shows the average number of markers in the same set-up.

4 Multi-level selection and language systematicity

The above markers occur systematically across patterns for marking the same participant roles. In this specific example, the agents succeeded in reaching coherence and systematicity after only 8.000 language games. When we compare the results to those of baseline experiment 3d, roughly the same level of generalization is reached.

Finally, Figure 4.19 looks inside the linguistic inventory of a single agent and offers a partial network of the agent's knowledge of its language. The figure concentrates on three constructions (in the middle) which are related to each other (indicated by the dotted line). The relation between the constructions indicate that construction-27 was created as a pattern of construction-2 and construction-10. The figure also shows all the lexical entries that are conventionally associated with these constructions. The links between the lexical entries and the constructions are used for optimizing processing: instead of trying out all the constructions in memory, only the linked constructions are considered. Links can be added as part of a problem-solving process during communication or pruned if the co-occurrence is not a successful one. Some redundant co-occurrence links may survive in the inventory. The links can also be seen as fusion links: they are annotated with information on how the participant roles can be fused with the semantic roles of the construction. This annotation is however not used by the agents themselves but for the clarity of interpretation for the experimenter. The actual fusion is taken care of by the unification of the potential valents of the lexical entry with the actual valency of the construction.

4.5.3.2 Discussion

The results of experiment 3 confirm the problem of systematicity that was uncovered in the other experiments. Here too, the strategy using multi-level selection was the only one to yield fully systematic languages. The systematicity rate was in each of the first four set-ups comparable to the rates in experiment 2. This may come as a surprise since the variation space is potentially smaller because the agents can extend the use of existing markers rather than inventing new ones all the time.

A closer look at the number of markers in the fourth set-up (multi-level selection with lateral inhibition), however, pointed to the reason for the small differences in systematicity rates: only a very small number of semantic roles survived the competition compared to a large number of specific markers. This means that the generalization rate is not really impressive so the number of variations is not much smaller in these simulations than was the case in experiment 2. The resulting number of specific markers versus semantic roles corresponds to the results

4.5 Experiment 3: multi-level selection with analogy

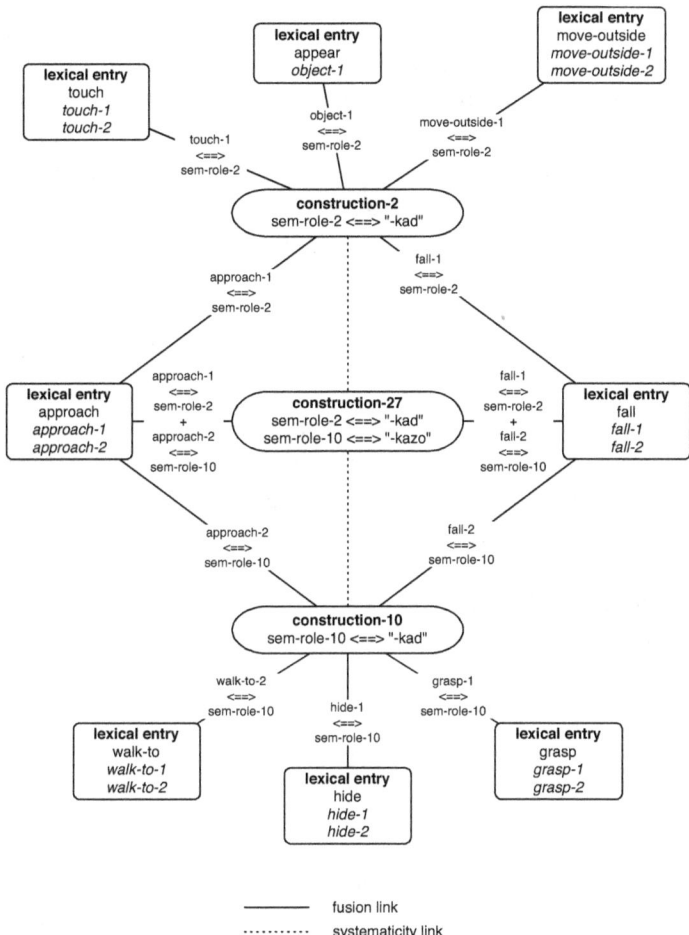

Figure 4.19: This figure gives a partial network for one agent in one of the simulations using multi-level selection with decay. In the middle there are three constructions which are systematically related to each other. The constructions are also linked with lexical entries. The links act both as co-occurrence links for optimizing processing and as fusion links for integrating the participant roles of the lexical entries with the semantic roles of the constructions. The networks are constructed in a stepwise fashion as a response to communicative needs.

149

obtained in baseline experiment 3c and also the reason for the result is the same: since the competition is held at the level of co-occurrence links and not at the level of constructions, the type frequency of a marker does not translate into a larger category gravity. Competition is held only in a local context so specific markers have an equally high chance of winning as more generalized semantic roles.

The results of the fifth set-up (multi-level selection with memory decay) also confirm the results of the baseline experiments and improve significantly in terms of generalization over the simulations using the fine-grained lateral inhibition dynamics. The number of specific categories has dropped by half and larger, more general semantic roles have a selectionist advantage because they occur more often. The generalization rate roughly matches the performance of baseline experiment 3d.

The consistency in number of generalized semantic roles and specific markers across the baseline experiments and the pattern experiments indicate that this is the maximum generalization rate that the agents can reach. Possible improvements would have to come from two sources:

1. The structure of the world: The capacity of analogical reasoning is heavily dependent on the structure of the world environment in which communication takes place. If the agents have to communicate about lots of events which show recurrent patterns in terms of visual primitives, they will be able to detect more analogies. If, however, the world is totally unstructured, the agents will come up with more specific markers than general semantic roles.

2. The capacity of analogical reasoning can be made more flexible. At the moment, the agents make a sharp distinction between what is analogous and what is not. A possible relaxation could be to only care about whether the mapping between a source role and a target role is discriminating enough for identifying the target role as well. Another possibility would be to use a similarity or a distance metric instead of the more rigid structural mapping that the agents currently use.

Experiment 3 also shows the potential power of the combination of analogical reasoning, pattern formation and multi-level selection respectively. First of all, analogical reasoning over the linguistic inventory can lead to an increasing generalization rate in the population, as is also shown in several instance-based approaches to language (Daelemans & Van den Bosch 2005; Skousen 1989). These

4.5 Experiment 3: multi-level selection with analogy

models also argue that a language can look rule-based from outside whereas in fact the generalization is distributed over the linguistic items in the inventory. This experiment shows that this observation also holds true for the case of the emergence of grammar if multi-level selection is applied. Finally, the formation of patterns to improve processing can have dramatic effects on the grammar: the patterns increase the survival chances of its related items; and they may potentially extend their use as well in later interactions.

So far, I did not spend much attention to the efficiency of the formalization of argument realization proposed in Chapter 2. In all the experiments presented in this Chapter and the previous one, the representation has proven to be flexible enough to deal with the enormous amount of **uncertainty** that is inherent to the emergence of new grammar conventions. In this case, the agents needed a flexible way of integrating lexical entries with constructions of various degrees of entrenchment. Instead of copying all the possible case frames into a new entry, the formalization allowed the agents to constantly 'mould' their lexical entries until a stable set of conventions had been negotiated. In this way, the competition of case markers could be held exclusively at the level of constructions instead of creating an additional competition on the lexical level for how these lexical entries should be integrated with the constructions. The lexical entries also integrated as easily with verb-specific constructions as with verb-class specific constructions.

The formalization was also flexible enough to deal with **multiple argument realization**: the agents were capable of integrating a single lexical entry into multiple patterns or constructions without the need for derivational rules or additional copies in the lexicon. Moreover, the lexical entries do not need to 'profile' their participant roles: the actual valency of a verb is determined by the construction it integrates with. Preferences for certain patterns of argument realization could be captured in this formalization by assigning a frequency score to the co-occurrence links of the lexical entries and the constructions that they are conventionally associated with.

One aspect that is still absent in the experiment is how the functions of the case markers start to influence each other once they start combining into patterns. At this moment, the meanings of the markers stay the same and patterning only influences their survival chances. Future work would thus have to include a way for the patterns themselves to evolve, which would also require the analogy to use the patterns as the source domain for innovation rather than focusing exclusively on single markers.

Including the patterns into the search domain could however lead to a huge hypothesis space and a complexity measure is needed to verify whether the algo-

4 Multi-level selection and language systematicity

rithm for analogy can scale up to larger worlds while maintaining a reasonable processing time. If not, a possible alternative could be a nearest-neighbour algorithm which has already been successfully applied to various tasks in natural language processing. In a comparison between Royal Skousen's *Analogical Modeling* (Skousen 1989) and *Memory-Based Language Processing* (Daelemans & Van den Bosch 2005), Daelemans (2002) shows that a relatively simple and efficient nearest-neighbour learner yields comparable and sometimes even better results than the costly algorithm of Analogical Modeling. This observation seriously challenges the more traditional approach to analogy and is highly relevant for the discussion of this work as well.

4.6 Towards syntactic cases

4.6.1 Overview

The experiments so far have dealt with stages 1 to 3 in the development of case markers (see Chapter 1). The next step is the introduction of syntactic roles that group together two or more semantic roles. In this section, I will introduce a first experiment that investigates how the transition to stage 4 can be achieved and what can be learned from the results. I will then use the grammatical square as a roadmap for future experiments.

4.6.2 A first experiment

As I argued in sections 1.2.5 and 1.2.6, syntactic roles impose even more abstraction on the conceptualization of specific events than semantic roles do. In natural languages, syntactic roles typically emerge when a category gradually starts extending its use until two cases merge into one class. In this first tentative experiment, I will scaffold the merger of cases and assume that a case marker can extend its use by subcategorization rather than by merging two roles. I will make this assumption more clear in the following paragraphs.

4.6.2.1 Experimental set-up

The experiment features the exact same set-up as the fourth set-up in experiment 3: the agents are capable of reusing a marker through analogy and combining the markers into larger patterns. They employ the alignment strategy of multi-level selection using lateral inhibition. The main question of the experiment is whether the agents are capable of aligning their grammars, which form an abstract inter-

4.6 Towards syntactic cases

mediary layer of semantic and syntactic roles which are not directly observable by the other agents.

The novelty of this particular set-up involves the idea of 'reusing as much as possible'. Roughly speaking, a speaker will reuse an existing marker even if it is not analogous to the target role, on the condition that the marker does not cover a conflicting participant role yet. The algorithm is operationalized as follows:

1. If the speaker diagnosed a problem of unexpressed variable equalities, he tries to repair the problem.

2. The speaker checks whether he already has a marker which can be reused:

    a) Take all known markers. Markers are ordered according to type frequency, that is, from more general (i.e. covering the most participant roles) to less general (i.e. covering the least participant roles). Loop through the markers until a solution is found:

        i. Take all the semantic roles that are covered by the marker, also ordered according to type frequency.

        ii. Loop through the semantic roles until a role is found which is analogous to the target role. If so, return the analogy.

    b) If a solution is found, return the analogy. If not...

        i. Take the most general marker which does not cover another participant role of the same event yet;

        ii. Create a new role for the target role and make it a subcategory of the chosen marker.

    c) If there are no markers yet or if no marker can be found that does not already cover a conflicting participant role, create a new marker.

3. The speaker creates the necessary rules and/or links in the inventory.

The hearer learns a marker in a similar way. If he observes a marker in a new situation, he will first try to retrieve an analogous role covered by that marker. If he cannot retrieve the analogy, he creates a new specific role and makes it a subcategory of the marker. It will often happen that the speaker used a marker which according to the hearer already covered a conflicting participant role. For example, the speaker uses *-bo* for marking 'approach-1', whereas the hearer has already observed this marker for covering 'approach-2'. In this case, the hearer will nevertheless create a new specific role for the new use as a possible subcategory of the marker. The fine-grained alignment strategy of the experimental set-up is flexible enough to rule out which participant role should win the competition (unless another marker takes over).

The main idea behind this innovation and learning strategy is that the speaker will be reluctant to invent a new marker. Rather, he will reuse a marker as long as it is discriminating a participant role in an event from the other roles. This means that, in principle, the agents should suffice in using three different markers. This experimental set-up has been implemented in a two-agent simulation and a five-agent simulation.

4.6.2.2 Results

The two-agent simulation features no variation in the population so the agents have no problems in aligning their grammars since they are endowed with the same algorithm of analogical reasoning. The resulting grammar is illustrated in Figure 4.20 which shows the mapping between participant, semantic and syntactic roles.

The diagram shows that the two agents indeed agree upon three case markers for covering all thirty participant roles. The results even seem to improve on the markers that were formed in baseline experiment 3a: ten semantic roles have been formed as opposed to six specific roles (which are also called 'sem-roles' in the experiment for convenience's sake). On the other hand, the baseline experiment featured two semantic roles which covered six and four participant roles respectively, whereas the semantic roles in this case reach a maximum of four.

In terms of inventory size, the agents require 16 single-argument, 16 two-argument and 3 three-argument constructions. The fact that the number of two- and three-argument constructions is almost the same as in the experiments using no analogy is due to the fact that only in two cases, a larger construction can also be fused with two different lexical entries. For example, *approach* and *fall* integrate with the same three constructions. So even though single-argument constructions can group several participant roles together, the patterns do not succeed in going beyond a verb-specific use.

The results of the two-agent simulation can now be taken as the baseline for the multi-agent simulations. A similar snapshot of the multi-agent simulation is presented in Figure 4.21 and Figure 4.22. These diagrams present the internal mappings between participant, semantic and syntactic roles from two different agents in the same population. Both agents (as well as the other agents in the population) converge on a coherent set of meaning-form mappings.

A closer look at the two diagrams shows that the agents have converged on five different case markers. Two of these markers are participant role-specific,

4.6 Towards syntactic cases

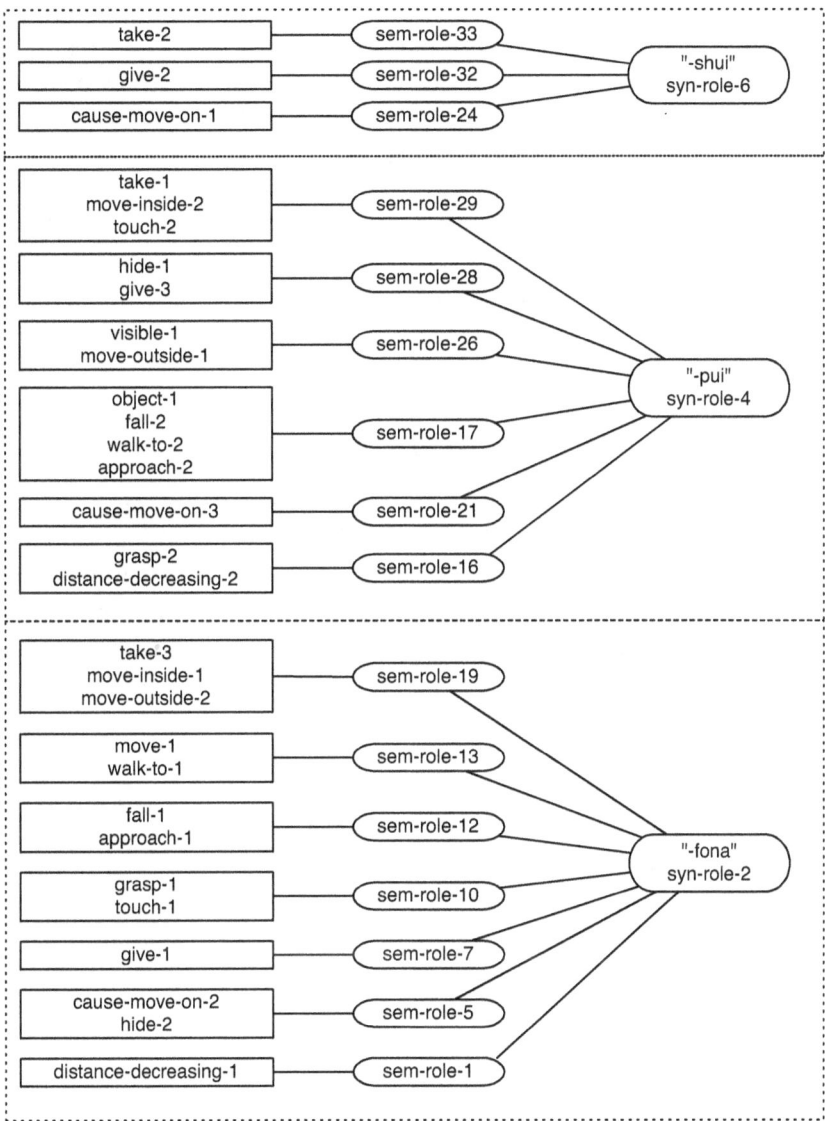

Figure 4.20: This diagram shows the mapping between participant roles and semantic roles; and between semantic roles and syntactic roles in the two-agent simulation on the emergence of syntactic roles. Since there are no variations in the simulation, both agents align their grammars perfectly. The results are taken as the baseline for the multi-agent simulations.

while the others group together multiple roles. Compared to the two-agent simulation, there is a significant loss in number of semantic roles: the first agent has constructed five semantic roles and the second agent has constructed six semantic roles. This leaves 18 and 17 specific roles respectively. Most of the semantic roles also only cover two participant roles.

A comparison of the semantic roles of both agents also shows that they do not align their internal categorization. For example, the agent in Figure 4.21 groups 'move-outside-2', 'walk-to-1', 'fall-2' and 'grasp-2' together. The other agent has a similar category but has constructed a separate role for 'fall-2'. The other agent has also created a semantic role for covering 'move-inside-2' and 'move', whereas these are two distinct categories for the first agent.

4.6.2.3 Discussion of the two-agent simulation

The agents in the two-agent simulation were capable of improving over baseline experiment 3a in terms of semantic roles, single-argument constructions and the number of markers. The improvement is due to the fact that the limited use of markers guides the search space more strongly during innovation. In the previous experiments, each semantic role had its own case marker so the chances that they had the same type frequency were quite high. In this case, the speaker would always randomly choose which semantic role to extend. In this new simulation, the type frequency of the syntactic role was more important which led to a faster divergence between the productivity rate of the cases. This means that semantic roles which would otherwise miss extension due to random choice now have more weight to categorize new participant roles.

An interesting side-effect of the innovation algorithm is that there are two syntactic roles which cover almost exclusively semantic roles while a third role acts as a waste basket category for three participant roles which are all three part of events featuring three participants. This maps onto the distinction between agents and patients (and subjects and objects) that is made by most of the languages in the world. Most theories of language assume a (near-)universal distinction between agents and patients to be given (either based on a universal conceptual space or on Universal Grammar). This first tentative experiment suggests an alternative hypothesis: the distinction could emerge as a side-effect of communicative goals because language users want to make grammatically and communicatively relevant distinctions. In most of the cases, two or three syntactic roles suffice. The extension of case markers and the merger of semantic role could thus spontaneously lead to 'core' cases.

4.6 Towards syntactic cases

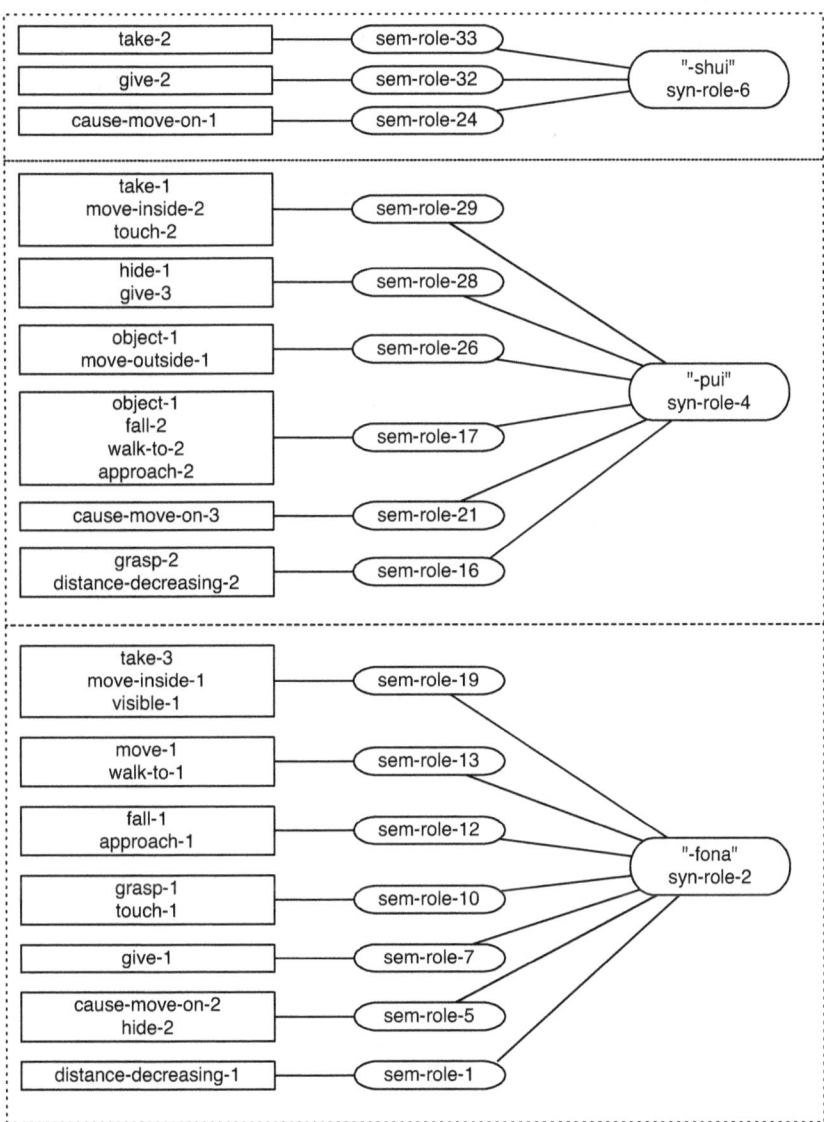

Figure 4.21: The mapping between participant, semantic and syntactic roles in a single agent in the multi-agent simulation.

4 Multi-level selection and language systematicity

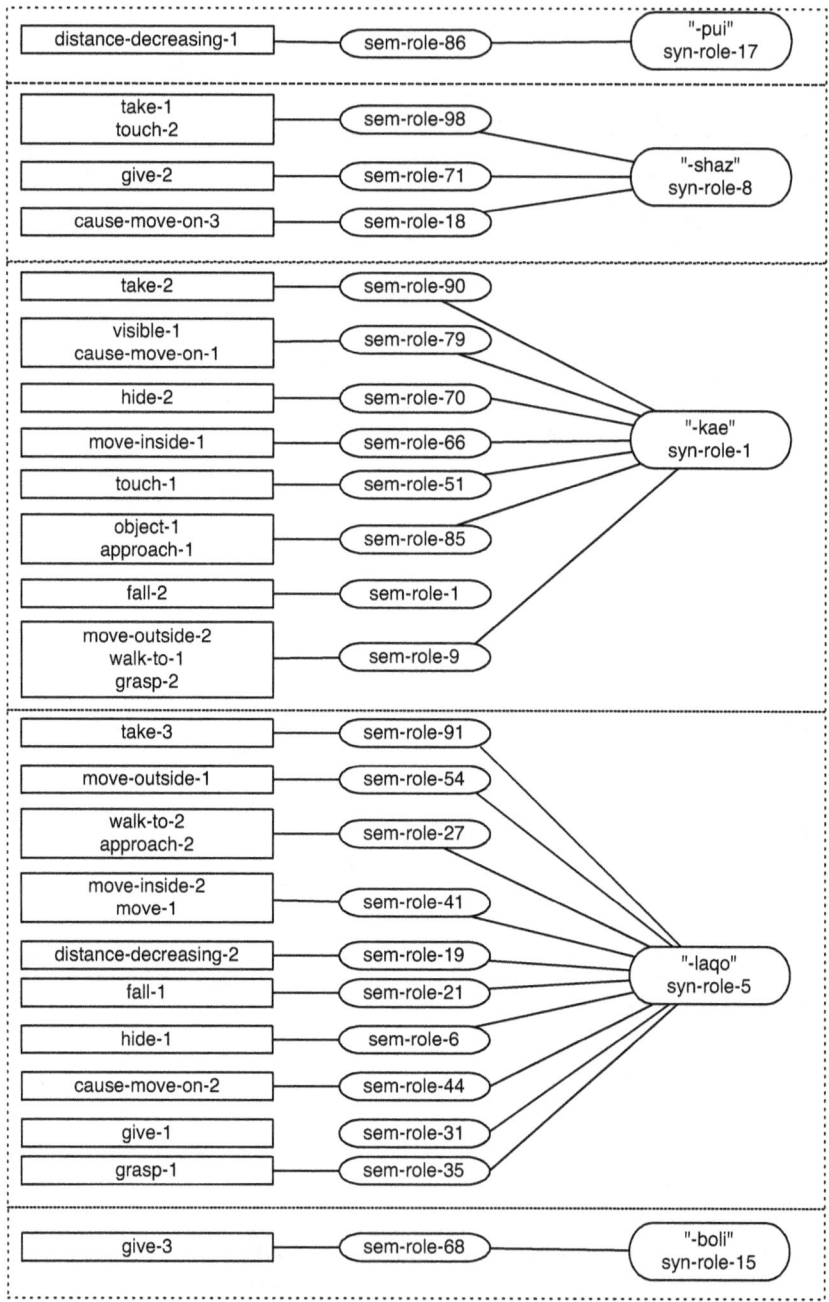

Figure 4.22: This diagram shows the internal mapping as known by another agent in the population.

4.6 Towards syntactic cases

A final remark considering the two-agent simulation is that there is no gain in terms of inventory size with respect to larger constructions. This is due to the fact that only a couple of constructions share the same semantic roles which combine into the same larger construction. As I suggested during the discussion of experiment 3, the newly formed patterns themselves should be considered by the analogy as well. This could further increase the generalization and productivity rate of the agents and could be an additional drive towards a prototypical agent-patient distinction.

4.6.2.4 Discussion of the multi-agent simulation

The results of the multi-agent simulation shows that the alignment of an indirect and multilayered grammatical mapping is no trivial issue: the number of semantic roles constructed by each agent drops significantly and there are differences in how the internal mapping of each agent is organized. This is basically a problem of feedback: there is too much variation floating around in the population for the agents to successfully retrieve the analogy meant by the speaker. Additional feedback could consist of alternative agnating structures that could be exploited for constructing semantic roles. This, however, would require the capacity of dynamically updating the function or meaning of the semantic roles, which the agents do not have (also see the concluding remarks in §3.5).

4.6.3 The grammar square: a roadmap for further work

The first experiments towards syntax showed that once the mapping between semantic roles and syntactic roles becomes indirect and polysemous, the agents are faced with a complex coordination problem: the abstract layer of semantic and syntactic roles is not directly observable from the outside and the agents have no means of finding a shared categorization. Yet the alignment of this internal categorization is crucial in order to preserve a good productivity and generalization rate for reaching communicative success in future interactions. In order to take this step, the experimental set-up needs to be expanded. We can use the grammar square (repeated in Figure 4.23), as a guidance for identifying which efforts need to be made in order to solve this coordination problem.

4 Multi-level selection and language systematicity

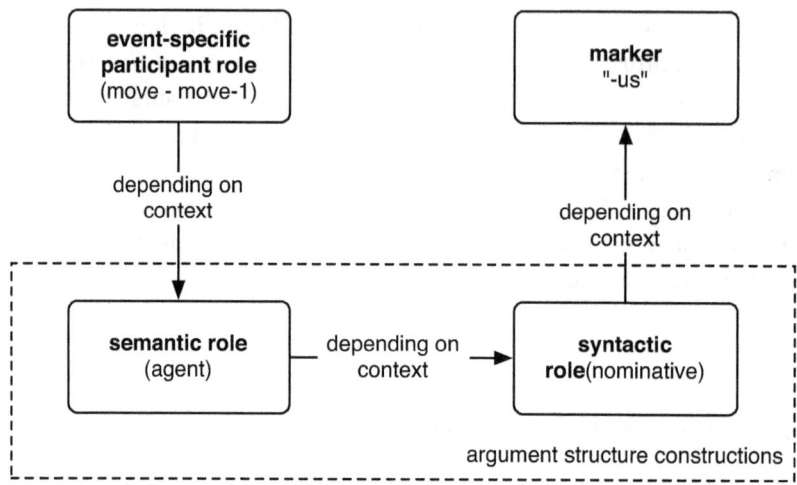

Figure 4.23: The grammar square can be read as a roadmap for future research. Each mapping in the square is dependent on the context, so experiments should investigate which mechanisms and conditions can lead to such an indirect mapping.

4.6.3.1 Mapping participant roles onto semantic roles

Participant roles of a particular event can map onto several semantic roles in natural languages. This is clear in the following sentences, in which *the window* first plays the role of patient, then some entity which undergoes a change of state, and finally some stative entity:

(17) He broke the window.

(18) The window broke.

(19) The window was broken.

In the experiments presented in this book, such functional variation was impossible: during conceptualization, the agents always profile the complete participant role in the event structure. This could lead to sentences similar as example 17. However, in the other two sentences, only a subpart of the participant role is profiled: example 18 profiles the change of state whereas example 19 profiles the resulting state of the participant.

In order to achieve the same functional variation, the agents would thus have to be able to include aspect (and tense) distinctions in their conceptualization. For this, the conceptualization algorithm and the algorithm for analogy would

4.6 Towards syntactic cases

have to be changed in order to include the hierarchical structure of the event descriptions and the time stamps provided by the event recognition system. On the level of the interaction pattern, the agents would somehow have to be able to get sufficient feedback in order to recognize and learn the relevant aspectual distinctions. The emergence of grammatical markers for aspect (and tense) is no trivial matter and goes well beyond the scope of this book.

4.6.3.2 Mapping semantic roles onto syntactic roles

The mapping between semantic roles and syntactic roles can already be multi-layered in nature without taking information structure into account: in examples 18 and 19, the distinction is not one of active versus passive, but rather one of aspect. In order to see such alternations emerging, the idea of reuse can be exploited again. As the agents develop their grammars, they increase their expressive power. From the moment they want to express aspectual distinctions as well, they could try to reuse the existing grammatical system instead of inventing some new strategy. This puts pressure on the existing conventions and may lead to additional abstractions in the form of syntactic roles.

Another way to investigate the emergence of syntactic roles would be to endow the agents with the capacity of dynamically updating the representation of their categories. If categories are not fixed but dynamic, there is a risk of 'category leakage' as observed in natural languages: some categories start expanding their use which could lead to the merger of two semantic roles into one case. Typically, the more frequent cases would start extending their usage which could gradually lead to prototypical agent and patient categories.

4.6.3.3 Mapping syntactic roles onto case markers

In the experiments, there is a one-to-one relation between syntactic roles and case markers. In natural case grammars, however, there are often paradigms of related markers that together cover a particular case. These marker alternations typically indicate grammatical distinctions in terms of gender and number. Evolving this kind of variation would thus require a need for marking grammatically relevant distinctions between arguments.

Even more intriguing are case systems where the same markers can be used to indicate different cases. For example, Latin uses the inflection *-um* to mark nominative case in neuter singular words (*bellum* 'war') and accusative case in masculine singular words (*dominum* 'master') (Blake 1994: 4–5). This means that case markers somehow manage to grow a paradigmatic case system which goes

4 Multi-level selection and language systematicity

beyond the borders of individual cases. Applied to the experiments, this would mean lifting the present assumption that competing case markers are always competing with each other for marking a particular participant role. Instead, agents should be allowed to accept competition and variation at each possible mapping in the grammatical square. This may lead to a credit assignment problem in which the agents can never have complete certainty about which mapping in the grammatical square was relevant during a particular innovation.

From the above discussion it should be clear that scaling up the experiments towards richer syntax and grammar is not a trivial matter. It would include research into the emergence of aspect and tense distinctions, a dynamic representation of linguistic categories, and allowing competition on all aspects of the grammatical square. A scale-up to include information structure as well would involve expansion of the language game model to larger dialogues, which creates the need for additional capacities such as episodic memory, scoping and coordination issues and possibly anaphora resolution.

5 Impact on artificial language evolution and linguistic theory

5.1 Introduction

The time has now come to weave through the theoretical foundations and experimental results to reflect on the contributions of this book to artificial language evolution and linguistics. §5.2 deals with the first part of this reflection by comparing the results of this book to those obtained in a recent study on case marking in the Iterated Learning Model, one of the most widely adopted approaches in the field of artificial language evolution. The comparison shows that the cognitive-functional approach outperforms the Iterated Learning Model and that the work in this book is a significant step forwards in the field.

The other three sections of this chapter deal with the contributions of this book to linguistics. More specifically, I believe this book can have an impact in three domains. First of all, the formalism proposed in Chapter 2 is the first computational implementation of argument structure ever in a construction grammar framework. In §5.3, I will compare it to an upcoming alternative in Sign-Based Construction Grammar. A second contribution has to do with the structure of the linguistic inventory. The problem of systematicity and multi-level selection is new to linguistics and may have an impact on how we should conceive the constructicon. I will discuss this matter from the viewpoint of construction grammars and usage-based models of language in §5.4. Finally, the experiments in this book and prior work in the field provide alternative evidence in recent debates in linguistic typology and grammaticalization. These debates concern the status of semantic maps and thematic hierarchies as universals of human cognition, and the appropriateness of reanalysis as a mechanism for explaining grammaticalization. §5.5 introduces the debates and illustrates how experiments on artificial language evolution can propose a novel way of thinking about the issues at hand.

5 Impact on artificial language evolution and linguistic theory

5.2 Pushing the state-of-the-art

5.2.1 Overview

The significance of scientific research can only be fully appreciated by comparing it to other studies in its domain. In this section, I will illustrate how the work in this book advances the state-of-the-art in artificial language evolution by comparing it to a recent study by Moy (2006) who investigated the emergence of a case grammar in the Iterated Learning Model (ILM), at present one of the most widely adopted models in the field. The comparison reveals some fundamental problems with the ILM and shows that a cognitive-functional approach is the most fruitful way for moving the experiments on artificial language evolution towards greater complexity, expressiveness and realism. In the following subsections, I will summarize four series of experiments reported by Moy and discuss how and why the work in this book yields better results. Finally, I will give a general overview of both approaches.

5.2.2 Experiment 1: A primitive case system?

The main objective of Moy's work is to expand the Iterated Learning Model as presented by Kirby (2002) in order to study the emergence of a case grammar. Kirby's original experiments investigated how a recursive word-order syntax can emerge as a side-effect of the cultural transmission of language from one generation to the next without the need for communicative pressures (the so-called "function independence principle", Brighton, Kirby & Smith 2005). Moy's first series of experiments are a replication of these simulations.

5.2.2.1 The experiment

The experiment features a population of two agents: one "adult" speaker and one "child" learner. The adult speaker has to produce a number of utterances that are observed by the learner. The adult speaker has an innovation strategy which allows him to invent a random holistic word for each new meaning if he does not know a word yet. The child learner is equipped with a Universal Grammar in the form of an induction algorithm and will try to induce as much grammatical rules as possible. The child will thus overgeneralize the input provided by the speaker which causes language change as illustrated in the child-based model in Chapter 1. After some time, the adult agent "dies" and the learner becomes the new adult speaker so its grammar becomes the new convention. A new child learner is then

5.2 Pushing the state-of-the-art

introduced into the population. This population turnover is iterated thousands of times.

The ILM hypothesizes that the development of grammar is triggered by the Poverty of the Stimulus or the learning bottleneck: since children cannot observe all possible utterances in a language, there is a pressure on language to become more learnable. The linguistic inventory should therefore evolve to an optimal size for a given meaning space. The meaning space consists here of five predicates and five objects, which can combine into simple two-argument events such as *loves(john, mary)*. In total there are 100 possible events. The optimal inventory size consists of 11 rewrite-rules: one abstract rule for word order, and ten rules for each word.

One challenge for a Universal Grammar mechanism is to provide the agents with a strategy for filtering the "correct" input from the "wrong" input. In these experiments, child learners will especially be confronted with conflicting input at the beginning because the language of the adult speaker is still holistic and unstructured. The ILM solves this problem by ignoring all variation. For the learner, this means that once a rule has been induced, all conflicting input is neglected. On top of that, the agents are endowed with a deterministic parser which always picks the first matching rule in the list. Competing rules are therefore never considered because they are lower in the list. This assures a one-to-one mapping between meaning and form, which is crucial for the ILM to work properly (Smith 2003b). The deterministic parser also allows the agents to rely on word order for distinguishing the semantic roles of events.

5.2.2.2 Results

The results of the simulations show that the agents start inventing holistic utterances, which leads to an unstructured language in the first generations. After several hundreds of generations, the language becomes more and more regular and thus learnable due to the overgeneralization of linguistic input by the child learners. These overgeneralizations become the new grammar of the language once the child replaces the adult speaker. Moy notes, however, that not all languages evolve to the optimal size of 11 rules, but that "a significant number of the runs converged on a larger grammar with 16 rules" (p. 113). These grammars contain two distinct noun categories: one for the agent and one for the patient. Here is an example of such a grammar which uses an SOV word order:

5 Impact on artificial language evolution and linguistic theory

(1)
$$
\begin{aligned}
s/[P, X, Y] &\rightarrow 3/X, i, 1/Y, 2/P \\
1/anna &\rightarrow i, p, l \\
1/kath &\rightarrow c, s \\
1/mary &\rightarrow t, a \\
1/john &\rightarrow j, e \\
1/pete &\rightarrow h \\
3/kath &\rightarrow a, k, f \\
3/pete &\rightarrow a, u, f \\
3/mary &\rightarrow t, s \\
3/anna &\rightarrow g \\
3/john &\rightarrow p \\
2/kisses &\rightarrow t \\
2/hates &\rightarrow z, s \\
2/loves &\rightarrow m, q, j \\
2/adores &\rightarrow u, i \\
2/sees &\rightarrow m, y
\end{aligned}
$$
(Moy 2006: 113)

In the above grammar, the agents have to use a different word for the same object depending on which semantic role it plays in the event:

(2) p   i   ta   mqj
   john [EMPTY] mary loves
   'John loves Mary.'

(3) ts   i   je   mqj
   mary [EMPTY] john loves
   'Mary loves John.'

This kind of "suboptimal" grammar is not exclusive to Moy's replication experiment: it also occurs in Kirby's original simulations. For example, Kirby (1999) suggests that the two distinct noun categories can be considered as case-marked nominals. In the discussion of the replicating experiment, Moy seems to follow this hypothesis:

> Could we view such a grammar as exhibiting some form of primitive case system, in that it is possible to distinguish subject forms of nouns from objects, rather than using the same form for both? This is analogous perhaps to highly irregular forms of case found in some languages, such as the English pronouns *I*, *me*, *we* and *us*, where the nominative forms, (*I* and *we*)

used to the [sic] represent the subject of a sentence, have no morphological relationship to the accusative forms used for objects (*me* and *us*). (Moy 2006: 114)

5.2.2.3 Discussion

As I argued in §4.3.4, considering the above grammar as some kind of primitive case system is an over-interpretation of experimental results. While there are many attested examples in natural languages in which a word form depends on the linguistic context (e.g. many Slavic languages such as Russian use different lexical entries for verbs depending on aspect), they do not come about as frozen accidents of the learning mechanism. As for the English pronouns, they are remnants of a stage in the development of English where the grammar had a fully productive case system. Both Moy and Kirby thus fail to identify the problem of systematicity that occurs in the experiments.

This observation illustrates the importance of a strong dialogue with linguistics. Most research in the field so far has contented itself with shallow comparisons to natural languages. It is however crucial to go into more empirical details in order to appreciate the enormous complexity involved in grammatical phenomena in natural languages. In this book, I tried to offer such an appreciation of case markers in the first Chapter. A better understanding of the developmental pathways of case markers helped to uncover the problem of systematicity in this book and prevented me from simply concluding that the lack of systematicity could be mapped onto some of the more exotic case alignment systems found in the world's languages (see Figure 5.5). Other first steps towards domain-specific dialogues exist for colour terms (Steels & Belpaeme 2005), spatial language (Loetzsch et al. 2008b) and vowel systems (de Boer 1999).

In this book, I solved the problem of frozen accidents through multi-level selection. I implemented multi-level selection as an alignment strategy which is therefore tightly coupled to communicative success. In the ILM, however, communicative success has no impact on the behaviour of the agents so multi-level selection cannot be readily applied here. Second, multi-level selection only makes sense if there is variation in the model, but the ILM avoids variation as much as possible so once a frozen accident occurs, it is hard to get rid of it.

Even though it is unwarranted to equate the frozen accidents in the ILM experiments with case systems in natural languages, Moy's work takes an interesting turn by asking how the ILM can be expanded so that it favours these "subopti-

5 Impact on artificial language evolution and linguistic theory

mal" languages. If Moy succeeds in demonstrating the factors that *systematically* lead to the emergence of such languages, the experiments could still come up with relevant pressures for evolving a case language.

5.2.3 Experiment 2: dealing with variation

In order to encourage the emergence of a primitive case system, Moy (2006: chapter 5) experiments with various modifications of Kirby's parser that make it less deterministic and which allows for variation in word order. The hypothesis is that if the agents can no longer rely on word order for distinguishing agents from patients in the events, they will start learning grammatical rules with case-like properties.

5.2.3.1 Experimental results

Moy first tries to introduce variation in the word order by allowing the agents to randomly choose among conflicting rules or by reshuffling the inventory. In all the simulations, however, the agents fail to converge on a compositional grammar: the linguistic inventories of the agents are very large and too much conflicts are known for reaching a regular language. Moy argues that this is due to the fact that compositionality can only emerge in the ILM if variation in meaning-form mappings is ignored: learners will not consider any new variation anymore once they have associated a certain meaning with a certain form, and the deterministic parser excludes the use of variations. The same conclusion has also been suggested by Smith (2003b), but as opposed to Moy who rejects this unrealistic assumption, Smith argues that natural languages have such a bias towards one-to-one mappings as well.

Moy thus points to a fundamental problem with the ILM: in order to allow variation in word order, the agents need to be capable of parsing and producing competing rules. Yet, in order for the grammar to emerge at all, the ILM expects that a single variation is maintained. Moy notes that in order to dampen the search space, the agents need a way to prefer some variations over other ones. She therefore endows the agents with an alignment strategy which takes the frequency of rules into account. The more frequent the rule, the higher the probability that the agent will select it for production. The alignment strategy allows the agents to reach a compositional language again. It does not, however, lead to an increase in the number of primitive case grammars. In additional experimental set-ups, Moy allows even more word order freedom by reshuffling sentences before they are actually produced, but this again does not lead to a preference for

5.2 Pushing the state-of-the-art

the primitive case grammar. Finally, manipulating the size of the transmission bottleneck (i.e. the number of utterances that the child learner observes during a lifetime) does not yield significant results either.

Moy concludes that the small effect of free word order and the bottleneck size is due to the fact that the agents do not have to reach mutual understanding: if the free word order cannot be parsed by the hearer, it will simply be ignored so it will not lead to a change in the linguistic inventory. In other words, the child agent does not really care about converging on the same language as that of the adult speaker but learns whatever hypotheses its induction algorithm comes up with. Moy argues that the agents thus have no need for disambiguating semantic roles, which prevents them from reaching a case-like grammar.

5.2.3.2 Discussion

Moy's experiments reveal a number of fundamental shortcomings of the ILM: first of all, the agents have no way of dealing with variation. This problem did not surface in Kirby's prior work because he implemented a bias towards one-to-one mappings that excludes the possibility of competitors. Moreover, the ILM is typically implemented using only two agents, so no competing rules can ever be introduced in the population. Moy's results clearly show that there is no connection whatsoever between the grammar that is acquired by the learner and the grammar of the speaker: in fact, the learner will apply a "first come, first serve" approach to learning grammar in which the first successful parse leads to a fixed entry in the inventory. This means that the agents in Kirby's models did not *learn* to mark the distinction between semantic roles, but that they have this distinction already built in.

Moy rightfully notices that the agents need some kind of (alignment) strategy in order to reach a regular language. She introduces an utterance-based strategy which counts the number of occurrences of rules. Equipped with this alignment strategy, the agents are capable of producing and parsing multiple word orders, but this has hardly any effect on the language of the agents. Moy then rightfully concludes that the agents need **communicative pressures**: since the child learner does not care about communicative success, any grammar induction will do. The experiments thus show that the ILM's "function independence principle" cannot lead to grammar (at least not a case grammar) unless by accident or through a Universal Grammar. The transmission bottleneck is therefore not a sufficient trigger for marking event structure through grammar.

5 Impact on artificial language evolution and linguistic theory

5.2.3.3 Problems with multi-agent simulations

Another way in which the problems of the ILM can be demonstrated is to scale up the experiments to multi-agent populations. This has indeed been attempted by Smith & Hurford (2003). Smith & Hurford reached the following conclusions:

1. The agents fail to align their grammars because they have no alignment strategy and different agents will come up with different innovations and generalizations;

2. As a result, learners are presented with inconsistent training data;

3. The eager abstraction algorithm has disastrous consequences for the performance of the agents.

Smith & Hurford consider the option of allowing the learners to keep multiple hypotheses. Since the agents are however "eager learners", their abstractions harm their performance: abstractions made by one agent are not always the same as the abstractions made by another one so the agents never reach a shared language. This means that the agents would have to maintain all possible grammars, which rapidly becomes intractable. Another problem is that the agents need to find out which grammar is "best". Smith & Hurford refute the possibility of a cost system (similar to the lateral inhibition strategies proposed in many problem-solving models) on the grounds that it is "rather ad hoc". The solution offered by Smith & Hurford is however at least ad hoc as most cost systems are: they implement strong production biases coupled to "smart pruning" in order to reduce the number of hypotheses.

However, variation is a fundamental property of language. Introducing additional production biases is a way to put less weight on the cultural evolution of language and more on the genetic endowment of the agents, which is exactly the contrary of what the ILMs try to show. Moreover, there now exist mathematical models of lateral inhibition dynamics which solve the "rather ad hoc" status of cost systems (Baronchelli et al. 2006; De Vylder 2007). Also the alignment strategy based on token frequency proposed in this book is rooted in proposals made in cognitive-functional models of language.

The real problem for the ILM is however that such a cost system only works in a bottom-up, instance per instance learning of the grammar. Otherwise it would indeed lead to an intractable search space containing all possible grammars. In order to avoid innate biases towards one-to-one mappings, it is therefore necessary to introduce **an utterance-based selectionist system** rather than

5.2 Pushing the state-of-the-art

a grammar-based selectionist system. The work in this book demonstrates how such a bottom-up approach can lead to systematic languages if analogy is used in combination with multi-level selection.

5.2.4 Experiment 3: implementing communicative pressures

Following the conclusion that the agents need additional communicative pressures in order to form a primitive case grammar, Moy (2006: chapter 6) presents a series of experiments in which ambiguous word orderings occur. The hypothesis is that this ambiguity will lead the agents to prefer rules that use different noun categories to mark the distinction between semantic roles.

5.2.4.1 Experimental results

In a first set-up, Moy implements an "inversion procedure" that swaps the ordering of words for which the agent already has a rule. This procedure thus guarantees ambiguity during learning. The results are however disastrous: most of the runs fail to reach any kind of regularity at all. Moy assigns the reason for this failure to the fact that the child learner indeed faces ambiguity, but that he still does not need to reach mutual understanding with the speaker. The hearer thus keeps ignoring the ambiguous utterances if they do not fit the grammar rules that have already been acquired.

In an attempt to fix this problem, Moy implements a learner that does not tolerate ambiguity and an interaction script that forces the speaker to introduce unambiguous utterances: the meaning that was parsed by the hearer is compared to the intended meaning of the speaker. If there is a mismatch, the speaker has to come up with an alternative verbalization. However, this implementation does not lead to success either: in most cases, the speaker does not have an alternative way to verbalize an utterance so he will invent a new holistic string. Since the ILM features meaning transfer, the hearer will each time learn this new utterance. The result is that there is constant innovation in the simulations so the agents never reach an "optimal" language. Additional attempts, such as punishing ambiguous utterances, do not yield improvement either.

5.2.4.2 Discussion

Even though Moy's experiments started from a correct observation, the "communicative pressures" that are needed for a case grammar were not operationalized and implemented in a satisfying way. The main problem is that the agents in

5 Impact on artificial language evolution and linguistic theory

her experiments are not truly communicating. First of all, the speaker's output was randomly changed by an artificial procedure in order to create ambiguities for the hearer. This is already highly problematic because it would require some malicious mind-reading from the speaker's part, but there are other more serious issues: the speaker does not have any communicative goal at all. He just produces an utterance but does not care about whether this utterance had the intended effect in the hearer's mind. Other simulations that emphasize the importance of communication have all come to the conclusion that the speaker must try to produce an utterance in such a way as to improve the chance of being understood by the hearer (Smith 2003a; Steels 2003b). In this book, this was operationalized in the form of re-entrance (see Chapter 3).

From the part of the hearer, there is the same problem. "Ambiguity" in Moy's model does not mean that the hearer did not understand what the speaker said because there is meaning transfer and the hearer can even compare his parsed meaning to the speaker's intended meaning. The problem is that the hearer does not attempt to align his grammar to that of the speaker at all: a mismatch in meanings means the rejection of the speaker's utterance. This means that the hearer stubbornly sticks to his induced grammar rules which may well be completely different than the grammar of the adult speaker because of the greedy induction algorithm. This problem does not occur in the experiments in this book because the agents try to find out what the speaker's intentions were and want to conform to the conventions of the population.

In short, none of the agents ever actually try to reach communicative success. As I argued in Chapter 3, language is an **inferential coding system** in which the language users are assumed to be intelligent enough to make innovations that can be understood by the hearers, and in which hearers can make **abductions** about the speaker's intended meaning. In Moy's experiments, the agents only want to get rid of internal inconsistencies rather than trying to converge on the same grammar.

5.2.5 Experiment 4: more innate knowledge

In a final series of experiments, Moy (2006: chapter 7) tries to address the problem of the "suboptimal" primitive case system in a different way. She starts from the observation that the grammar inducer "is not capable of *effectively* learning inflectional grammars" (p. 206). For example, the default inducer would fail to notice the inflectional markers in an utterance such as *johnalovesmaryb*: instead of recognizing *-a* as an indicator of the subject and *-b* as an indicator of the object, the learner will induce them as an integral part of the word form. Moy

5.2 Pushing the state-of-the-art

therefore proposes several implementations that attempt to solve this problem. I will discuss one of these attempts in which he implements a richer meaning representation.

5.2.5.1 Experimental results

In all of the previous experiments, the semantic roles of agent and patient were implicit in the meaning so the inducer wasn't able to extract them. Moy therefore decides to make the meaning representation richer by explicitly adding the roles of "actor" and "actedon". The meaning [loves, john, mary] would thus become [[act, loves], [actor, john], [actedon mary]] (p. 217). The "optimal" case marking language should have 15 rules: one top-level rule, ten lexical entries, two markers and two rules to combine the markers with the noun categories. Despite the explicit representation of semantic roles, however, not all simulations led to satisfying results. There were two kinds of problematic cases:

- One type of grammar again features two completely distinct noun categories with different words for the same meaning. The inducer failed to recognize inflectional markers for the agent and the patient.

- A second type of languages *did* have inflectional markers, but they also featured two different lexical entries for the nouns. An example of such a grammar is:

(4)
```
s/ [P, X, Y]      →   1/Y, 13/X, 6/P
13/ [A, B]        →   16/B, 15/A
1/ [C, D]         →   3/C, 8/D
15/ actor         →   i
3/ actedon        →   h
16/ john          →   v, s
16/ jane          →   k, h
8/ john           →   e, v, s, n
8/jane            →   s
6/ [E, F]         →   14/F, 7/E
7/ act            →   i, b
14/ adores        →   y, n, k
14/loves          →   j, v
14/sees           →   h, m, l
```
(Moy 2006: 230)

5 Impact on artificial language evolution and linguistic theory

This would lead to sentences such as:

(5) h   evsn kh i   jv   ib
     actedon john jane actor loves act
     'Jane loves John.'

(6) h   s   vs i   jv   ib
     actedon jane john actor loves act
     'John loves Jane.'

5.2.5.2 Discussion

Moy's experiments suggest that the Iterated Learning Model cannot overcome its bias towards one-to-one mappings, which is confirmed in the fact that experimenters working with the model increasingly turn to innate constraints for explaining grammar emergence: Moy explicitly includes two semantic roles in the meaning space, and Smith (2003b) and Smith & Hurford (2003) implement explicit biases towards one-to-one mappings. This is highly problematic since grammatical categories are clearly multifunctional. It also means that the ILM studies have given up on their original objectives: instead of demonstrating that grammar can evolve through *cultural* selection, a strong Language Acquisition Device is built in.

The experiments in this book do not presuppose such a bias towards one-to-one mappings and in fact offer **the first multi-agent simulations ever featuring polysemous categories**. By taking communicative pressures seriously and by providing the agents with a richer cognitive apparatus including analogy and multi-level selection, this book demonstrated how agents can deal with the variety and uncertainty that is inherent to multi-agent simulations, how they can self-organize and coordinate a grammar involving multifunctional semantic roles, and how they can reuse the same linguistic items in multiple patterns of argument realization.

What is also striking about Moy's results is the fact that even though there are only two agents at each given time and even though the learner is equipped with a highly specialized learning mechanism, the grammars can still get stuck in a state which is not fully systematic. This suggests that (a) a learning bottleneck is not a sufficient pressure for reaching a systematic language, and that (b) an innate mechanism that seriously restricts the space of possible grammars is not sufficient for dealing with variation. The only way to avoid this unsystematic state, as I argued in Chapter 4, is to assume a cognitive-functional view on gram-

5.2 Pushing the state-of-the-art

mar in which agents are given credit for possessing the right skills and alignment strategies to arrive at a shared and systematic communication system.

5.2.6 Summary: case markers serve communication

The ILM and the problem-solving approach both argue that grammar evolves through cultural evolution but both models diverge significantly in terms of assumptions and hypotheses (see Table 5.1). The most important difference is that the ILM tries to explain as much grammatical structure as possible as a side-effect of the cultural transmission of language from one generation to the next, whereas the problem-solving approach assumes that grammatical development is triggered by the need to optimize communicative success. This leads to two different types of learners: in the ILM the learner needs strong innate constraints

Table 5.1: This table summarizes the main differences between Moy (2006) and the work in this book.

	Iterated Learning	This book
Triggers of grammar	- Poverty of the Stimulus - Learning bottleneck - Function independence	- Communicative success - Reducing cognitive effort - Increasing expressiveness
Learner	- Eager learner - Greedy induction - Top-down	- Lazy learner - Careful abstraction - Bottom-up
Language change	- Hearer-based innovation - Mismatch in learning	- Speaker-based innovation - Adoption by hearer - Propagation in population
Grammaticalization	- Analysis only - Holistic strategy - Start without language	- Analogy and patterns - Continuity principle (reuse) - Start from lexicon
Inventory	- Rewrite rules - Ordered but unstructured	- Constructions - Structured through usage
Meanings	- Two-way contrast - Semantic roles given	- Event-specific meaning - No prior semantic roles
Population	- Two-agent simulation - Generational turnover - Speakers vs learners	- Multi-agent simulation - Single generation - Peer-to-peer interactions

5 Impact on artificial language evolution and linguistic theory

as opposed the problem-solving approach where the learner is equipped with a rich cognitive apparatus for detecting and solving communicative problems.

Since the learner in the ILM is endowed with some kind of Universal Grammar, the model has a lot of difficulties with handling inconsistent input data and variation. The problem-solving model of this book, on the other hand, does not face those difficulties. It features a redundant and bottom-up approach to language and an utterance-based selectionist system in which careful abstraction is possible despite the enormous uncertainty about the conventions in the speech community. The agents in this book do not assume one-to-one mappings and the experiments offer the first multi-agent simulations ever which involve polysemous categories.

Another achievement of this book is that it detected and solved the problem of systematicity. I showed that the problem also occurs in Iterated Learning Models (and other models, see Chapter 4) but that it remained unnoticed so far. I argued that this was due to an underestimation of the complexity of natural language phenomena and a shallow comparison between natural and artificial languages. The work in this book is more firmly rooted in linguistic theory and offers a model which is closer to attested cases of grammaticalization.

It should be noted that both approaches are not mutually exclusive. The problem-solving approach naturally incorporates all the learning constraints that are focused upon in the ILM but goes much further in terms of learning and innovation strategies in order to optimize communicative success. Expanding the model to multi-generational population dynamics is indeed technically quite trivial and has already been successfully demonstrated in many experiments (e.g. De Beule 2008; Steels & McIntyre 1999). Expanding the ILM to a multi-agent population, however, is much more problematic.

5.3 Argument structure and construction grammar

5.3.1 Overview

In Chapter 2 and van Trijp (2008b), I proposed a formalization of argument realization in Fluid Construction Grammar. Even though my proposal was explicitly implemented for supporting experiments on artificial language evolution, its ideas are relevant for formalisms of natural languages as well. Within the family of construction grammars, however, no alternative computational implementation has been reported yet in a peer-reviewed publication that can handle both parsing and production. As such, van Trijp (2008b) offers the first computational implementation of argument structure constructions within a construction grammar framework.

This doesn't mean that no other work has been done yet: at the moment this book was written, a different proposal was still in the process of being worked out (but not implemented) in Sign-Based Construction Grammar (SBCG, Fillmore et al. unpubl.), a formalism that combines HPSG (Pollard & Sag 1994) with Berkeley Construction Grammar (BCG, Kay & Fillmore 1999). Since the draft proposals are closely related to the more construction-oriented approaches in HPSG, I will assume here that SBCG can be implemented and applied in a *computational* formalism as well. In the remainders of this section, I will briefly illustrate how SBCG deals with argument structure (based on Fillmore et al. unpubl. Kay 2005; Michaelis 2012; Sag 2013). I will then illustrate this for the English ditransitive based on Kay (2005) and then compare it to my own representation of argument structure.

5.3.2 Argument structure in BCG and SBCG

Early representations of argument structure in a construction grammar framework (such as Goldberg 1995) and the representation used in this book propose argument structure constructions in which the meaning can be seen as a skeletal or schematic event type such as X-CAUSES-Y-TO-MOVE. These constructions then have to unify or fuse with the lexical entry of the verb. In later versions of BCG and in SBCG, however, argument structure constructions are implemented as two-level derivational rules that have a "mother"-component (MTR) and a "daughter"-component (DTR). The DTR unifies with the lexical entry of the verb and is complemented by the MTR. The SBCG proposal looks very much like lexical rules in lexicalist accounts.

The SBCG approach is in the same spirit as Goldberg (1995) in the sense that minimal lexical entries are assumed for verbs which have to be complemented by argument structure constructions. SBCG however goes a step further and allows argument structure constructions to *override* the default behaviour of a verb (Michaelis 2012; Sag 2013). Sag (2013) writes that SBCG has a feature called "argument structure" (ARG-ST) which encodes the valence of a verb. This feature is a structured list which is coupled to the "Accessibility Hierarchy" of Keenan & Comrie (1977): the first argument maps onto subject, the second onto the direct object, etc. The rank-based listing of arguments is chosen to eliminate the need for explicit features such as "subject" and "object".

Different argument realization patterns, such as the active-passive alternation, are represented through different values for the ARG-ST list. SBCG has two different ways to implement these differences: either a derivational construction overrides the default ARG-ST of the verb (as is the case in passivization) or there is lexical under-specification (for example in locative alternations). In addition to the feature ARG-ST, SBCG also has a feature VAL(ence) which is a list of the syntactic elements that a linguistic expression yet has to combine with. Sag gives the example of the verb phrase *persuaded me to go*, which takes the VAL list < NP > because it still needs to combine with a subject NP. The clause *my dad persuaded me to go* takes an empty VAL list because it doesn't need to combine with any other argument anymore. Only lexical constructions have both ARG-ST and VAL features. Phrases, clauses, NPs, and other items only have empty VAL lists.

5.3.3 An example: the ditransitive construction

I will now illustrate argument structure constructions in SBCG based on Kay (2005)'s analysis of the English ditransitive. Kay's proposal is somewhat different than the most recent developments of the SBCG architecture, but the underlying ideas are the same (Kay, pers. comm.). It shares many aspects with the approach offered by Goldberg (1995), such as the assumption that there is a default and minimal lexical entry for each verb. For example, the lexical entry of the verb *to bake* contains two minimally required arguments (a baker and a thing that is baked). Argument structure constructions can add arguments such as the beneficiary in *He baked him a cake*.

Goldberg sees argument structure constructions as larger patterns carrying grammatical meanings which have to be "fused" with the meaning of the lexical entries. Kay, however, proposes argument structure constructions which are more like lexical constructions with a "mother constituent" and a single daughter. The daughter unifies with a lexical entry and is elaborated by the mother constituent. Applied to the English ditransitive construction, Kay proposes three "maximal recipient constructions" which all three inherit from a more schematic "Abstract Recipient Construction":

(7)

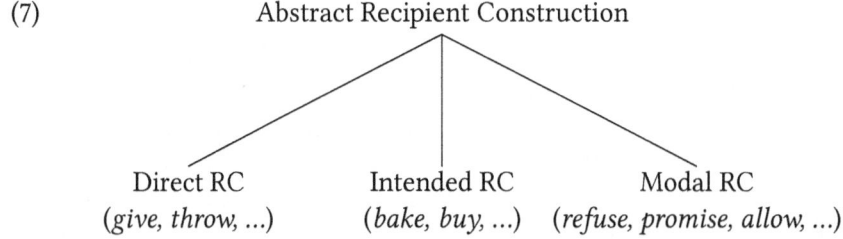

5.3 Argument structure and construction grammar

These constructions are represented in a unification-based grammar as detailed in Kay & Fillmore (1999), and which is similar to analyses of argument structure in HPSG (Pollard & Sag 1994). The Abstract Recipient Construction is shown in Figure 5.1. The construction shows all information which is common to all English ditransitive constructions. The lower box represents the DTR constituent, which needs to unify with the lexical entry of the verb. As can be seen, its valence list contains an NP (which plays the role of "actor") and an underspecified argument (…). The top box represents the MTR constituent which complements the lexical entry of the verb with the "recipient" role. The 'list'-feature displays the construction's primary semantic frame (*an intentional act* which has an actor and an undergoer) and additionally an *intended result* which still needs to be specified by another frame. Kay proposes that the intended result in the Direct RC is the 'receive frame' (see below) whereas in the other sub-constructions it is not.

The Direct RC corresponds to Goldberg (1995)'s "central sense" of the ditransitive as in *He gave him a book*. The main frame of the MTR component is a CAUSE-MOVE act which is defined as a subtype of an intentional act. The receive frame is unified with the intended result of the main frame indicating that there was an actual transfer of possession. The daughter's valence list indicates that it takes verbs which have at least two arguments (an actor and an undergoer). The Direct RC is illustrated in Figure 5.2.

In the Intended RC, for handling utterances such as *He baked him a cake*, there is no actual transfer of possession entailed but only the intention of transfer. A second reason for positing a different construction for the Intended RC is that it cannot occur in the passive. Kay therefore includes an explicit stipulation in the construction which states that it cannot combine with a derivational passive construction. All the remaining senses of the ditransitive are grouped together in the Modal RC. This construction is similar to the Intended RC in that it does not entail actual transfer either, but it is different in the sense that it doesn't require *beneficiary* semantics. Kay argues that specific meanings are contributed by the verbs themselves so no additional constructions need to be posited.

5.3.4 Discussion and comparison

5.3.4.1 Derivational versus non-derivational constructions.

The most remarkable distinction between argument realization in Sign-Based Construction Grammar and Fluid Construction Grammar is that FCG adopts the cognitive-functional tradition of construction-based approaches in which argu-

5 Impact on artificial language evolution and linguistic theory

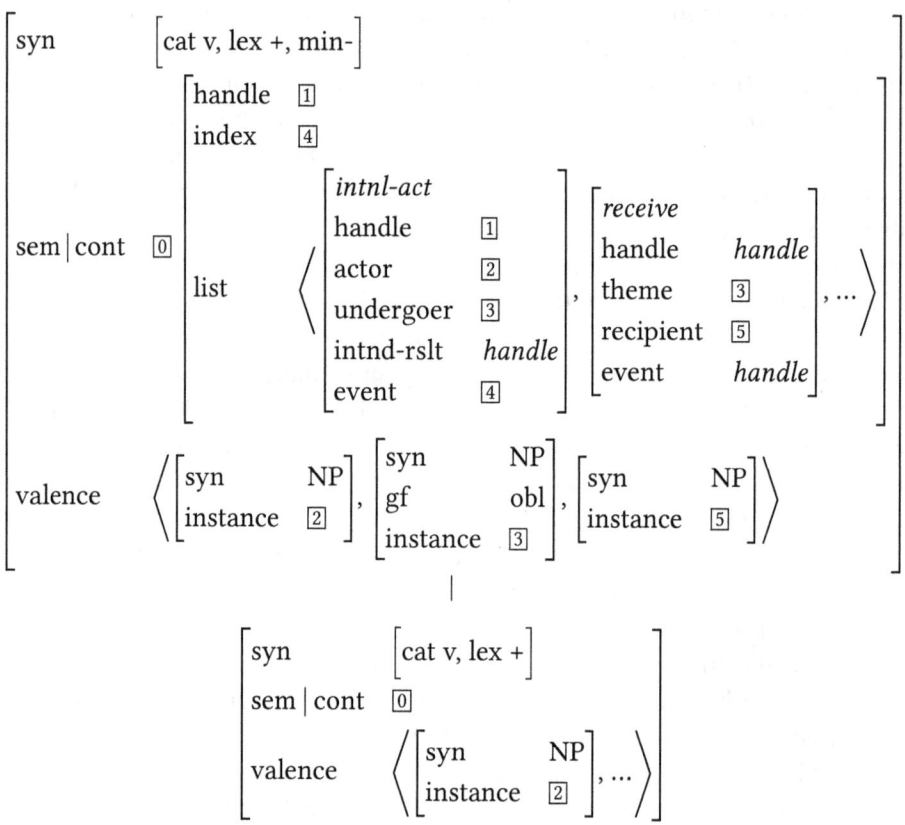

Figure 5.1: The Abstract Recipient Construction proposed by Kay (2005).

ment structure constructions have skeletal meanings that need to unify or fuse with the semantics of the lexical entries of the verbs. FCG could thus be said to implement a "fusion" process similar to proposals made by Goldberg (1995). SBCG, on the other hand, has given up on this kind of analysis and moved closer towards HPSG by using (almost lexical) derivational rules which feature two components: a mother and a daughter.

These different approaches are the result of different solutions to the same problem: multiple argument realization. Both SBCG and FCG try to solve the problem through the notion of "potential syntactico-semantic arguments" (Sag 2013) or what I called "potential valents" in Chapter 2. This word "potential" refers to the fact that a lexical entry can combine with multiple argument realization patterns. However, the implementation of this "potential" is fundamentally different in both formalisms.

5.3 Argument structure and construction grammar

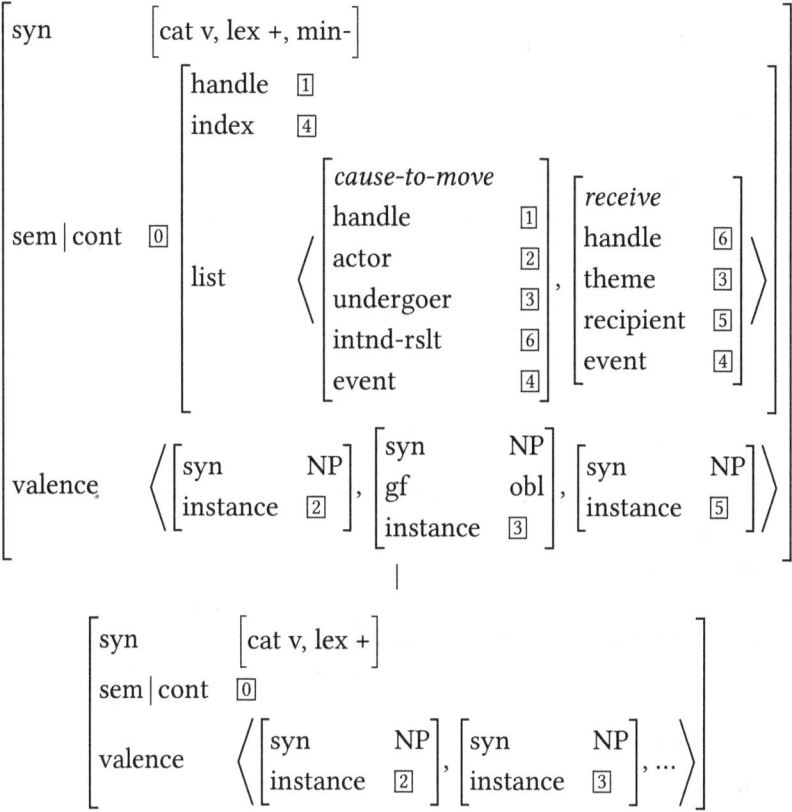

Figure 5.2: The Direct Recipient Construction proposed by Kay (2005).

SBCG starts from the traditional assumption that lexical entries have a fixed predicate-frame which is implemented in the verb's VAL(ence) list. In order to still cope with multiple argument realization patterns, this VAL list either needs to be under-specified or overridden by derivational rules. This capacity of overwriting the predicate-frame of a verb is in fact the only difference with traditional lexicalist accounts. FCG, on the other hand, does not assume a minimal lexical entry: a linguistic item merely lists its potential from which more grammatical constructions can select the actual valency. In other words, the meaning of the verb strongly influences its morpho-syntactic realization but its actual valency is still dependent on the other constructions that combine with it.

The difference can be easily explained through an analogy to mathematics which I borrowed and adapted from Michaelis (2012). Michaelis writes that constructions have the possibility to change the associations within an arithmetic sequence like *2 x (3 + 4)* to the sequence *(2 x 3) + 4*, which would yield different results (*14* and *10*). The individual numbers, however, denote the same value in each sequence. Michaelis' analogy does not quite fit, however, since in SBCG a number would be listed with a minimal ARG-ST (for example saying that "2" has to be used in a sum). SBCG therefore does more than storing the entry "2" with its denotation and would need a derivational rule which overrides the specification of "2". FCG, on the other hand, would list the number "2" and state that it can be potentially used in sums, divisions and other functions without actually committing to a single operation. The construction would then pick what it needs from the number.

5.3.4.2 Evidence from corpus-linguistics

Technically speaking, the implementation differences between SBCG and FCG do not really matter. The main problem with derivational constructions, however, is the assumption that some senses of lexical items are more central or more basic than others. Traditionally, these "minimal entries" are however based on intuition rather than empirical data. For example, what is the minimal entry for a verb such as *to give* if the following examples are taken into account:

(8) He gave him the book.
(9) He was given the book.
(10) He gave blood.
(11) Give it!
(12) Give it to me!
(13) Give me the book!

More examples can easily be found. The point is however that FCG would have no real preference for either pattern (except perhaps as the result of frequency and priming effects) since the lexical entry does not contain a fixed predicate-frame. SBCG would list *give* as a three-place predicate even though numerous sentences can be observed in which not all three arguments are present. Both formalisms thus make different predictions as to the frequency of argument realization patterns: FCG allows for different frequency patterns for each verb individually (which is captured through co-occurrence links between lexical entries and constructions), whereas SBCG predicts a most basic use of a verb with derived and therefore less frequent uses.

5.3 Argument structure and construction grammar

These predictions can be verified through careful corpus studies. A good example is the active-passive alternation. In FCG, the passive is an argument structure construction in its own right which stands on equal footing with active argument structure constructions. In SBCG, on the other hand, the passive construction is a derivational construction, which needs to overwrite the default active VAL.

The relationship between active and passive has been investigated by Stefanowitsch & Gries (2003) in a "collostructional analysis". Collostructional analysis combines statistical data of co-occurrences between words with a close attention to the constructions in which these words occur. This method allows for a detailed analysis of the relations between words and constructions. Stefanowitsch & Gries use a slightly extended collostructional analysis for investigating various alternations among which the active-passive one. The results of their study shows that there are clear semantically motivated classes of distinctive collexemes for both the active and the passive. The most distinctive collexemes with respect to the active voice were *to have* along with emotional-mental stative verbs such as *think, say, want* and *mean*. With respect to the passive voice, there is a clear class of verbs that "overwhelmingly encode processes that cause the patient to come to be in a relatively permanent end state" (p. 110), such as *base, concern* and *use*.

Stefanowitsch & Gries thus confirm prior claims by Pinker (1989) and conclude that the passive construction is primarily a semantic construction rather than a construction that is mainly used for marking differences in information structure. In other words, there are no empirical grounds for assuming that the active construction is basic and that the passive construction has to be derived from it. This observation is highly problematic for the lexical derivations in SBCG but can be captured nicely by FCG.

5.3.4.3 Thematic hierarchy

The above observations also make the ranked ordering of the ARG-ST of SBCG highly problematic: many verbs apparently prefer the passive construction and therefore violate the ranking more frequently than they follow it. Moreover, the universality of the thematic hierarchy has become a matter of big debate due to the serious empirical problems with such hierarchies (Levin & Rappaport Hovav 2005). In fact, many researchers in HPSG have turned to macro-roles or other constructs to get rid of the unsatisfactory thematic hierarchies (Davis & Koenig 2000).

FCG does not assume any notion of thematic hierarchies, macro-roles or universal linking rules. Instead, preference patterns for argument linking and real-

5 Impact on artificial language evolution and linguistic theory

ization emerge as a side-effect of analogy in innovation and multi-level selection: analogical reasoning explains why existing linguistic items get reused in new situations and multi-level selection assures a growing systematicity in which linguistic items combine into a structured linguistic inventory. Recurrent patterns are hypothesized to be captured by the distributed constructions which show systematicity in their classification behaviour. I will come back to this matter in more detail in the other sections of this chapter.

5.3.4.4 The emergence of argument structure constructions.

A third problem with the architecture of SBCG is that it would be very hard to implement in the scenario of an emergent language or in which the first emergence of grammar takes place. If there is no grammar yet, there are simply no conventions to build a grammar upon. Language users would nevertheless have to agree on the "basic" argument structure of a lexical entry despite the many conflicting variations floating around in the population (which are often more frequent than what would be intuitively speaking the "minimal" entry). Then they would have to agree somehow that all possible alternations are in fact derivational constructions. On top of that, these derivational constructions have to be nicely ordered: for example, the passive alternation comes after the ditransitive derivation which comes after the lexical entry. Again, FCG seems to be more flexible in this respect.

5.4 Analogy, multi-level selection and the constructicon

5.4.1 Overview

In generative grammar, the problem of systematicity has never been an issue since all categories and grammar rules are assumed to be innate. In construction grammars and usage-based models of language, however, the linguistic inventory is supposed to be acquired in a bottom-up fashion so more attention has been given to how this inventory should be structured. In this section, I will give a brief overview of the most important proposals in construction grammar based on Croft & Cruse (2004: 262–290). Next, I will argue that construction grammars need to take multi-level selection into account in how they conceive the relations between constructions in the linguistic inventory or the "constructicon".

5.4 Analogy, multi-level selection and the constructicon

5.4.2 The organization of the linguistic inventory

Croft & Cruse (2004) write that the structured, linguistic inventory of a speaker

> is usually represented by construction grammars in terms of a **taxonomic network** of constructions. Each construction constitutes a **node** in the taxonomic network of constructions. (Croft & Cruse 2004: 262)

In other words, constructions are related to each other through taxonomy links or instance links which describe a relationship of schematicity between two constructions. The following example shows a taxonomic relation between the idiom *The X-er, the Y-er* and an *instance* of that more schematic construction:

(14)   [The X-er, the Y-er]
                                   |
           [The bigger they come, the harder they fall.]
      (Croft & Cruse 2004: 263, example 3)

The rule of thumb for deciding when a construction has its independent node in the network is when not all aspects of the construction's semantics or syntax can be derived from its subparts or from more schematic constructions. For example, the idiom *to kick the bucket* has its own representation in the network because its meaning cannot be derived from the individual words in combination with a schematic transitive construction. Most but not all theories assume that *to kick the bucket* is also part of the inheritance network but which locally overrides the default behaviour of the more schematic constructions:

(15)   [VerbPhrase]   (Croft & Cruse 2004: 263, example 4)
                    |
             [Verb Obj]
                    |
             [[*kick* Obj]
                   |
         [*kick* [*the bucket*]]

Depending on how much redundancy the theory allows, frequent instances can be kept as well even though a more schematic construction may already exist. Finally, sentences usually feature *multiple inheritance*: constructions often only offer a "partial specification" of the grammatical structures of their daughter constructions. Croft & Cruse give the example *I didn't sleep*, which inherits from both the [Subject - Intransitive Verb] construction and the [Subject Auxiliary-n't Verb] construction (p. 264, example 6).

5 Impact on artificial language evolution and linguistic theory

The most influential construction grammars all assume the above organization of the linguistic inventory. Croft & Cruse discuss four of them: Berkeley Construction Grammar (Kay & Fillmore 1999), the Lakoff/Goldberg model (Goldberg 1995), Cognitive Grammar (Langacker 1987) and Radical Construction Grammar (Croft 2001). The latter three are also considered to be usage-based models of language. Croft & Cruse compare the different models based on a couple of questions, of which the following two are directly relevant for our discussion (p. 265, questions (iii) and (iv)):

1. What sorts of relations are found between constructions?

2. How is grammatical information stored in the construction taxonomy?

5.4.3 Construction grammars

5.4.3.1 Berkeley Construction Grammar

In the discussion of Berkeley Construction Grammar (BCG) in §5.3.2 I already briefly mentioned that BCG features an inheritance network for organizing the linguistic inventory. Unlike examples 14 and 15, however, BCG does not allow for any kind of redundancy. It is a complete inheritance model in which information is only represented once and at the highest, most schematic level possible. This also means that BCG does not require all constructions to be symbolic units (i.e. form-meaning mappings): they can be entirely syntactic or semantic as well.

BCG therefore captures all information in terms of taxonomy links. Since no information is stored more than once, parts of constructions can in fact be children of other parent constructions. The network thus not only has instance links between constructions, but also between parents and parts of other constructions.

5.4.3.2 The Lakoff/Goldberg model.

The model proposed by Lakoff (1987) and Goldberg (1995) focuses more on the categorization relations that may exist between constructions. Next to the taxonomy/instance links, Goldberg also proposes a meronomic or subpart link (p. 78) and a "polysemy" link (p. 38). The subpart link is different from the BCG subpart links: in BCG, a subpart is a complete instance of a more schematic construction, whereas Goldberg sees subpart links as constructions which are subparts of larger constructions but nevertheless have an independent representation in

5.4 Analogy, multi-level selection and the constructicon

the inventory. The "polysemy" links are links between constructions that have the same syntactic specification but different semantics.

One important aspect of the Lakoff/Goldberg model is the notion of a prototype and (metaphorical) extension. For example, if constructions are related through polysemy links, there is always a "central sense" assumed. For the English ditransitive, this is the sense of actual transfer as in *I gave him a book*. Goldberg and Lakoff propose a somewhat different model when it comes to metaphorical extension: Goldberg assumes that metaphorical extension involves a superordinate schema from which the central sense and the extenstion(s) are instances; Lakoff does not assume such a schema.

The type of inheritance in the Lakoff/Goldberg model is different from BCG in the sense that an instance is allowed to locally overwrite some information that is normally inherited from a higher schema. For example, a schematic category such as BIRD may contain the feature FLIES, but this is not true for penguins. In the penguin-category, the inheritance of FLIES is therefore blocked by local specifications. This solution is also handy when there is conflicting information in the case of multiple inheritance: the instance is then assumed to be represented as a full entry in the inventory.

5.4.3.3 Cognitive Grammar.

Langacker's Cognitive Grammar (CG) is regarded by most cognitive linguists as some form of construction grammar because it shares many of its assumptions and objectives. Langacker assumes that a category typically has a prototypical member or a set of members and that new instances are categorized by extension from the prototypes. Next to this model of prototypes and extension, CG also allows for a more schematic unit which subsumes the prototype and its extensions. This view comes closest to the model of extension through analogy that I operationalized in Chapter 3.

The organization of the linguistic inventory is dependent on language use. The entrenchment or independent representation of a linguistic item is hypothesized to depend on its token frequency: if a unit occurs frequently enough, it is stored in memory. Productivity of a linguistic unit goes hand in hand with its extension through language use: if a (prototypical) category gets extended to new situations, it increases its type frequency and hence its productivity. As said before, categories can form a network based on prototypical members (instances) and non-prototypical members, but there are also abstractions which are related to their members through taxonomy links.

5.4.3.4 Radical Construction Grammar

The word "radical" in Radical Construction Grammar (RCG) comes from the fact that RCG does not assume constructions to be built from atomic categories such as nouns or verbs, but rather that the construction is the atomic unit of language. All other categories are defined in terms of the constructions they occur in. Categories are thus assumed to be construction- and language-specific. For example, the transitive construction and intransitive construction are hypothesized to contain two different verb categories: the transitive verb and the intransitive verb. The superordinate category Verb is seen as a linguistic abstraction over those two categories (Croft & Cruse 2004: 287–288):

(16)

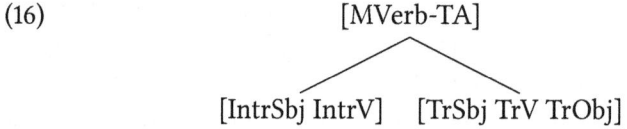

In the above example, the label MVerb is used to indicate that this is a morphological construction (TA stands for Tense and Aspect). The superordinate abstraction can only be made if it is linguistically motivated. For example, both transitive and intransitive verbs can be marked for tense and aspect so both categories should be able to occur in those Tense-Aspect constructions. In short, RCG is a strongly non-reductionist approach as opposed to BCG.

RCG features the same taxonomy links as other construction grammars and also allows for redundant information according to the principles of usage-based models of language. One other important aspect of RCG is that it is based on the "semantic map" model (see §5.5). In this model, all constructions are hypothesized to map onto contiguous regions in "conceptual space" which is assumed to be universal. Finally, syntactic structures are defined as language-specific units but in relation to "syntactic space" which aims at typologically comparing the world's languages.

5.4.4 The inventory in Fluid Construction Grammar

5.4.4.1 Design stance

Before I start the comparison between Fluid Construction Grammar and the above theories, I would like to emphasize again that FCG takes a design stance towards the emergence of grammar and that it therefore only implements mechanisms that are experimentally demonstrated to be necessary requirements. The fact that FCG does not make the same abstractions or does not feature the same

5.4 Analogy, multi-level selection and the constructicon

complex mechanisms for organizing the linguistic network therefore does not mean that they are refuted, but only that they are not necessary (yet) for the level of complexity that is reached in current simulations. On the other hand, FCG can show which proposals stand the computationally rigid test in less complex languages. Secondly, by demonstrating novel but necessary mechanisms in those less complex languages, FCG can show which ideas are currently being overlooked by linguistic theories.

5.4.4.2 The emergence of linguistic categories

With respect to the "atomic" building blocks of a grammar in emergence, FCG is closest related to Radical Construction Grammar. From an evolutionary point-of-view, it is more natural to think of constructions or form-meaning mappings as the atomic units in language and that other categories are dependent on the organization of these constructions. For example, the experiments do not feature an explicit category for nouns or verbs, yet all words can be used without any problem in argument structure constructions. Further categorizations should be functionally motivated. For example, if the agents should also worry about tense and aspect marking, they might need additional generalizations over their existing constructions.

This scenario is attractive in many ways. First, the agents do not need to agree on a set of building blocks such as nouns or verbs before they can start combining them into sentences. Instead they keep on constructing new categories on the fly but only when this optimizes communication and thus when it is functionally motivated. This approach also seems to fit natural languages better since it is impossible to come up with an abstract rule that can be applied to all parts of speech of a language. Finally, this approach also suits my proposal of potential valents for linguistic items: the freer and typically lexical items can be potentially used in many different constructions, whereas the more grammaticalized, tightened constructions typically decide on the actual valency of a linguistic expression.

FCG therefore rejects the reductionist approach of BCG (and SBCG). Reductionist approaches are still dominant in linguistics as a result of a desire for maximizing "storage parsimony" in the linguistic inventory. Croft & Cruse (2004: 278), however, point to psychological evidence that suggests that storage parsimony is a cognitively implausible criterion for modeling the linguistic inventory. Language users rather seem to store a lot of redundant information which requires more memory but which optimizes "computing parsimony" because not all information has to be computed online.

5.4.4.3 Innovation through analogy and pattern formation.

Fluid Construction Grammar also subscribes the usage-based model and argues that innovation occurs through analogical reasoning. In the experiments of this book, I implemented an innovation strategy in which the productivity of a category is related to its type frequency and which is therefore similar to proposals made in Cognitive Grammar. FCG also allows for careful abstraction in which an instance link is created between the more abstract category and the specific instances that are compatible with it. A second drive for innovation is pattern formation: frequently co-occurring utterances are stored as independent units in memory. This is also completely in line with usage-based models that take token frequency as an indicator of entrenchment. The newly formed patterns themselves may be extended through analogy as well.

One salient feature of FCG is that all innovation occurs in a stepwise fashion. If a careful abstraction is made, it is at that moment only valid for the instances that were used in creating the abstraction. The newly formed category therefore does not automatically extend its use to other situations: an explicit link in the network has to be created during other interactions. For pattern formation as well, links are kept between the newly created pattern and its subparts. All the links in the inventory are used for optimizing linguistic processing: instead of considering the entire memory, only linked constructions are unified and merged. Only when this strategy leads to communicative problems, the language user will try to adapt the inventory through analogy.

5.4.4.4 Multi-level selection in the emergence of language systematicity.

The work in this book has also uncovered the problem of systematicity which has so far been overlooked by all linguistic theories. The usage-based models presented in the previous section mainly focus on a top-down inheritance network and seem to assume that this suffices for reaching and maintaining systematicity if the network is combined with an innovation strategy based on type frequency and productivity.

The experiments in Chapter 4, however, demonstrate that this is not the case. Next to an innovation strategy which systematically reuses productive and successful items of the inventory, language users need an alignment strategy based on multi-level selection to further streamline their inventories and keep the generalization rate of their language high. The experiments demonstrated that a top-down strategy does not suffice but that the success and evolution of specific instances must also have a way to influence the more schematic constructions in the network. The networks therefore need **systematicity links** rather than (only) taxonomy links.

5.4.4.5 On the status of inheritance networks.

The experiments on multi-level selection show how a linguistic network similar to the one proposed in Radical Construction Grammar could gradually emerge: a nonreductionist approach is taken in which each construction has its specific categories. However, FCG does not make explicit generalizations over these constructions as is done in RCG, but rather keeps systematicity links which are used by the multi-level selection alignment strategy. There is no need for an inheritance network and all utterances are licensed by unifying and merging fully specified constructions.

This architecture suffices for the kinds of experiments performed in this book and only further work can show whether additional abstractions and perhaps inheritance networks are really needed. A serious challenge to these kinds of abstractions and inheritance networks is posed by the successful application of instance-based models in natural language processing such as Memory-Based Language Processing (Daelemans & Van den Bosch 2005) and Analogical Modeling (Skousen 1989). Another challenge for inheritance networks, I believe, is that they might require abstractions that are too greedy and therefore harmful to the communicative success of language users, especially in experiments on the emergence of grammar. As becomes very clear in such experiments, agents have to deal with an enormous amount of uncertainty about the conventions in their population. It might very well turn out to be that a fully redundant model (with or without careful abstraction) using multi-level selection is a more adequate model.

5.5 Linguistic typology and grammaticalization

5.5.1 Overview

The previous two sections mainly dealt with the relations between construction grammar and the experiments in this book. In this section, I will discuss how the methodology of artificial language evolution can provide novel insights to the fields of grammaticalization and linguistic typology.

5 Impact on artificial language evolution and linguistic theory

5.5.2 The status of semantic maps

5.5.2.1 Introduction

Semantic maps have offered linguists an appealing and empirically rooted methodology for visualizing the multifunctional nature of grammatical categories and for describing recurrent structural patterns in how these functions relate to each other. Consider the following examples in which various functions of the English preposition *to* are illustrated along with some corresponding examples from the French preposition *à* and the German dative case (taken from Haspelmath 2003: example 2, p. 212 and example sentences on p. 213–215):

(17) English preposition *to*:

    a. Goethe went to Leipzig as a student. (direction)
    b. Eve gave the apple to Adam. (recipient)
    c. This seems outrageous to me. (experiencer)
    d. I left the party early to get home in time. (purpose)
    e. This dog is (mine/*to me). (predicative possessor)
    d. I'll buy a bike (for/*to) you. (beneficiary)
    e. That's too warm (for/*to) me. (dative judicantis)

(18) French preposition *à*:
Ce chien est   à moi.
this dog is.3SG to me
'This dog is mine.' (predicative possessor)

(19) German dative case:
Es ist   mir   zu warm.
it is.3SG 1SG.DAT too warm
'It's too warm for me.' (dative judicantis)

5.5.2.2 The universality of semantic maps.

Instead of listing the various functions of a grammatical morpheme or "gram", semantic maps offer a

> 'geometrical representation of functions in "conceptual/semantic" ' space that are linked by connecting lines and thus constitute a network. (Haspelmath 2003: 213)

5.5 Linguistic typology and grammaticalization

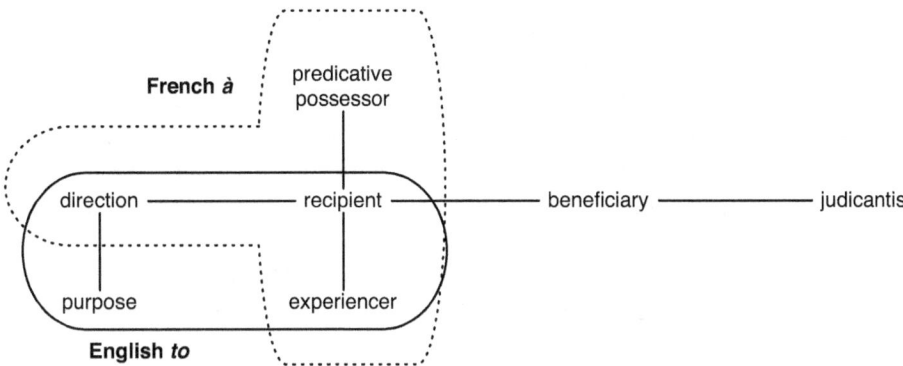

Figure 5.3: This partial semantic map compares the French preposition *à* to the English preposition *to* with respect to which typical dative functions they cover. Non-dative functions are ignored in this map (adapted from Haspelmath 2003: figures 8.1 and 8.2, p. 213 and 215).

Figure 5.3 gives an example of a semantic map which shows some typcal functions for the dative case. This map features a network of seven nodes which each represent a grammatical function. The Figure also illustrates that the English preposition *to* covers four of these functions (as was shown in example 17): purpose, direction, recipient and experiencer. It does not cover the functions beneficiary, predicative possessor (if prepositional verbs are not counted as in *the dog belongs to me*) and dative judicantis.

Semantic maps depend crucially on cross-linguistic research. For example, a node in the network is only added if at least one language is found which makes the distinction. Haspelmath gives the example of direction versus recipient (p. 217). Based on English and French, which use one preposition for both functions, this distinction could not be made. However, German uses *zu* or *nach* for direction, whereas it uses the dative case for recipient. A large sample set of languages is therefore needed to uncover all the uses of a gram.

Another important aspect of semantic maps is the connection between nodes in the network. The map must represent these nodes in a contiguous area on the map. Haspelmath writes that based on the English preposition *to*, for example, the following three orders could be possible for purpose, direction and recipient (p. 217, example 4):

(20) a. purpose – direction – recipient
 b. direction – purpose – recipient
 c. direction – recipient – purpose

193

5 Impact on artificial language evolution and linguistic theory

Again, data from other languages are taken into account for choosing which option can be eliminated. Since the French preposition *à* cannot be used for marking purpose, option (b) cannot represent a contiguous space in the network. The German preposition *zu* eliminates option (c) because it can express purpose and direction, but not recipient. The direct connections between functions on the semantic map are important because they are hypothesized to be universal:

> Semantic maps not only provide an easy way of formulating and visualizing differences and similarities between individual languages, but they can also be seen as a powerful tool for discovering universal semantic features that characterize the human language capacity. Once a semantic map has been tested on a sufficiently large number of languages [...] from different parts of the world, we can be reasonably confident that it will indeed turn out to be universal. (Haspelmath 2003: 232)

This view is shared by many other linguists, among whom Bill Croft. Croft's *Semantic Map Connectivity Hypothesis* (Croft 2001: 96) states that the functions of a particular construction will always cover functions that are connected regions in *conceptual space*. In other words, grammatical categories are language-particular, but they are based on a universal conceptual/semantic space.

The universality of semantic maps is however an issue of debate. For example, Cysouw (2007) reports on his attempts at making a satisfying map for person marking. He concludes that there is no single "universal" semantic map. Instead, different semantic maps are possible depending on the level and granularity of the analysis. Cysouw therefore calls for using semantic maps as a tool for modeling attested linguistic variety and as a way to predict *probable* languages rather than *possible* languages by weighting the function nodes in the network depending on the number of attested cases.

Cysouw thus points to a serious problem of the semantic map hypothesis: what grain-size is acceptable for making semantic maps? For example, Haspelmath (2003) uses functions such as "recipient" and "beneficiary" as primitive categories for his analysis. However, these functions are language-specific and no grammatical category has been demonstrated to cover all possible instantiations of such a function. Instead, languages tend to have many exceptions, irregularities or a redundant overlap in categories that mark that function. For example, "recipient" and "beneficiary" not only occur with the prepositions *to* and *for* respectively, they can also take the first object position in the English ditransitive.

The universality hypothesis therefore faces a problem of circularity. On the one hand, semantic maps are hypothesized to represent universal conceptual

5.5 Linguistic typology and grammaticalization

space; on the other hand, that conceptual space is based on an analysis which ignores language-internal differences and irregularities, and the languages that do not mark any differences are still assumed to have the same underlying functions.

Artificial language evolution could demonstrate an alternative hypothesis to explain the universal tendencies in grammatical marking. In problem-solving models such as this book, grammatical evolution is a consequence of distributed processes whereby language users shape and reshape their language. The main challenge is therefore to find out what these processes are and under what circumstances they could create the kind of semantic maps that are observed for human languages. The hypothesis is that these processes suffice for the emergence of semantic maps and that conceptual space is dynamically configured in co-evolution with grammar. Semantic maps of different languages will naturally show similarities and differences depending on whether they followed the same evolutionary pathways or not.

5.5.2.3 Prior work on concept emergence.

As mentioned in §1.4, prior work in the field has already demonstrated how a population of agents could self-organize a shared ontology through communicative interactions. Steels (1997a) reports the first experiments in which conceptualization and lexicon emergence are coupled to each other. In the experiment, a population of artificial agents take turns in playing "guessing games": the speaker chooses one of the objects in the context to talk about and wants to draw the hearer's attention to it by saying a word. The game is a success if the hearer points to the correct object. If the game fails, the speaker will point to the intended topic and the hearer tries to guess what the speaker might have meant with his word. The agents start without any language and even without an ontology. Instead, they are equipped with several sensory channels for perceiving the objects in their environment. At the start of a game, two agents are randomly chosen from the population to act as a speaker and as a hearer. The speaker chooses an object from the context to talk about and needs to conceptualize a meaning which discriminates the topic from the other objects in the context. For example, if the topic is a green ball and there are also three red balls in the context, then the topic's colour would be a good discriminating feature. At the beginning of the experiment, the agents have no concepts yet so the speaker has to create a new one. He will do so by taking the minimal set of features that can discriminate the topic from the other objects. The speaker will then invent a new word for this concept or meaning and transmit it to the hearer.

5 Impact on artificial language evolution and linguistic theory

The hearer will in turn experience a communicative problem: He does not know the word that was used by the speaker. The game thus fails, but the speaker points to the intended object. The hearer then tries to retrieve the intended meaning through the same discrimination game. Often there are many different sets of discriminating features possible, but if the agents play a sufficient amount of language games with each other, they come to an agreement on what the form-meaning pairs are in their language and thus also reach a shared conceptual space. Similar experiments have been successfully performed in the domains of colour terms (Steels & Belpaeme 2005) and spatial language (Steels & Loetzsch 2008), and they have been scaled up to large meaning spaces (Wellens 2008).

5.5.2.4 The contribution of this book

All of the above experiments confirm that communicative success can be a driving force for constructing an ontology of meaningful distinctions and that language can be used as a way to agree on a shared ontology among a population of autonomous embodied artificial agents. These experiments, however, have only focused on concept-and-lexicon emergence so far, and the systematic relations between words have not been investigated yet. The experiments in this book, however, have polysemous semantic roles so they form an ideal starting point for testing the alternative hypothesis.

Figure 5.4 illustrates how analogical reasoning can be responsible for constructing coherent classes of semantic roles. The diagrams shows two semantic maps for two languages that were formed in the last set-up of experiment 3 as described in §4.5 (multi-level selection with memory decay and pattern formation). Both diagrams show that it is possible to draw a primitive semantic map which compares the semantic roles of both languages. For example, in one language the marker *-mepui* can be used for covering four participant roles. Three of them (grasp-1, touch-1 and take-2) overlap with a semantic role of a different language. A similar observation counts for the two semantic roles in the second semantic map.

A comparison of the formed artificial languages suggests that grammaticalization processes can be visualized as a movement or change in connected regions of a continuous domain as a side-effect of analogical reasoning: extension of a category happens when new situations are encountered which are closely related to the existing categories. This shows that semantic maps could in principle be the result of dynamic processes involving analogy rather than starting from universal conceptual space.

5.5 Linguistic typology and grammaticalization

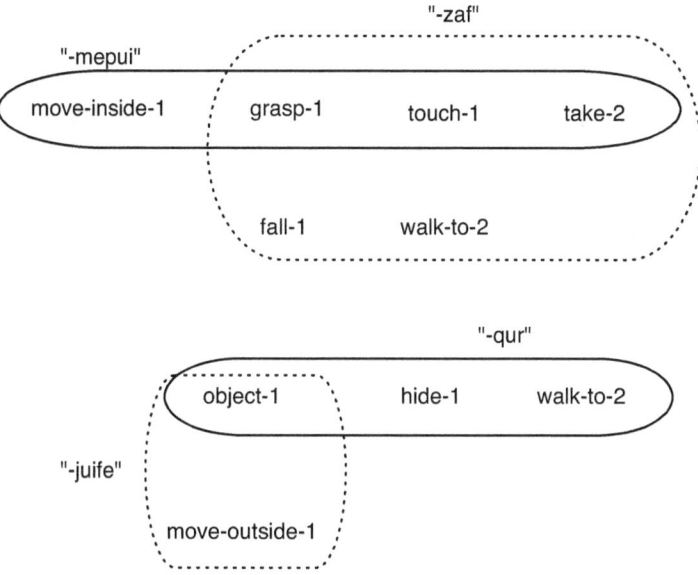

Figure 5.4: This diagram compares two different artificial grammars with respect to two categories in each of them. The languages were formed using the final set-up of experiment 3 (§4.5). Even though the agents did not have a continuous conceptual space in advance, it is nevertheless possible to draw a primitive semantic map afterwards.

The alternative proposed here needs further investigation and essentially requires a significant scale-up in terms of the meaning space and world environment as well as the conceptualization capabilities of the agents. The present results are however encouraging and the proposed alternative has the advantage that it is more adaptive and open-ended to a changing environment: a universal conceptual space would still require some mechanism of mapping culture-specific developments (such as buying and selling, driving cars, and steering airplanes) onto a prewired structure. If the alternative hypothesis is followed, semantic maps would thus not point to a universal map of human cognition but rather to recurrent patterns in human experience and preferred developmental pathways followed by dynamic categorization mechanisms.

197

5 Impact on artificial language evolution and linguistic theory

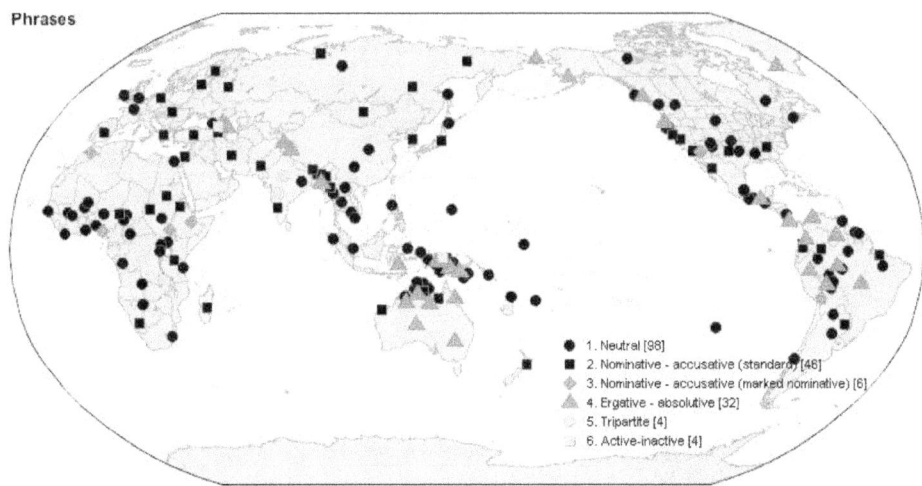

Figure 5.5: The alignment of case marking of full nounphrases (Comrie 2005: 98).

5.5.3 Thematic hierarchies in case systems

Many linguistic theories assume that argument linking is governed by a universal thematic hierarchy (e.g. Dik 1997; Fillmore 1968; Givón 2001; Jackendoff 1990; Keenan & Comrie 1977). However, empirical evidence shows that such hierarchies can offer tendencies at best, and that they cannot be considered as innate knowledge (Levin & Rappaport Hovav 2005). Even for language-specific argument linking patterns, no satisfying hierarchy has been found yet.

The question of how language systematicity can ever arise becomes a big issue if no universal hierarchy can be found, especially if no Universal Grammar is assumed. The map in Figure 5.5, for example, shows the alignment of case marking of full noun phrases across 190 languages. It clearly demonstrates strong systematicity in the marking of "core arguments" in these languages. Comrie (2005) distinguishes five different systems (I count the two variants of nominative-accusative systems as one):

- Neutral: the subject of intransitive clauses (S) is marked in the same way as both the subject (A) and object (P) of transitive clauses. Example: Mandarin.

- Nominative-accusative: A and S are marked in the same way (nominative marking). P is marked differently (accusative marking). Example: Latvian.

5.5 Linguistic typology and grammaticalization

- Ergative-absolutive: S and P are marked in the same way (ergative marking), A is marked differently (absolutive marking). Example: Hunzib.

- Tripartite: S, A and P are all marked differently. Example: Hindi.

- Active-inactive: There is a different marker for an agentive S (aligning with A) and a patientive S (aligning with P). Example: Georgian.

The answer for most linguists is again sought in universals. For example, Croft (1998) assumes a universal conceptual space and universal linking rules for mapping arguments to core syntactic cases. The problem here is again that the proposals only work for analyses that do not go beyond the crude representation of case marking systems as presented in Figure 5.5. Closer studies show that the proposed systems are again only tendencies in each language and that there are lots of exceptions to the "default" alignment of case marking. Also the typological variation across languages is greater than suggested by the traditional SAP-system of core arguments (Mithun 2005).

5.5.3.1 Analogy, pattern formation and multi-level selection.

In the case of thematic hierarchies, a similar alternative can be devised based on the distributed processes whereby language users shape and reshape their language for communication. As I argued in Chapter 3, generalization of grammatical categories arises as a side-effect within inferential coding systems: language users want to increase their communicative success and when speakers have to solve a problem or innovate, they will try to do this in such a way that the intended communicative effect is still reached. By exploiting analogy, the speaker can hook the new situation up to previous conventions which are probably known by the hearer as well. The hearer can then retrieve the intended meaning through the same mechanisms of analogical reasoning.

As categories get reused more often, they increase their type frequency and hence their productivity. An additional factor that boosts the success of such a category is when it starts to form patterns or groups with other elements in the inventory. A multi-level selection alignment strategy then assures that certain categories can also survive and reoccur in multiple levels of the linguistic network which again increases their frequency and chances of survival. Multi-level selection could thus explain how different constructions align their categories with each other as demonstrated in the map in Figure 5.5.

Preferences in argument linking, as predicted by thematic hierarchies, could thus gradually emerge as a side-effect of these mechanisms: as certain categories become more and more dominant and productive, they can start to extend their use across patterns and eventually evolve into prototypical subject and object categories (as I also suggested in §1.2.6). The many subregularities that are observed in languages are no problem in this model and are in fact predicted because everything has to emerge in a bottom-up fashion. Further experiments on the emergence of syntactic cases could thus be the starting point for modeling this alternative to thematic hierarchies.

5.5.4 A redundant approach to grammaticalization

A third debate in which artificial language evolution can offer novel insights is grammaticalization theory. As I already mentioned in §1.2.4, one of the problems of grammaticalization is that linguists can usually only detect language change once the processes of grammaticalization have already taken place. It is therefore difficult to hypothesize what mechanisms should be proposed to explain such changes especially since the consequences of communicative interactions in larger populations are often overlooked. Multi-agent simulations can thus demonstrate which mechanisms are better suited for dealing with innovations, variations, and propagations of linguistic conventions.

5.5.4.1 Reanalysis and actualization

Diachronic reanalysis has taken a foreground position in traditional grammaticalization theory. For example, Hopper & Traugott (1993) write: "Unquestionably, reanalysis is the most important mechanism for grammaticalization" (p. 32). Reanalysis is understood as a "change in the structure of an expression or class of expressions that does not involve any immediate or intrinsic modification of its surface manifestation" (Langacker 1977: 59). In other words, reanalysis is not noticeable from the surface form but only has consequences for the grammar at a later stage. Many theories therefore posit another mechanism called "actualization" that maps out the consequences of reanalysis (Timberlake 1977).

Reanalysis is typically illustrated by the grammaticalization of *be going to* into *gonna* (Hopper & Traugott 1993: 2–4). In an older use of *be going to*, *to* was part of a purposive directional complement as in *I am going to marry Bill* meaning 'I am going/travelling in order to marry Bill'. At a later stage, *to* is hypothesized to be reanalysed as belonging to *be going* instead of to the complement. In other words, rebracketing of the structure has taken place from [[I] [am going] [to marry Bill]] to [[I] [am going to] [marry Bill]].

5.5 Linguistic typology and grammaticalization

Reanalysis has recently been challenged. Haspelmath (1998) writes that reanalysis does not entail a loss of autonomy which is typical for grammaticalization and that grammaticalization is (almost exclusively) unidirectional instead of bidirectional as predicted by reanalysis. Haspelmath also rejects the combination of reanalysis with actualization which is often used as a way to assign gradualness to reanalysis (p. 340–341). Actualization makes "reanalysis" as a mechanism impossible to verify and it requires speakers to know at least two analyses of the same construction to account for both the old and the new behaviour. Actualization also does not explain how innovations might propagate. Haspelmath's comparison of "grammaticalization" and "reanalysis" is summarized in Table 5.2.

Table 5.2: This table shows the major differences between grammaticalization and reanalysis (Haspelmath 1998: 327, Table 1).

Grammaticalization	Reanalysis
loss of autonomy / substance	no loss of autonomy / substance
gradual	abrupt
unidirectional	bidirectional
no ambiguity	ambiguity in the input structure
due to language use	due to language acquisition

Despite the problems of reanalysis, it seems hard to conceive an alternative process that could explain certain changes. Haspelmath suggests that formal theories should implement the gradience of membership of word classes in some way such as "$V_{1.0}$ for ordinary verbs, $V_{.7}/P_{.3}$ for preposition-like verbs (e.g. *considering*) and so on" (p. 330). Even though gradience is indeed an important matter, such a proposal cannot capture the fact that the old use of a linguistic item and its new function can co-exist for hundreds of years in a language. The alternative that I would propose is redundancy and pattern formation along the lines of my example for French predicate negation in Chapter 4. Applied to the example of *gonna*, this alternative would simply state that the frequent co-occurrence of the words *be going to* led to the creation of a pattern for optimizing linguistic processing. Once this pattern is created, it may start evolving on its own which allows it to gradually drift away from the original use of the words.

5 Impact on artificial language evolution and linguistic theory

5.5.4.2 Example: the English verbal gerund.

To illustrate this alternative approach, I will briefly take a look at the English verbal gerund which historically developed from a deverbal nominalization and which later acquired more and more verbal properties. I will show examples of this development taken from Fanego (2004) and summarize how he describes this grammaticalization process in terms of "reanalysis" and "actualization". Next, I will argue for a simpler model based on redundancy and pattern formation.

The English gerund is a unique category in European languages in the sense that it is a third type of verbal complement besides to-infinitives (example 21) and finite clauses (22). The present-day English gerund has the following verbal properties: it can take a direct object (23), it can be modified by adverbs (24), it can mark tense, aspect and voice distinctions (25), it can be negated using the predicate negator *not* (26) and it can take a subject in a case other than the genitive (27).

(21) I just called *to say* 'I love you'.

(22) Just tell him *we're not interested anymore.*

(23) By writing *a book*, he managed to face all his inner demons.

(24) My *quietly* leaving before anyone noticed.

(25) The necessity of *being loved* is a driving force in our lives.

(26) My *not* leaving the room caused a stir.

(27) We should prevent *the treaty* taking effect.

Studies on the emergence and evolution of the gerund suggest that it developed from a deverbal nominalization construction, similar to phrases such as *the writing of a book* (Tajima 1985). This nominalization lacked the aforementioned verbal properties, which can be illustrated with a similar nominalization construction in Dutch: example 28 shows that the nominalized *bewerking* "adaptation" cannot be complemented by a direct object (as is possible with the English gerund). Instead, it requires the genitival preposition *van* 'of' (a). Example (c) shows that speakers of Dutch need to combine a prepositional noun phrase with some kind of to-infinitive to express one of the functions carried by the English gerund.

(28)   a.   de bewerking van het stuk
                the adaptation of   the piece
          'the adaptation of the play'

5.5 Linguistic typology and grammaticalization

    b.   *door bewerking het stuk
          by   adaptation the piece

    c.   door het stuk te bewerken
          by   the piece to adapt
          'by adapting the play'

From this kind of deverbal nominalization, the English gerund probably evolved according to the following steps (Tajima (1985); summary and examples taken from Fanego (2004)):

1. Around 1200, the deverbal nominalization *-ing* began taking adverbial modifiers of all kinds:

    (29)   Of þi comyng at domesday
             'Of your coming *at doomsday*.'

2. The first examples with direct objects have been attested around 1300.

    (30)   yn feblyng þe body with moche fastyng
             'in weakening the body by too much abstinence'

3. In the Early Modern English period, other verbal features are increasingly found, such as distinctions of voice and tense. From Late Modern English on, gerunds also start to take subjects:

    (31)   he was war of hem comyng and of here malice
             'he was informed of them coming and of their wickedness'

Fanego (2004) argues that these changes are best understood as reanalysis of a nominal structure to a (more) verbal one (p. 26). This requires the speaker's ability to recognize multiple structural analyses since the "old" and the "new" use co-existed for a long time. The following examples show how the nominal analysis and the more verbal structure could be used together around 1300, whereas nowadays the nominal structure is unacceptable unless there is a determiner:

(32)   Sain Jon was ... bisi In ordaining of priestes, and clerkers, And in planning kirc werkes.
       'Saint John was ... busy ordaining priests and clerics, and in planning church works.'

5 Impact on artificial language evolution and linguistic theory

(33) the ordaining of priests / the planning of works

(34) ordaining priests / planning works

(35) *ordaining of priests / *planning of works

In order to account for the gradualness of the change, Fanego suggests a reanalysis-plus-actualization model. He acknowledges Haspelmath (1998)'s criticism on this model that it is still not gradual enough and he proposes that the gerund should be regarded as a hybrid category which is partly noun and partly verb. To summarize, Fanego suggests that the development of the various uses of the English gerund involved (a) reanalysis and (b) actualization using Haspelmath's proposal for gradient categories.

5.5.4.3 Problems with Fanego's account.

Fanego's analysis of the development of English requires complex cognitive operations from the part of the speaker that do not seem entirely justified. First of all, in order to reconcile reanalysis with the data, he needs to call on the process of actualization. However, as Haspelmath (1998) already noted, actualization "waters down the notion of reanalysis, because it allows one to posit non-manifested reanalysis as one pleases" (p. 341). It also seems contradictory to propose reanalysis, which is essentially an abrupt and discrete process, together with Haspelmath's gradient categories. Mechanisms such as semantic bleaching, analogy and extension could explain a gradual shift from a nominal category to a more verb-like category just as well without evoking reanalysis.

A second problem has to do with the idea of a gradient category, that is, analyzing the gerund as some hybrid category which is let's say 20% nominal and 80% verbal. This kind of analysis treats the Gerund as a single category in the grammar whereas Fanego himself distinguishes at least three different types existing today, each with their own particular syntactic behaviours:

- Type 1: gerunds lacking determiners (e.g. *by writing it*)

- Type 2: gerunds taking determiners (e.g. *the writing of the letter*)

- Type 3: verbal gerund (e.g. *the people living in this town*)

5.5.4.4 A model based on redundancy

Reanalysis is a mechanism which is based on mismatches in learning. In the case of the English gerund, Fanego writes that the first gerunds to take verbal traits

5.5 Linguistic typology and grammaticalization

were the ones occurring in constructions without determiners (p. 19–20). However, the lack of determiners is in itself not necessarily a reason for reanalyzing a grammatical structure, especially since determiners were not at all obligatory in many noun phrases in Old and Middle English (Traugott 1992: 172–174). One can therefore reverse the question and ask why some uses of the gerund resisted the spread of determiners. In other words: is there a *functional* explanation for the development of the gerund?

A first step in the alternative hypothesis is to accept redundancy: language users store many instances in memory so rather than looking for a single category which leads to multiple structural analyses, speakers are assumed to store many instances in memory. Actual change in the system only takes place if one of these redundant instances gets extended. No layering or complex mechanisms for disambiguity are needed since there are still enough instances left that cover the older use of a particular form. Redundancy thus requires a far more simple cognitive model than the reanalysis-and-actualization approach and treats each use of the gerund as a construction in its own right.

Instead of reanalysis and mismatches in learning, the alternative hypothesis assumes that some patterns or instances extend their usage for a communicative reason. Fanego lists several possible sources (p. 11–17): first of all, the *-ing*-form of nominalizations was in competition with the Old English present participle *-ende* (which still exists in Dutch, for example). *-ing* became dominant by the fifteenth century and thus increased its frequency. Along with this competition, the productivity of *-ing* also increased from a limited number of verbs to an almost fully productive schema. A third possible source could be the fact that the English to-infinitive has resisted the combinations with other prepositions than *to* and *for to*. This created a gap in the usage of the infinitive which could be filled by the gerund (or conversely, the expansion of the gerund prevented the infinitive from filling this gap itself). Other sources are influences from French and the co-occurrence of the gerund with a genitive phrase.

The point here is not to find *the* source for the development of the English gerund but rather to illustrate that many possible sources can be identified and that they all probably played some role. It is therefore fruitful to see language as a selectionist system in which all linguistic items compete for a place in the inventory. Due to multi-level selection, categories can become more dominant across patterns which is what seemed to have happened with the gerund: it increased its productivity, won the competition against *-ende* for marking participles and hence became more frequent and successful.

Haspelmath (1998) also criticized reanalysis for failing to explain the strong unidirectional tendency of grammaticalization. In a system of multi-level selec-

5 Impact on artificial language evolution and linguistic theory

tion, this could be explained due to the fact that once linguistic items become part of larger patterns or occur in multiple constructions, they are no longer fully independent of those constructions. The benefit of belonging to larger groups is that each item's individual survival chances increase, but the possible downside could be that the original use becomes structurally ambiguous or that it loses its distinctiveness. This would weaken its position and leaves the possibility for other items to conquer its space. In other words, there are always two factors influencing survival of a linguistic item: frequency and function.

5.5.4.5 Back to the computational model

The above analysis is only an illustration of how computational modeling could inspire linguists to come up with alternative hypotheses. The grammaticalization model of redundancy that I presented here mainly comes from the observation that variation in a population is an extremely challenging problem and that it is very difficult for a population to reach a shared and coherent language without losing generalization accuracy. Moreover, the design stance can offer mechanisms and operationalizations that are simpler than the processes that are often proposed in verbal theories.

That said, the experiments presented in this book have not yet offered any proof that an analysis such as the one proposed here can actually work. However, they did show that a redundant and bottom-up approach *can* deal with high degrees of uncertainty in the development of a grammar whereas no such model exists (yet) for reanalysis. The comparison between the Iterated Learning Model (which essentially relies on reanalysis) and this book has shown that a usage-based approach performs significantly better than a reanalysis model. This does not mean that reanalysis does not exist or that it cannot be operationalized, but it poses some serious challenges to the effectiveness and explanatory power of the mechanism.

Postscriptum

This book is a trimmed version of my doctoral dissertation in which I investigated how case systems may emerge as the consequence of locally situated interactions in a population of autonomous artificial agents that shape and reshape their language in order to optimize their communicative success (van Trijp 2008a). When I submitted my thesis, I felt that I had just finished the first part of a longer saga, and the past six years have proven that feeling to be right. This postscriptum therefore summarizes the directions that my research has taken since 2008.

Fluid Construction Grammar

If there is one important aspect that sets the experiments in this book apart from previous experiments in artificial language evolution, it is the fact that they are more strongly connected to empirical evidence of real-life language evolution. Earlier experiments typically involved abstract models, whereas I *reverse-engineered* a processing model of English argument structure constructions in Fluid Construction Grammar. This methodological innovation[1] ensures that the agents have sufficiently sophisticated representation and processing techniques for handling linguistic structures of natural language-like complexity, and it offers a "target structure" that helps the experimenter to identify adequate learning and innovation operators. It also led to the first computational and bidirectional construction grammar implementation of argument structure (van Trijp 2008b), which demonstrates that it is perfectly feasible to operationalize constructional analyses in a formally precise way.

The formalization of argument structure in this book stretched the expressive power of the "2005–2007-implementation" of FCG. My colleagues and I therefore

---

[1] I do not claim to be the inventor of this innovation: the choice of reverse-engineering an actual language was in the first place made possible by the vision of Luc Steels, who realized that more sophisticated language technologies were required for moving the field of artificial language evolution forward (Steels 2004a), and by my colleagues (particularly Joachim De Beule, Martin Loetzsch, Michael Spranger and Pieter Wellens) who further developed Steels' implementation into the FCG-system and experimental framework that support the experiments in this book (Loetzsch et al. 2008a).

Postscriptum

came together in a groundbreaking FCG workshop in Ellezelles (Belgium, 30 June – 4 July 2008) in which almost all of FCG's present-day features were devised and implemented.[2] FCG is now regarded as an innovative and mature grammar formalism (van Trijp 2013a) that has been applied for reverse-engineering grammars of English, French, Russian, German, Hungarian, Polish, Spanish, and so on (Steels 2011; 2012; Steels & Hild 2012). Many of those grammars have served as a basis for understanding the evolution of intricate phenomena such as colours (Bleys 2011), spatial terms (Spranger 2011) and quantifiers (Pauw 2013).

The increased expressive power of FCG has allowed me to tackle many non-trivial problems concerning argument structure and language processing. First of all, this book's proposal for handling argument structure has turned out to be a recurrent "design pattern" for argument realization and has been further refined by van Trijp (2011a). The implementation has been extended with solutions for feature indeterminacy and ambiguity (van Trijp 2011c), and long-distance dependencies (van Trijp 2014b); and it has been grounded on humanoid robots (Steels et al. 2012). I have also been particularly concerned with fluid and robust language processing (Steels & van Trijp 2011), integrating diagnostics and repairs in the FCG-system (Beuls, van Trijp & Wellens 2012) and exploring reflective architectures for open-ended processing (van Trijp 2012a).

Artificial language evolution

Most experiments in artificial language evolution involve direct one-to-one mappings between meaning and form. The experiments reported in this book have significantly pushed the state-of-the-art by showing how polysemous categories may emerge in a multi-agent population (for more recent results, see van Trijp 2010a; 2011b; 2012d,e). Moreover, the experiments have identified multi-level selection as a crucial step in the transition from lexical to grammatical languages. The relation between multi-level selection and language systematicity has been explored in more detail by van Trijp & Steels (2012).

The experiments have also taken an exciting turn in recent years by applying the model to real-life language phenomena, which is made possible thanks to the aforementioned advances in Fluid Construction Grammar. The first experiment of this kind is presented by van Trijp (2010b), who investigates an ongoing evolution in the pronoun system of Spanish. More specifically, the experiment

---

[2] The workshop participants included Luc Steels, Joris Bleys, Thomas Cederborg, Pascal Costanza, Joachim De Beule, Katja Gerasymova, Martin Loetzsch, Vanessa Micelli, Simon Pauw, Michael Spranger, Pieter Wellens and myself.

demonstrates how a population of language users are able to shift a case-based system of pronouns to a gender-based system without loss in communicative success (despite competing variants in the population).

Another recent case study focuses on German definite articles (van Trijp 2012c,b; 2013b; 2014a), which are notorious for their case syncretism (i.e. the same form maps onto multiple, often conflicting functions). These syncretic forms have long been regarded as non-systematic, historical accidents. The agent-based models however demonstrate that the system of definite articles has evolved to become easier to process by comparing a reverse-engineered processing model of the current German grammar to a model of its oldest attested historical predecessor (Old High German).

Acknowledgements

And finally I arrive at the last sentences of this book, and undoubtedly the most difficult ones to write because here I have to find the right words to express my gratitude to so many people who have supported me through all these years.

The first person I want to thank is Luc Steels, founder of the SONY Computer Science Laboratory Paris, and the best mentor imaginable for a young researcher such as myself. Not only has he provided me with a secure position in a superb research environment, he also still manages to surprise me with his groundbreaking ideas and his relentless energy. Luc is able to write a research proposal in the morning, conduct an experiment in the afternoon, and compose an opera in the evening. I hope that one day I can discover his secret. I also wish to thank Walter Daelemans and Guy De Pauw for their guidance and input; and for introducing me to Luc and thereby landing me my first job in science. I always enjoy my visits to Antwerp for the interesting discussions and fresh perspective.

I would also like to thank Stefan Müller and Martin Haspelmath and their colleagues for making Language Science Press possible and for giving this book series a forum. I thank Sebastian Nordhoff in particular, whose hard work has been indispensable in getting this book published.

In the past years, I have been extremely fortunate to work with some of the brightest people I have ever met. So I would like to thank my colleagues in Paris (in order of appearance): Benjamin K. Bergen, Martin Loetzsch, Wouter Van den Broeck, Michael Spranger, Vanessa Micelli, Katja Gerasymova, Simon Pauw, Damien Munch, Nancy Chang, Manfred Hild, Fabrizio Lo Scudo, Miquel Cornudella Gaya and Paul Van Eecke; as well as Sophie Boucher, Peter Hanappe, Frédéric Kaplan, Pierre-Yves Oudeyer, François Pachet, Pierre Roy and Nicolas

Postscriptum

Duval. I would also like to thank my colleagues from Barcelona and Brussels Joachim De Beule, Joris Bleys, Bart De Vylder, Pieter Wellens, Wout Monteyne, Frederik Himpe, Carl Jacobs, Thomas Cederborg, Katrien Beuls, Kevin Stadler, Lara Mennes, Bart de Boer, Emília Garcia Casademont and Yana Knight.

I would be nowhere in life if I hadn't grown up in the most wonderful family one can imagine. I want to thank my parents for working so hard for me, for their love and for giving me all the happiness and opportunities that most people can only dream of. Thanks to my brother and sisters, Bianca, Davy and Tiny; their spouses Paul, Ann and Peter; and their children Lorenz, Stef, Laura, my godchild Zoë, Isabo and Amber. Thanks to all my friends who found a way to stay in touch despite the distance and my "arch-nemesis" Filip who designed an alternative cover for my book. Missing all of you has been the hardest part of my life.

Finally, I would like to thank my beautiful daughter Elise, who has turned my world upside down and made it so much better in every way. Despite her young age, she never ceases to amaze me with her joy and creativity, and just by being herself she makes me the proudest father on the planet. I dedicate this book to you. Having you in my life is more than any man deserves. I love you.

Paris, 10 April 2014

Appendix: Measures

The simulations reported in this thesis make use of a number of measures for assessing the progress made during the experiments. This appendix collects and explains them all both in order to provide the reader with a clear understanding of what is being measured and in order to provide the research community with clear definitions of measures for future experiments.

Communicative success

Communicative success as a local measure. Communicative success can be measured by the agents themselves and it can influence their linguistic behaviour. In the description games played in the experiments in this thesis, a game is a success if the hearer signals agreement with the speaker's description and a failure if the hearer signals disagreement. The hearer will agree if interpretation yields a single set of bindings between the parsed meaning and the facts in the memory. The hearer will disagree if interpretation is ambiguous (i.e. more than one hypothesis was returned) or if interpretation failed.

Plotting communicative success. Communicative success can also be plotted for a series of interactions by recording the success or failure of every language game. This is a global measure which is not observable by the agents themselves and thus has no influence on their linguistic behaviour. Each successful game is counted as 1 and each failed game is counted as 0. The sum of these results is then divided by the size of a certain interval into a single number between 0 and 1. The interval in all the reported simulations is set to 10.

$$\text{Result of game}_i = \begin{cases} 1 & \text{if game}_i \text{ is successful} \\ 0 & \text{if game}_i \text{ is successful} \end{cases}$$

$$\text{Communicative success}_m^n = \frac{1}{(n-m)} \sum_{i=m}^{n} \text{Result of game}_i$$

Appendix: Measures

Cognitive effort

Cognitive effort as a local measure. Local cognitive effort is defined in this thesis as the number of inferences the hearer has to make during interpretation (i.e. the number of variables that need to be made equal). Since the event types in the simulations take a maximum of three participant roles, this measure ranges from 0 to 3. This number is recalculated onto a scale between 0 and 1 by taking the effort and dividing it by the maximum number of inferences (which is 3). One inference thus returns 0.33, two inferences 0.66 and three inferences 1. Failed language games count as 1, which is the maximum effort score. The agents use cognitive effort as one of the triggers for expanding their language.

Plotting cognitive effort. Cognitive effort can be plotted for a series of interactions by recording the hearer's effort during each interaction. Again, this is a global measure which is only accessible for the experimenter but not for the agents themselves. As with communicative success, cognitive effort in each game returns a value between 0 and 1. Global cognitive effort is measured by dividing the sum of the results by the size of a certain interval (which here is 10). This returns a measure between 0 and 1. In the following formulae CG_i stands for 'the hearer's cognitive effort during game$_i$'.

$$CG_i = \begin{cases} \text{Success}_i &= \dfrac{\text{number of inferences}}{\text{maximum number of inferences}} \\ \text{Failure}_i &= 1 \end{cases}$$

$$\text{Cognitive effort}_m^n = \frac{1}{(n-m)} \sum_{i=m}^{n} CG_i$$

Average preferred lexicon

The average preferred lexicon is used by various measures in this thesis. This lexicon is derived by taking the most frequent form for every possible meaning in the population. For example, if six agents in a population of ten prefer the marker *-bo* for the participant role 'move-1' as opposed to four agents that prefer the marker *-ka*, then *-bo* is listed in the average preferred lexicon with a frequency of 0.6. This lexicon is calculated for each individual participant role and for each possible combination of participant roles. For the experiments in this thesis, the complete meaning space of participant roles consists of the following meanings (of which the numbers correspond to the numbers in Figures 4.6, 4.7, 4.13 and 4.14):

1. object-1
2. move-1
3. visible-1
4. approach-1
5. approach-2
6. distance-decreasing-1
7. distance-decreasing-2
8. fall-1
9. fall-2
10. grasp-1
11. grasp-2
12. hide-1
13. hide-2
14. move-inside-1
15. move-inside-2
16. move-outside-1
17. move-outside-1
18. touch-1
19. touch-2
20. walk-to-1
21. walk-to-2
22. cause-move-on-1
23. cause-move-on-2
24. cause-move-on-3
25. give-1
26. give-2
27. give-3
28. take-1
29. take-2
30. take-3
31. approach-1 approach-2
32. distance-decreasing-1 distance-decreasing-2
33. fall-1 fall-2
34. grasp-1 grasp-2
35. hide-1 hide-2
36. move-inside-1 move-inside-2
37. move-outside-1 move-outside-2
38. touch-1 touch-2
39. walk-to-1 walk-to-2
40. cause-move-on-1 cause-move-on-2
41. cause-move-on-1 cause-move-on-3
42. cause-move-on-2 cause-move-on-3

Appendix: Measures

43. give-1 give-2
44. give-1 give-3
45. give-2 give-3
46. take-1 take-2
47. take-1 take-3
48. take-2 take-3
49. cause-move-on-1 cause-move-on-2 cause-move-on-3
50. give-1 give-2 give-3
51. take-1 take-2 take-3

Meaning-form coherence

Meaning-form coherence is a global measure which is not accessible to the agents. It takes the most frequent form for a particular meaning (i.e. the form which is preferred by most agents in the population) from the average preferred lexicon. For example, if the marker *-bo* is preferred by six agents in a population of ten agents, it is listed in the preferred average lexicon with a frequency score of 0.6. Meaning-form coherence calculates the average of all these individual frequency scores:

$$\text{MF coherence} = \frac{\text{sum of all frequency scores in preferred average lexicon}}{\text{number of entries in preferred average lexicon}}$$

Systematicity

Systematicity is again a global measure which is not accessible to the agents. It is calculated by taking each meaning in the average preferred lexicon and comparing it to the combinations of meanings in which it occurs. If the combination uses the same marker as the relevant meaning, then a score of 1 is counted. If it is not, a score of 0 is counted. The sum of all these scores is divided by the number of meanings that had to be checked in the average lexicon, which yields a score between 0 (no systematicity) and 1 (maximum systematicity).

For example, suppose that the meaning 'appear-1' is most frequently marked by *-bo*, 'appear-2' by *-ka* and the combination of the two as *-bo -si*. First we take 'appear-1' and check whether its marker also occurs in the combination with appear-2: this is indeed the case so the form-meaning mapping is systematic in both constructions, which is counted as '1'. For appear-2, however, the pattern uses a different marker *-si* so no systematic relation exists across patterns, which is counted as 0. The combination itself does not occur in a larger pattern so it is not considered by the systematicity measure.

References

Amberber, Mengistu & Helen de Hoop (eds.). 2005. *Competition and variation in natural languages: The case for case.* Oxford: Oxford University Press.

Baillie, Jean-Christophe & Jean-Gabriel Ganascia. 2000. Action categorization from video sequences. In Werner Horn (ed.), *Proceedings of the 14th European Conference on Artificial Intelligence (ECAI)*, 643–647. Berlin, Germany: IOS Press.

Barðdal, Johanna. 2009. The development of case in Germanic. In Johanna Barðdal & Shobhana Chelliah (eds.), *The role of semantic, pragmatic and discourse factors in the development of case*, 123–159. Amsterdam: John Benjamins.

Barðdal, Johanna & Shobhana Chelliah (eds.). 2009. *The role of semantic, pragmatic and discourse factors in the development of case.* Amsterdam: John Benjamins.

Baronchelli, Andrea, Maddalena Felici, Vittorio Loreto, Emanuele Caglioti & Luc Steels. 2006. Sharp transition towards shared vocabularies in multi-agent systems. *Journal of Statistical Mechanics* P06014.

Batali, John. 1998. Computational simulations of the emergence of grammar. In James R. Hurford, Michael Studdert-Kennedy & Chris Knight (eds.), *Approaches to the evolution of language: Social and cognitive bases*, 405–426. Edinburgh: Edinburgh University Press.

Batali, John. 2002. The negotiation and acquisition of recursive grammars as a result of competition among exemplars. In T. Briscoe (ed.), *Linguistic evolution through language acquisition: Formal and computational models*, 111–172. Cambridge: Cambridge University Press.

Belpaeme, Tony. 2002. *Factors influencing the origins of colour categories.* Vrije Universiteit Brussel PhD thesis.

Belpaeme, Tony & Joris Bleys. 2005. Colourful language and colour categories. In Caroline Lyon, Angelo Cangelosi & Chrystopher L. Nehaniv (eds.), *AISB'05: Proceedings of Second International Symposium on the Emergence and Evolution of Linguistic Communication (EELC'05).* Hatfield, UK.

Bergen, Benjamin K. & Nancy Chang. 2005. Embodied Construction Grammar. In Jan-Ola Östman & Mirjam Fried (eds.), *Construction grammars: Cognitive grounding and theoretical extensions*, 147–190. Amsterdam: John Benjamins.

References

Beuls, Katrien, Remi van Trijp & Pieter Wellens. 2012. Diagnostics and repairs in Fluid Construction Grammar. In Luc Steels & Manfred Hild (eds.), *Language grounding in robots*, 215–234. Berlin/New York: Springer.

Blake, Barry J. 1994. *Case* (Cambridge Textbook in Linguistics). Cambridge: Cambridge University Press.

Bleys, Joris. 2008. The origins of recursive rules: A usage-based account. In Andrew D. M. Smith, Kenny Smith & Ramon Ferrer i Cancho (eds.), *The evolution of language. Proceedings of the 7th international conference (EVOLANG 7)*, 34–41. Singapore: World Scientific Press.

Bleys, Joris. 2011. *Language strategies for the domain of colour*. Brussels: Vrije Universiteit Brussel PhD thesis.

Boas, Hans C. & Ivan A. Sag (eds.). 2013. *Sign-Based Construction Grammar*. Stanford: CSLI Publications.

Bresnan, Joan. 1982. *The mental representation of grammatical relations*. Cambridge, MA: MIT Press.

Brighton, Henry, Simon Kirby & Kenny Smith. 2005. Cultural selection for learnability: Three principles underlying the view that language adapts to be learnable. In Maggie Tallerman (ed.), *Language origins: Perspectives on evolution*, Chapter 13. Oxford: Oxford University Press.

Briscoe, E. J. 2000. Grammatical acquisition: Inductive bias and coevolution of language and the language acquisition device. *Language* 76(2). 245–296.

Butt, Miriam. 2006. *Theories of case* (Cambridge Textbooks in Linguistics). Cambridge: Cambridge University Press.

Bybee, Joan & Sandra A. Thompson. 2000. Three frequency effects in syntax. In, vol. 23 (Berkeley Linguistics Society), 65–85. Dwinelle Hall, Berkeley CA: University of California, Berkeley.

Christiansen, Morten & Simon Kirby. 2003. Language evolution: The hardest problem in science? In Morten Christiansen & Simon Kirby (eds.), *Language evolution*, 1–15. Oxford: Oxford University Press.

Comrie, Bernard. 2005. Alignment of case marking. In Martin Haspelmath, Matthew S. Dryer, David Gil & Bernard Comrie (eds.), *The world atlas of language structures*, chap. 98–99, Oxford: Oxford University Press.

Croft, William. 1991. *Syntactic categories and grammatical relations. The cognitive organization of information*. Chicago: Chicago UP.

Croft, William. 1998. Event structure in argument linking. In Miriam Butt & Wilhelm Geuder (eds.), *The projection of arguments: Lexical and compositional factors*, 21–63. Stanford: CSLI Publications.

Croft, William. 2000. *Explaining language change: An evolutionary approach.* Harlow Essex: Longman.

Croft, William. 2001. *Radical construction grammar: Syntactic theory in typological perspective.* Oxford: Oxford UP.

Croft, William. 2004. The relevance of an evolutionary model to historical linguistics. In Ole Nedergaard Thomsen (ed.), *Different models of linguistic change*, 91–132. Amsterdam: John Benjamins.

Croft, William. 2005. Logical and typological arguments for radical construction grammar. In Jan-Ola Östman & Mirjam Fried (eds.), *Construction grammars: Cognitive grounding and theoretical extensions*, 273–314. Amsterdam: John Benjamins.

Croft, William & D. Alan Cruse. 2004. *Cognitive linguistics* (Cambridge Textbooks in Linguistics). Cambridge: Cambridge University Press.

Cysouw, Michael. 2007. Building semantic maps: The case of person marking. In Matti Miestamo & Bernhard Wälchli (eds.), *New challenges in typology*, 225–248. Berlin: Mouton De Gruyter.

Daelemans, Walter. 2002. A comparison of analogical modeling of language to memory-based language processing. In R. Skousen, D. Lonsdale & D. Parkinson (eds.), *Analogical modeling*, 157–179. Amsterdam: John Benjamins.

Daelemans, Walter & Antal Van den Bosch. 2005. *Memory-based language processing* (Studies in Natural Language Processing). Cambridge: Cambridge University Press.

Davidse, Kristin. 1996. Functional dimensions of the dative in English. In William Van Belle & Willy Van Langendonck (eds.), *The dative. Volume 1: Descriptive studies* (Case and Grammatical Relations Across Languages), 289–338. Amsterdam: John Benjamins.

Davis, Anthony & Jean-Pierre Koenig. 2000. Linking as constraints on word classes in a hierarchical lexicon. *Language* 76(1). 59–91.

De Beule, Joachim. 2007. *Compositionality, hierarchy and recursion in language. A case study in Fluid Construction Grammar.* Vrije Universiteit Brussel PhD thesis.

De Beule, Joachim. 2008. The emergence of compositionality, hierarchy and recursion in peer-to-peer interactions. In Andrew D. M. Smith, Kenny Smith & Ramon Ferrer i Cancho (eds.), *The evolution of language. Proceedings of the 7th international conference (EVOLANG 7)*, 75–82. Singapore: World Scientific Press.

References

De Beule, Joachim & Benjamin K. Bergen. 2006. On the emergence of compositionality. In A. Cangelosi, A. Smith & K. Smith (eds.), *The evolution of language*. Singapore: World Scientific.

De Beule, Joachim & Luc Steels. 2005. Hierarchy in Fluid Construction Grammar. In Ulrich Furbach (ed.), *KI 2005: Advances in artificial intelligence. Proceedings of the 28th German conference on AI* (Lecture Notes in Artificial Intelligence 3698), 1–15. Berlin: Springer.

de Boer, Bart. 1999. *Self-organisation in vowel systems*. Brussels: Vrije Universiteit Brussel PhD thesis.

de Boer, Bart. 2000. Self organization in vowel systems. *Journal of Phonetics* 28(4). 441–465.

De Pauw, Guy. 2002. *An agent-based evolutionary computing approach to memory-based syntactic parsing of natural language*. Antwerp: Universiteit van Antwerpen PhD thesis.

De Vylder, Bart. 2007. *The evolution of conventions in multi-agent systems*. Brussels: Vrije Universiteit Brussel PhD thesis.

Dik, Simon. 1997. *The theory of functional grammar*. Berlin: Mouton de Gruyter.

Fanego, Teresa. 2004. On reanalysis and actualization in syntactic change: The rise and development of English verbal gerunds. *Diachronica* 21(21). 5–55.

Fillmore, Charles J. 1968. The case for case. In E. Bach & R. Harms (eds.), *Universals in linguistic theory*, 1–88. New York: Holt, Rhinehart & Winston.

Fillmore, Charles J., Paul Kay, Laura Michaelis & Ivan Sag. unpubl. *Construction grammar*. Unpublished manuscript. Chapter 7 available online at http://lingo.stanford.edu/sag/SBCG/7.pdf. Last accessed on 1 May 2008. Chicago: Chicago University Press.

Galantucci, Bruno. 2005. An experimental study of the emergence of human communication systems. *Cognitive Science* 29(5). 737–767.

Gil, David. 2008. How much grammar does it take to sail a boat? (or, what can material artifacts tell us about the evolution of language. In Andrew D. M. Smith, Kenny Smith & Ramon Ferrer i Cancho (eds.), *The evolution of language. Proceedings of the 7th international conference (EVOLANG 7)*, 123–130. Singapore: World Scientific Press.

Givón, Talmy. 1997. Grammatical relations: An introduction. In Talmy Givón (ed.), *Grammatical relations: A functional perspective* (Typological Studies in Language 35), 1–84. Amsterdam: John Benjamins.

Givón, Talmy. 2001. *Syntax*. Vol. 1. Amsterdam: John Benjamins.

Gleason, Henry A. 1965. *Linguistics and English grammar*. New York: Holt, Rinehart & Winston.

Goldberg, Adele E. 1995. *A construction grammar approach to argument structure.* Chicago: Chicago UP.

Haspelmath, Martin. 1998. Does grammaticalization need reanalysis? *Studies in Language* 20(3). 315–350.

Haspelmath, Martin. 2003. The geometry of grammatical meaning: Semantic maps and cross-linguistic comparison. In Michael Tomasello (ed.), *The new psychology of language*, vol. 2, 211–242. Mahwah, New Jersey: Lawrence Erlbaum.

Hawkin, Stephen. 1988. *A brief history of time. From the big bang to black holes.* Introduction by Carl Sagan. London: Bantam Books.

Hoefler, Stefan & Andrew D. M. Smith. 2008. Reanalysis vs metaphor: What grammaticalisation can tell us about language evolution. In Andrew D. M. Smith, Kenny Smith & Ramon Ferrer i Cancho (eds.), *The evolution of language. Proceedings of the 7th international conference (EVOLANG 7)*, 34–41. Singapore: World Scientific Press.

Hopper, Paul & Elizabeth Closs Traugott. 1993. *Grammaticalization.* Cambridge: Cambridge University Press.

Jackendoff, Ray. 1990. *Semantic structures.* Cambridge, MA: MIT Press.

Kaplan, Frédéric, Angus McIntyre & Luc Steels. 1998. An architecture for evolving robust shared communication systems in noisy environments. In *Proceedings of Sony Research Forum 1998*.

Kay, Paul. 2005. Argument structure constructions and the argument-adjunct distinction. In Miriam Fried & Hans C. Boas (eds.), *Grammatical constructions: Back to the roots*, 71–98. Amsterdam: John Benjamins.

Kay, Paul & Charles J. Fillmore. 1999. Grammatical constructions and linguistic generalizations: The what's X doing Y? Construction. *Language* 75. 1–33.

Keenan, Edward & Bernard Comrie. 1977. Noun phrase accessibility and universal grammar. *Linguistic Inquiry* 8(1). 63–99.

King, Robert D. 1969. *Historical linguistics and generative grammar.* New York: Prentice Hall.

Kirby, Simon. 1999. Syntax out of learning: The cultural evolution of structured communication in a population of induction algorithms. In D. Floreano, J. D. Nicoud & F. Mondada (eds.), *Advances in artificial life: Proceedings of the 5th European Conference on Artificial Life*, 694–703. Berlin: Springer.

Kirby, Simon. 2000. Syntax without natural selection: How compositionality emerges from vocabulary in a population of learners. In Chris Knight, James Hurford & Michael Studdert-Kennedy (eds.), *The evolutionary emergence of language: Social function and the origins of linguistic form*, 303–323. Cambridge: Cambridge University Press.

References

Kirby, Simon. 2001. Spontaneous evolution of linguistic structure: An iterated learning model of the emergence of regularity and irregularity. *IEEE Transactions on Evolutionary Computation* 5(2). 102–110.

Kirby, Simon. 2002. Learning, bottlenecks and the evolution of recursive syntax. In Ted Briscoe (ed.), *Linguistic evolution through language acquisition: Formal and computational models*, 173–204. Cambridge: Cambridge University Press.

Kirby, Simon & James Hurford. 2002. The emergence of linguistic structure: An overview of the iterated learning model. In Angelo Cangelosi & Domenico Parisi (eds.), *Simulating the evolution of language*, 121–148. London: Springer Verlag.

Kirby, Simon, Kenny Smith & Henry Brighton. 2004. From UG to universals: Linguistic adaptation through iterated learning. *Studies in Language* 28(3). 587–607.

Kulikov, Leonid, Andrej Malchukov & Peter de Swart (eds.). 2006. *Case systems in a diachronic perspective: A typological sketch*. Amsterdam: John Benjamins.

Lakoff, George. 1987. *Women, fire, and dangerous things: What categories reveal about the mind*. Chicago: The University of Chicago Press.

Langacker, Ronald W. 1977. Syntactic reanalysis. In Charles N. Li (ed.), *Mechanisms of syntactic change*, 59–139. Austin: University of Texas Press.

Langacker, Ronald W. 1987. *Foundations of cognitive grammar. Volume 1*. Stanford: Stanford University Press.

Langacker, Ronald W. 2000. A dynamic usage-based model. In Michael Barlow & Suzanne Kemmer (eds.), *Usage-based models of language*, 1–63. Chicago: Chicago University Press.

Levin, Beth & Malka Rappaport Hovav. 1999. Two structures for compositionally derived events. In *Proceedings of SALT 9*, 127–144. Ithaca, NY: Cornell Linguistics Circle Publications.

Levin, Beth & Malka Rappaport Hovav. 2005. *Argument realization* (Research Surveys in Linguistics). Cambridge: Cambridge University Press.

Li, Charles N. & Sandra A. Thompson. 1976. Subject and topic: A new typology of language. In Charles N. Li (ed.), *Subject and topic*, 458–489. New York: Academic Press.

Loetzsch, Martin, Pieter Wellens, Joachim De Beule, Joris Bleys & Remi van Trijp. 2008a. *The Babel2 Manual*. Tech. rep. AI-Memo 01-08. Brussels: AI-Lab VUB.

Loetzsch, Martin, Remi van Trijp, & Luc Steels. 2008b. Typological and computational investigations of spatial perspective. In I. Wachsmuth & G. Knoblich (eds.), *Modeling communication with robots and virtual humans* (LNCS 4930), 125–142. Berlin: Springer.

Malchukov, Andrej & Andrew Spencer (eds.). 2009. *The Oxford handbook of case*. Oxford: Oxford University Press.

Michaelis, Laura A. 2012. Complementation by construction. In Marc Hauser (ed.), *Proceedings of the Thirty-Second Annual Meeting of the Berkeley Linguistics Society*. Berkeley: BLS.

Mitchell, Tom M. 1997. *Machine learning* (McGraw-Hill Series in Computer Science). New York: WCB/McGraw-Hill.

Mithun, Marianne. 2005. Beyond the core: Typological variation in the identification of participants. *International Journal of Linguistics* 71(4). 445–472.

Moy, Joanna. 2006. *Word order and case in models of simulated language evolution*. York: University of York PhD thesis.

Nowak, Martin A., Natalia L. Komarova & Partha Niyogi. 2001. Evolution of Universal Grammar. *Science* 291. 114–118.

Nowak, Martin A. & David C. Krakauer. 1999. The evolution of language. *Proceedings of the National Academy of Sciences of the United Stated of America* 96(14). 8028–8033.

Oudeyer, Pierre-Yves. 2005. The self-organization of speech sounds. *Journal of Theoretical Biology* 233(3). 435–449.

Palmer, F. R. 1994. *Grammatical roles and relations*. Cambridge: Cambridge UP.

Pauw, Simon. 2013. *Size matters: Grounding quantifiers in spatial perception*. Amsterdam: University of Amsterdam PhD thesis.

Pinker, Steven. 1989. *Learnability and cognition: The acquisition of argument structure*. Cambridge: Cambridge UP.

Pollard, Carl & Ivan A. Sag. 1994. *Head-Driven Phrase Structure Grammar*. Chicago: University of Chicago Press.

Sag, Ivan A. 2013. Sign-based construction grammar: An informal synopsis. In Hans C. Boas & Ivan A. Sag (eds.), *Sign-Based Construction Grammar*, 69–202. Stanford: CSLI Publications.

Siskind, Jeffrey Mark. 2000. Visual event classification via force dynamics. In *Proceedings of the National Conference on Artificial Intelligence (AAAI)*, 149–155.

Skousen, Royal. 1989. *Analogical modeling of language*. Dordrecht: Kluwer.

Smith, Andrew D. M. 2003a. Intelligent meaning creation in a clumpy world helps communication. *Artificial Life* 9(2). 175–190.

Smith, Kenny. 2003b. *The transmission of language: Models of biological and cultural evolution*. Edinburgh: University of Edinburgh PhD thesis.

Smith, Kenny & James R. Hurford. 2003. Language Evolution in populations: Extending the iterated learning model. In W. Banzhaf, J. Ziegler, P. Dittrich, J.

References

T. Kim & T. Christaller (eds.), *Advances in artificial life: Proceedings of the 7th European Conferenceon Artificial Life*, 507–516. 2003: Springer.

Smith, Kenny, Simon Kirby & Henry Brighton. 2003. Iterated learning: A framework for the emergence of language. *Artificial Life* 9(4). 371–386.

Sperber, D. & D. S. Wilson. 1986. *Relevance: Communication and cognition*. Cambridge, MA: Harvard University Press.

Spranger, Michael. 2011. *The evolution of grounded spatial language*. Brussels: Vrije Universiteit Brussel PhD thesis.

Steedman, Mark. 2000. *The syntactic process*. Cambridge, MA: MIT Press.

Steels, Luc. 1996a. A self-organizing spatial vocabulary. *Artificial Life* 2(3). 319–332.

Steels, Luc. 1996b. Emergent adaptive lexicons. In Pattie Maes, Maja J. Mataric, Jean-Arcady Meyer, Jordan Pollack & Stewart W. Wilson (eds.), *From animals to animats 4: Proceedings of the Fourth International Conference On Simulation of Adaptive Behavior*, 562–567. Cambridge Ma.: The MIT Press.

Steels, Luc. 1996c. Perceptually grounded meaning creation. In Mario Tokoro (ed.), *Proceedings of the Second International Conference on Multi-Agent Systems*, 338–344. Menlo Park: AAAI Press.

Steels, Luc. 1997a. Constructing and sharing perceptual distinctions. In Maarten W. van Someren & Gerhard Widmer (eds.), *Proceedings of the European conference on machine learning*, 4–13. Prague, Czech Republic: Springer.

Steels, Luc. 1997b. Language learning and language contact. In Walter Daelemans, Antal van den Bosh & Ton Weijters (eds.), *Workshop Notes of the ECML/MLnet Familiarization Workshop on Empirical Learning of Natural Language Processing Tasks*. Prague, Czech Republic: ECML/MLnet.

Steels, Luc. 1997c. Self-organizing vocabularies. In Christopher G. Langton (ed.), *Proceeding of alife v*.

Steels, Luc. 1997d. The origins of ontologies and communication conventions in multi-agent systems. *Journal of Agents and Multi-Agent Systems* 1(1). 169–194.

Steels, Luc. 1997e. The origins of syntax in visually grounded robotic agents. In Martha E. Pollack (ed.), *Proceedings of the Fifteenth International Joint Conference on Artificial Intelligence*, 1632–1641. San Francisco, CA: Morgan Kaufmann.

Steels, Luc. 1998a. Structural coupling of cognitive memories through adaptive language games. In Rolf Pfeifer, Bruce Blumberg, Jean-Arcady Meyer & Stewart W. Wilson (eds.), *From animals to animats 5: Proceedings of the Fifth International Conference on Simulation of Adaptive Behavior*, 263–269. Cambridge Ma.: The MIT Press.

Steels, Luc. 1998b. Synthesising the origins of language and meaning using co-evolution, self-organisation and level formation. In James R. Hurford, Michael Studdert-Kennedy & Chris Knight (eds.), *Approaches to the evolution of language: Social and cognitive bases*, 384–404. Edinburgh: Edinburgh University Press.

Steels, Luc. 1999a. How language bootstraps cognition. In Ipke Wachsmuth & Bernhard Jung (eds.), *Proceedings der 4. Fachtagung der Gesellschaft für Kognitionswissenschaft*, 1–3. Bielefeld.

Steels, Luc. 1999b. The spontaneous self-organization of an adaptive language. In Stephen Muggleton (ed.), *Machine intelligence 15*, 205–224. Oxford: Oxford University Press.

Steels, Luc. 1999c. *The Talking Heads Experiment. Volume 1. Words and meanings*. Special pre-edition for LABORATORIUM, Antwerpen. Brussels: VUB Artificial Intelligence Laboratory.

Steels, Luc. 2000a. The emergence of grammar in communicating autonomous robotic agents. In Werner Horn (ed.), *Proceedings of the 14th European Conference on Artificial Intelligence (ECAI)*, 764–769. Berlin, Germany: IOS Press.

Steels, Luc. 2000b. The puzzle of language evolution. *Kognitionswissenschaft* 8(4). 153–150.

Steels, Luc. 2001a. Language games for autonomous robots. *IEEE Intelligent Systems* 16 (5). 16–22.

Steels, Luc. 2001b. The role of language in learning grounded representations. In P. R. Cohen & T. Oates (eds.), *Papers from the 2001 AAI Spring Symposium*. Menlo Park, CA: AAAI Press.

Steels, Luc. 2002a. Grounding symbols through evolutionary language games. In Angelo Cangelosi & Domenico Parisi (eds.), *Simulating the evolution of language*, 211–226. London: Springer Verlag.

Steels, Luc. 2002b. Simulating the evolution of a grammar for case. In *Proceedings of the Evolution of Language Conference*. Harvard.

Steels, Luc. 2003a. Intelligence with representation. *Philosophical Transactions of the Royal Society A* 361(1811). 2381–2395.

Steels, Luc. 2003b. Language re-entrance and the 'inner voice'. *Journal of Consciousness Studies* 10(4-5). 173–185.

Steels, Luc. 2004a. Constructivist development of grounded construction grammars. In Walter Daelemans (ed.), *Proceedings 42nd Annual Meeting of the Association for Computational Linguistics*, 9–19. Barcelona.

Steels, Luc. 2004b. The architecture of flow. In Mario Tokoro & Luc Steels (eds.), *A learning zone of One's own*, 135–150. Amsterdam: IOS Press.

References

Steels, Luc. 2004c. The autotelic principle. In I. Fumiya, R. Pfeifer, L. Steels & K. Kunyoshi (eds.), *Embodied artificial intelligence* (LNAI 3139), 231–242. Berlin: Springer.

Steels, Luc. 2005a. The emergence and evolution of linguistic structure: From lexical to grammatical communication systems. *Connection Science* 17(3/4). 213–230.

Steels, Luc. 2005b. What triggers the emergence of grammar? In A. Cangelosi & C. L. Nehaniv (eds.), *AISB'05: Proceedings of EELC'05*, 143–150. Hatfield: AISB.

Steels, Luc. 2006. How to do experiments in artificial language evolution and why. In Angelo Cangelosi, Andrew Smith & Kenny Smith (eds.), *Proceedings of the 6th International Conference on the Evolution of Language*. London: World Scientific Publishing.

Steels, Luc. 2007. The recruitment theory of language origins. In C. Lyon, C. Nehaniv & A. Cangelosi (eds.), *The emergence of communication and language*, 129–151. Berlin: Springer Verlag.

Steels, Luc (ed.). 2011. *Design patterns in Fluid Construction Grammar*. Amsterdam: John Benjamins.

Steels, Luc (ed.). 2012. *Computational issues in Fluid Construction Grammar*. Heidelberg/Berlin: Springer.

Steels, Luc & Jean-Christophe Baillie. 2003. Shared grounding of event descriptions by autonomous robots. *Robotics and Autonomous Systems* 43(2-3). 163–173.

Steels, Luc & Tony Belpaeme. 2005. Coordinating perceptually grounded categories through language: A case study for colour. *Behavioral and Brain Sciences* 28. 469–529.

Steels, Luc & Joris Bleys. 2005. Planning what to say: Second order semantics for Fluid Construction Grammars. In Alberto J. Bugarín Diz & José Santos Reyes (eds.), *Proceedings CAEPIA 2005, 11th conference of the Spanish association for Artififcial Intelligence* (Lecture Notes in Artificial Intelligence). Santiago de Compostela: Springer.

Steels, Luc & Rodney A. Brooks (eds.). 1995. *The 'artificial life' route to artificial intelligence: Building embodied, situated agents*. New Haven: Lawrence Erlbaum Ass.

Steels, Luc & Joachim De Beule. 2006. Unify and merge in Fluid Construction Grammar. In P. Vogt, Y. Sugita, E. Tuci & C. Nehaniv (eds.), *Symbol grounding and beyond*. (LNAI 4211), 197–223. Berlin: Springer.

Steels, Luc, Joachim De Beule & Nicolas Neubauer. 2005. Linking in Fluid Construction Grammar. In *Proceedings of the 17th Belgium-netherlands conference on artificial intelligence (bnaic '05)*, 11–18. Brussels, Belgium.

Steels, Luc & Manfred Hild (eds.). 2012. *Language grounding in robots*. Berlin/New York: Springer.

Steels, Luc & Frédéric Kaplan. 1998a. Spontaneous lexicon change. In *Proceedings COLING-ACL 1998*, 1243–1250. San Francisco, CA: Morgan Kaufmann.

Steels, Luc & Frédéric Kaplan. 1998b. Stochasticity as a source of innovation in language games. In Christoph Adami, Richard K. Belew, Hiroaki Kitano & Charles E. Taylor (eds.), *Proceedings of the sixth international conference on artificial life*. MIT Press.

Steels, Luc & Frédéric Kaplan. 1999a. Collective learning and semiotic dynamics. In Dario Floreano, Jean-Daniel Nicoud & Francesco Mondada (eds.), *Advances in Artificial Life. Proceedings of the Fifth European Conference, ECAL '99* (Lecture Notes in Computer Science 1674), 679–688. Lausanne, Switzerland: Springer.

Steels, Luc & Frédéric Kaplan. 1999b. Situated grounded word semantics. In Thomas Dean (ed.), *Proceedings of the Sixteenth International Joint Conference on Artificial Intelligence (IJCAI'99)*, 862–867. Stockholm, Sweden: Morgan Kaufmann.

Steels, Luc & Frédéric Kaplan. 2002. Bootstrapping grounded word semantics. In T. Briscoe (ed.), *Linguistic evolution through language acquisition: Formal and computational models*, 53–73. Cambridge: Cambridge University Press.

Steels, Luc & Martin Loetzsch. 2008. Perspective alignment in spatial language. In Kenny R. Coventry, Thora Tenbrink & John. A Bateman (eds.), *Spatial language and dialogue*, 70–88. Oxford: Oxford University Press.

Steels, Luc & Angus McIntyre. 1999. Spatially distributed naming games. *Advances in Complex Systems* 1(4). 301–323.

Steels, Luc & Remi van Trijp. 2011. How to make construction grammars fluid and robust. In Luc Steels (ed.), *Design patterns in Fluid Construction Grammar*, 301–330. Amsterdam: John Benjamins.

Steels, Luc, Remi van Trijp & Pieter Wellens. 2007. Multi-level selection in the emergence of language systematicity. In Fernando Almeida e Costa, Luis M. Rocha, Ernesto Costa & Inman Harvey (eds.), *Advances in Artificial Life (ECAL 2007)* (LNAI 4648), 421–434. Berlin: Springer.

Steels, Luc & Paul Vogt. 1997. Grounding adaptive language games in robotic agents. In Phil Husbands & Inman Harvey (eds.), *Proceedings of the 4th European conference on artificial life*, 473–484. Brighton, U.K.: The MIT Press.

Steels, Luc & Pieter Wellens. 2006. How grammar emerges to dampen combinatorial search in parsing. In P. Vogt, Y. Sugita, E. Tuci & C. Nehaniv (eds.),

References

Symbol Grounding and Beyond. Proceedings of the Third EELC (LNAI 4211), 76–88. Berlin: Springer-Verlag.

Steels, Luc & Pieter Wellens. 2007. Scaffolding language emergence using the autotelic principle. In *IEEE Symposium on Artificial Life 2007 (Alife'07)*, 325–332. Honolulu, HI: Wiley – IEEE Press.

Steels, Luc, Frédéric Kaplan, Angus McIntyre & Joris Van Looveren. 2002. Crucial factors in the origins of word-meaning. In Alison Wray (ed.), *The transition to language*, 252–271. Oxford, UK: Oxford University Press.

Steels, Luc, Michael Spranger, Remi van Trijp, Sebastian Höfer & Manfred Hild. 2012. Emergent action language on real robots. In Luc Steels & Manfred Hild (eds.), *Language grounding in robots*, 255–276. Berlin/New York: Springer.

Stefanowitsch, Anatol & Stefan Th. Gries. 2003. Collostructions: Investigating the interaction of words and constructions. *International Journal of Corpus Linguistics* 2(8). 209–243.

Tajima, M. 1985. *The syntactic development of the gerund in middle English*. Tokyo: Nan'un-do.

Timberlake, Alan. 1977. Reanalysis and actualization in syntactic change. In Charles N. Li (ed.), *Mechanisms of syntactic change*, 141–177. Austin: University of Texas Press.

Tomasello, Michael. 1995. Joint attention as social cognition. In Chris Moore & Philip J. Dunham (eds.), *Joint attention: Its origins and role in development*, 103–130. Hillsdale, NJ: Lawrence Erlbaum Associates.

Traugott, Elizabeth Closs. 1992. Syntax. In Richard M. Hogg (ed.), *The cambridge history of the English language. The beginnings to 1066*, vol. 1, 168–289. Cambridge: Cambridge University Press.

Van den Broeck, Wouter. 2007. A constraint-based model of grounded compositional semantics. In L. S. Lopes, T. Belpaeme & S. J. Cowley (eds.), *Language and robots: Proceedings of the symposium*. Aveiro: Universidade de Aveiro.

Van den Broeck, Wouter. 2008. Constraint-based compositional semantics. In Andrew D. M. Smith, Kenny Smith & Ramon Ferrer i Cancho (eds.), *The evolution of language. Proceedings of the 7th international conference (EVOLANG 7)*, 338–345. Singapore: World Scientific Press.

Van Looveren, Joris. 2005. *Design and performance of pre-grammatical language games*. Brussels: Vrije Universiteit Brussel PhD thesis.

van Trijp, Remi. 2008a. *Analogy and multi-level selection in the formation of a case grammar. A case study in fluid construction grammar*. Universiteit Antwerpen PhD thesis.

van Trijp, Remi. 2008b. Argumentsstruktur in der Fluid Construction Grammar. In Kerstin Fischer & Anatol Stefanowitsch (eds.), *Konstruktionsgrammatik II: Von der Konstruktion zur Grammatik* (Stauffenburg Linguistik 47). Tübingen: Stauffenburg Verlag.

van Trijp, Remi. 2008c. The emergence of semantic roles in Fluid Construction Grammar. In Andrew D. M. Smith, Kenny Smith & Ramon Ferrer i Cancho (eds.), *The evolution of language. Proceedings of the 7th international conference (EVOLANG 7)*, 346–353. Singapore: World Scientific Press.

van Trijp, Remi. 2010a. Grammaticalization and semantic maps: Evidence from artificial language Evolution. *Linguistic Discovery* 8(1). 310–326.

van Trijp, Remi. 2010b. Strategy competition in the evolution of pronouns: a case-study of spanish leísmo, laísmo and loísmo. In A.D.M. Smith, M. Schouwstra, B. de Boer & K. Smith (eds.), *The evolution of language (EVOLANG 8)*, 336–343. Singapore: World Scientific.

van Trijp, Remi. 2011a. A design pattern for argument structure constructions. In Luc Steels (ed.), *Design patterns in Fluid Construction Grammar*, 115–145. Amsterdam: John Benjamins.

van Trijp, Remi. 2011b. Can iterated learning explain the emergence of case marking in language? In P. De Causmaecker, J. Maervoet, T. Messelis, K. Verbeeck & T. Vermeulen (eds.), *Proceedings of the 23rd Benelux Conference on Artificial Intelligence (BNAIC 2011)*, 288–295. Ghent: KAHO Sint-Lieven.

van Trijp, Remi. 2011c. Feature matrices and agreement: A case study for German case. In Luc Steels (ed.), *Design patterns in Fluid Construction Grammar*, 205–235. Amsterdam: John Benjamins.

van Trijp, Remi. 2012a. A reflective architecture for robust language processing and learning. In Luc Steels (ed.), *Computational issues in Fluid Construction Grammar*, 51–74. Heidelberg/Berlin: Springer.

van Trijp, Remi. 2012b. Not as awful as it seems: explaining German case through computational experiments in Fluid Construction Grammar. In *Proceedings of the 13th Conference of the European Chapter of the Association for Computational Linguistics*, 829–839. Avignon: ACL.

van Trijp, Remi. 2012c. Self-assessing agents for explaining language change: a case study in German. In L. De Raedt, C. Bessiere, D. Dubois, P. Doherty, P. Frasconi, F. Heintz & P. Lucas (eds.), *ECAI2012: The 20th European Conference on Artificial Intelligence* (Frontiers in Artificial Intelligence and Applications 242), 798–803. Amsterdam: IOS Press.

References

van Trijp, Remi. 2012d. The emergence of morphosyntactic case systems. In T.C. Scott-Phillips, M. Tamariz, E.A. Cartmill & J.R. Hurford (eds.), *The evolution of language (EVOLANG 9)*, 360–368. Singapore: World Scientific.

van Trijp, Remi. 2012e. The evolution of case systems for marking event structure. In Luc Steels (ed.), *Experiments in cultural language evolution*, 169–205. Amsterdam: John Benjamins.

van Trijp, Remi. 2013a. A comparison between Fluid Construction Grammar and Sign-Based Construction Grammar. *Constructions and Frames* 5. 88–116.

van Trijp, Remi. 2013b. Linguistic assessment criteria for explaining language change: a case study on syncretism in German definite articles. *Language Dynamics and Change* 3. 105–132.

van Trijp, Remi. 2014a. Fitness landscapes in cultural language evolution: A case study on German definite articles. In *The evolution of language (Evolang-X)*. Singapore: World Scientific.

van Trijp, Remi. 2014b. Long-distance dependencies without filler-gaps: A cognitive-functional alternative in Fluid Construction Grammar. *Language and Cognition* 6 (02). 242–270. DOI:10.1017/langcog.2014.8

van Trijp, Remi & Luc Steels. 2012. Multilevel alignment maintains language systematicity. *Advances in Complex Systems* 15(3–4).

Vogt, Paul. 2000. *Lexicon grounding on mobile robots*. Vrije Universiteit Brussel PhD thesis.

Vogt, Paul. 2007. Group size effects on the emergence of compositional structures in language. In Fernando Almeida e Costa, Luis M. Rocha, Ernesto Costa & Inman Harvey (eds.), *Advances in artificial life (ECAL 2007)* (LNAI 4648), 403–414. Berlin: Springer.

Wellens, Pieter. 2008. Coping with combinatorial uncertainty in word learning: A flexible usage-based model. In Andrew D. M. Smith, Kenny Smith & Ramon Ferrer i Cancho (eds.), *The evolution of language. Proceedings of the 7th international conference (EVOLANG 7)*, 370–377. Singapore: World Scientific Press.

Wellens, Pieter, Martin Loetzsch & Luc Steels. 2008. Flexible word meaning in embodied agents. *Connection Science* 20(2). 173–191.

Wilson, D. S. & E. Sober. 1994. Reintroducing group selection to the human behavioral sciences. *Behavioral and Brain Sciences* 17(4). 585–654.

Wray, Alison. 1998. Protolanguage as a holistic system for social interaction. *Language & Communication* 18. 47–67.

Wray, Alison (ed.). 2002. *The transition to language*. Oxford, UK: Oxford University Press.

Name index

Amberber, Mengistu, 1

Baillie, Jean-Christophe, 55
Baronchelli, Andrea, 18, 170
Barðdal, Johanna, 1
Batali, John, 17, 127, 128, 130
Belpaeme, Tony, 18, 167, 196
Bergen, Benjamin K., 20, 23, 131
Beuls, Katrien, 208
Blake, Barry J., 1, 2, 4, 5, 10, 109, 161
Bleys, Joris, 18, 20, 21, 208
Boas, Hans C., 23
Bresnan, Joan, 23
Brighton, Henry, 11, 131, 164
Briscoe, E. J., 11
Brooks, Rodney A., 16
Butt, Miriam, 1
Bybee, Joan, 90

Chang, Nancy, 23
Chelliah, Shobhana, 1
Christiansen, Morten, 13
Comrie, Bernard, 177, 198
Croft, William, 1, 8, 12, 20, 57, 115, 184–186, 188, 189, 194, 199
Cruse, D. Alan, 115, 184, 185, 188, 189
Cysouw, Michael, 194

Daelemans, Walter, 92, 150, 152, 191
Davidse, Kristin, 1
Davis, Anthony, 183
De Beule, Joachim, 20, 24, 28, 30, 131, 176

de Boer, Bart, 15, 20, 167
de Hoop, Helen, 1
De Pauw, Guy, 60, 129, 130
de Swart, Peter, 1
De Vylder, Bart, 18, 79, 170
Dik, Simon, 198

Fanego, Teresa, 202, 203
Fillmore, Charles J., 23, 177, 179, 186, 198

Galantucci, Bruno, 12
Ganascia, Jean-Gabriel, 55
Gil, David, 4, 61
Givón, Talmy, 5, 8, 198
Gleason, Henry A., 6
Goldberg, Adele E., 9, 40, 177–180, 186
Gries, Stefan Th., 183

Haspelmath, Martin, 60, 114, 116, 192–194, 201, 204, 205
Hawkin, Stephen, 14
Hild, Manfred, 208
Hoefler, Stefan, 50, 60
Hopper, Paul, 112, 114, 116, 200
Hurford, James, 11
Hurford, James R., 170, 174

Jackendoff, Ray, 198

Kaplan, Frédéric, 18, 59
Kay, Paul, 23, 177–181, 186

Name index

Keenan, Edward, 177, 198
King, Robert D., 12
Kirby, Simon, 11, 13, 131, 164, 166
Koenig, Jean-Pierre, 183
Komarova, Natalia L., 11
Krakauer, David C., 131
Kulikov, Leonid, 1

Lakoff, George, 186
Langacker, Ronald W., 64, 113, 186, 200
Levin, Beth, 25, 183, 198
Li, Charles N., 3
Loetzsch, Martin, 6, 18, 60, 167, 196, 207

Malchukov, Andrej, 1
McIntyre, Angus, 18, 176
Michaelis, Laura A., 177, 181
Mitchell, Tom M., 92
Mithun, Marianne, 199
Moy, Joanna, 131, 164, 166–168, 171–173, 175

Neubauer, Nicolas, 20, 24
Niyogi, Partha, 11
Nowak, Martin A., 11, 131

Oudeyer, Pierre-Yves, 15, 20

Palmer, F. R., 4, 8
Pauw, Simon, 208
Pinker, Steven, 183
Pollard, Carl, 23, 177, 179

Rappaport Hovav, Malka, 25, 183, 198

Sag, Ivan A., 23, 177, 179, 180
Siskind, Jeffrey Mark, 55
Skousen, Royal, 150, 152, 191

Smith, Andrew D. M., 20, 50, 60, 71, 172
Smith, Kenny, 11, 131, 164, 165, 168, 170, 174
Sober, E., 132
Spencer, Andrew, 1
Sperber, D., 64
Spranger, Michael, 208
Steedman, Mark, 23
Steels, Luc, 4, 6, 14, 16–21, 24, 28, 30, 49, 51, 52, 55, 58–60, 71, 74, 79, 95, 131, 140, 167, 172, 176, 195, 196, 207, 208
Stefanowitsch, Anatol, 183

Tajima, M., 202, 203
Thompson, Sandra A., 3, 90
Timberlake, Alan, 200
Tomasello, Michael, 52
Traugott, Elizabeth Closs, 112, 114, 116, 200, 205

Van den Bosch, Antal, 92, 150, 152, 191
Van Looveren, Joris, 19, 81
van Trijp, Remi, 19, 20, 140, 176, 207–209
Van den Broeck, Wouter, 21
Vogt, Paul, 12, 18

Wellens, Pieter, 6, 18–20, 24, 52, 60, 110, 131, 140, 196, 208
Wilson, D. S., 64, 132
Wray, Alison, 60

Subject index

abduction, 87, 172
abstraction, 9, 92, 108, 127, 131, 152, 161, 170, 175, 176, 187, 188, 190, 191
Académie française, 17
acceptability, 7, 194, 203
Accessibility Hierarchy, 177
acquisition, 59, 201
active-stative languages, 199
actualization, 200, 201, 204
adposition, 5, 59
adverb, 4, 202, 203
agnation, 6, 159
agreement, 1
alignment strategy, 49–51, 78, 92, 98, 99, 101–103, 107–109, 111, 120, 122, 123, 126, 129, 132–141, 143, 144, 152, 153, 167–170, 175, 190, 191, 199
ambiguity, 15, 19, 70, 72, 73, 77, 79, 86, 171, 201, 205
Analogical Modeling, 152
analogy, 6, 7, 50, 51, 57, 77, 86–90, 92, 97, 107–113, 115, 120, 132, 141, 150–154, 159, 160, 166, 171, 174, 175, 181, 182, 184, 187, 190, 191, 196, 199, 204
anaphora resolution, 162
animacy, 45, 129
argument realization, 25, 57, 174, 176, 177, 179–182

Artificial Intelligence, 16
artificial language evolution, 13, 14, 60, 131, 163, 164, 176, 191, 195, 200
Artificial Life, 13
aspect, 5, 14, 57, 160–162, 167, 188, 189, 202
    state, 7
assumption, 8, 14, 15, 19, 51, 59, 69, 108, 127, 129, 152, 162, 168, 175, 178, 181, 182, 187
autotelic principle, 20

bidirectionality, 20, 28, 30, 201
bottleneck, 165, 169, 174, 175

case
    accusative, 3, 167, 198
    allative, 6, 112
    case grammar, 49, 60, 161, 164, 168, 169, 171
    case marking, ix, 1–10, 39, 49–51, 59–61, 70, 72–74, 76–88, 90, 92, 93, 95–112, 116, 120, 122–125, 129, 137, 139, 141, 143–148, 150–154, 156, 161–163, 167, 172, 173, 175, 196, 198, 199
    case paradigm, ix, 161
    case split, 10
    case system, ix, 10, 161, 166–168, 172, 198, 199

Subject index

dative, 8, 109, 192, 193
genitive, 202, 205
instrumental, 10
locative, 10
nominative, 166, 198
tripartite case system, 199
catallaxy, 17
category gravity, 150
category leakage, 161
causality, 40, 43, 45, 47, 57, 183
child language acquisition, 59
co-existence, 115, 201, 203
co-occurrence, 47, 93, 94, 101, 108, 109, 129, 130, 141, 142, 148–151, 182, 183, 190, 201, 205
cognitive effort, 15, 51, 68–70, 79–81, 84–86, 98, 99, 102, 103, 105, 122, 144, 147, 175
cognitive-functional approach, 12, 64, 163, 164, 170, 174
collexemes, 183
collostructional analysis, 183
colour, 18, 56, 58, 123, 124, 167, 195, 196
communicative success, 15, 19, 51, 52, 54, 64, 67–71, 79–81, 84–87, 93, 94, 98, 99, 101–103, 105, 122, 128, 144, 147, 159, 167, 169, 172, 175, 176, 191, 196, 199
competition, 16, 78, 79, 81, 84, 100, 101, 103, 106, 107, 109, 115, 120–122, 125, 132–134, 137, 140–142, 144, 146, 148, 150, 151, 154, 162, 169, 205
complement, 200, 202
complex adaptive system, 16, 20
concept formation, 54, 195

conceptual space, 188, 194–197, 199
conceptual/intentional system, 53
conceptualization, 20, 21, 53–57, 65, 152, 160, 195, 197
confidence, 15, 27, 47, 48, 56, 78, 81, 84, 92–94, 99, 101, 103, 104, 107–109, 120, 125, 127, 133, 142
consolidation, 70, 78, 79, 84, 92–94, 103, 109, 119, 122, 134
construction
active construction, 37, 161, 177, 183, 199
adjective-noun construction, 24, 25
argument structure construction, 9, 37, 177, 178, 183, 184, 189
caused motion construction, 40, 43, 45, 47
passive construction, 37, 161, 177, 179, 183, 184
Recipient Construction, 178
the X-er, the Y-er construction, 185
verb-class-specific construction, 9
verb-specific construction, 74, 78, 90, 92, 151
construction grammar
Berkeley Construction Grammar, 177, 186–189
Cognitive Grammar, 186, 187, 190
Fluid Construction Grammar, 20, 21, 27, 28, 30, 32, 33, 43, 59, 176, 179–184, 188–191
Lakoff/Goldberg model, 186, 187
Radical Construction Grammar, 188, 191

Subject index

Sign-Based Construction Grammar, 163, 177–184, 189
vanilla construction grammar, 20
convention, 7, 10, 37, 47–50, 52, 59, 72, 78, 103, 108, 115, 125, 144, 148, 151, 161, 164, 172, 176, 184, 191, 199, 200
coordination problem, 159
credit assignment problem, 162
cross-generational, 68
crossover, 11
crystalization, 17

derivation, 37, 131, 151, 177–185
design stance, 188, 206
determiner, 21, 203–205
diachronic, 125, 130
dialogue, 17, 69, 162, 167
discrimination game, 17, 18, 58, 196
displacement, 2
dissociation, 10, 39
ditransitive clause, 6, 47, 177–179, 184, 187, 194
Dutch, 10, 202, 205

eager learner, 92, 131
egocentric perspective transformation, 15
Embodied Construction Grammar, 23
emergence, 4, 12–15, 18–21, 151, 155, 161, 162, 164, 168, 174, 184, 190, 195, 202
English, 6, 10, 13, 24, 25, 47, 56, 125, 127, 166, 167, 177–179, 187, 192–194, 202–205
entailment, 6, 179, 201
entrenchment, 10, 20, 47, 72, 87, 108, 142, 151, 187, 190
episodic memory, 162

event profile, 43, 54, 57, 65, 160
event recognition, 20, 56, 161
event structure, ix, 3, 9, 35, 37, 49–52, 57, 60, 61, 86–89, 107, 128, 129, 160, 163, 169, 177–179, 183, 184, 189
event token, 55, 69
event type, 55, 57, 61–63, 66, 68, 69, 79, 81–83, 120, 141, 177
evolution
    cultural evolution, 5, 12, 13, 127, 170, 175, 190, 195, 202
exemplar-based models, 92, 127, 139, 150, 191
expressiveness, 7, 164, 175
extension, 7, 10, 37, 47, 51, 90–92, 107, 113, 115, 116, 118, 125, 141, 148, 151, 152, 156, 161, 187, 190, 196, 200, 204, 205

feature structure, 27–29
    coupled feature structure, 27–30, 32, 38, 39, 43, 44, 66, 67, 73, 74, 76, 116, 118
finiteness, 5, 110, 202
Fluid Construction Grammar, x
formation, 4, 16, 17, 19, 49, 51, 54, 59, 60, 65, 66, 84, 98, 110, 111, 113, 114, 116, 120, 129, 130, 132, 141, 151, 190, 196, 199, 201, 202
frame
    semantic frame, 36, 43, 90–92, 179
    syntactic frame, 43
French, 8, 10, 24, 112–114, 192–194, 201, 205
frequency, 7, 55, 68, 79, 81–83, 90, 93, 94, 103, 104, 106–109, 116, 120,

233

Subject index

127, 140–142, 150, 151, 153, 156, 168, 170, 182, 187, 190, 199, 205, 206
function independence principle, 164, 169
fusion, 148, 149, 180

gender, ix, 3, 10, 161
generalization, 116, 129, 144, 150, 164, 170, 189–191, 199, 206
generative grammar, 184
Georgian, 199
German, 3, 59, 192–194
gerund, 202–205
grammatical square, 49, 152, 159, 160, 162
grammaticalization, 5, 6, 10, 60, 61, 163, 176, 191, 196, 200–202, 205, 206

Head-Driven Phrase Structure Grammar, 37, 177, 179, 180, 183
Hebbian learning, 93
hierarchy, 20, 52, 56, 198
Hindi, 199
holistic versus compositional languages, 60, 62, 164, 165, 171
Hunzib, 199

idiom, 112, 115, 116, 132, 133, 185
IMA language, 61
Indo-Aryan, 10
induction, 50, 129, 164, 169, 172, 175
inferential coding system, 64, 71, 107, 108, 172, 199
inflection, 9, 90, 161, 172, 173
information structure, 3, 9, 10, 161, 162, 183
inheritance, 119, 185–187, 190, 191

innovation, 7, 12, 50, 64, 70, 72, 76, 78, 81, 82, 86, 92, 104, 105, 108, 109, 125, 127, 131, 139, 151, 154, 156, 162, 164, 170–172, 175, 176, 184, 190, 199–201
instance link, 185, 186, 190
intransitive clause, 198
Italian, 8
Iterated Learning Model (ILM), 11, 60, 131, 163–165, 167–171, 174–176, 206

Jespersen's cycle, 112
joint attention, 52

Language Acquisition Device, 174
language change, 50, 116, 164, 175, 200
language contact, 18, 125, 127
language faculty, 52
language game, 15–19, 51–53, 64, 68, 69, 79, 81–85, 95, 98, 99, 101, 102, 105, 118, 121–126, 129, 134–136, 138, 139, 142, 144, 145, 148, 162, 196
    description game, 52, 68, 79, 120, 128, 141
    guessing game, 195
    multiword naming game, 19, 81
    naming game, 18
lateral inhibition, 78, 81, 94, 101, 104, 107, 109, 122, 127, 133, 141–144, 146, 148, 150, 152, 170
Latin, 161
Latvian, 198
lazy learner, 92, 131
learning bias, 168–170, 174
learning strategies

diagnostics, 49, 51, 72, 77, 79, 111, 112, 116, 119, 120, 141
repair strategies, 49, 51, 71–73, 75, 77, 79, 84, 86, 111, 112, 116, 119, 120, 141, 153
level formation, 16
lexical entry, 25, 33–37, 39, 44, 45, 47, 48, 60, 61, 73, 74, 91–93, 108, 110, 167, 173, 177–182, 184
lexical rule, 37, 177
lexicalist, 35, 177, 181
lexicon, 18, 19, 59, 60, 68, 70, 78, 98, 128, 129, 132, 151, 175, 195, 196
license, 75, 116, 117, 191
linguistic inventory, 54, 70, 78, 83, 101, 114, 116, 118, 121, 131, 132, 140, 148, 150, 163, 165, 168, 169, 184–189
linguistic perspective, 10
linguistic typology, 163, 191
locative alternation, 178
logic variable, 33

machine learning, 130
macro-roles, 183
measure
global measure, 16
local measure, 15, 51
memory decay, 94, 105, 107–109, 142, 143, 150, 196
Memory-Based Language Processing, 152
meronomy, 186
minimal lexical entry, 177, 178, 181, 182
Minimalist Program, 28
modality, 5, 14
molecular self-assembly, 17

monitoring, 19, 71
mother and daughter components, 177, 178, 180
multi-level selection, 111, 127, 132–144, 146–152, 163, 167, 171, 174, 184, 190, 191, 196, 199, 205, 206
multiple word utterances, 19
mutation, 11

natural language processing, 152, 191
navigation, 12
nearest-neighbour, 152
negation, 112, 114, 115, 201
negotiation, 7, 12, 17, 20, 69, 129, 151
neural network, 17
nominalization, 202, 203, 205
noun, 4, 24, 61, 113–116, 165, 166, 171, 173, 188, 189, 198, 202, 204, 205
number, ix, 3, 10, 161
singular, 21, 161

Ockham's razor, 60
origins, 13, 127

parsimony, 189
participant role, 7–9, 25, 37, 49, 51, 57, 61–63, 67, 72, 79, 81, 84–88, 90, 93–99, 101–107, 109, 196
pattern formation, 19, 110–117, 120, 141, 150, 190, 196, 199, 201, 202
PERACT system, 55–57
performance, 74, 134, 135, 144, 150, 170
phonological reduction, 59, 110
polysemy, 49, 110, 186, 187
Poverty of the Stimulus, 165, 175
predicate-frame, 181, 182

Subject index

preposition, 5, 6, 10, 112, 192–194, 201, 202, 205
priming, 182
problem-solving, 12, 50, 64, 127, 148, 170, 175, 176, 195
productivity, 86, 90, 97, 103, 108, 156, 159, 187, 190, 199, 205
pronoun, 166, 167
propagation, 5, 21, 49, 50, 55, 81, 114, 200, 201
prototype, 21, 187

re-entrance, 19, 20, 70, 71, 92, 172
reaction network, 27–29, 32–35, 37, 39, 41, 43, 45, 65, 66, 74–76, 93, 116–118
reanalysis, 50, 112–116, 163, 200–206
rebracketing, 200
recursion, 20, 127, 134, 164
reductionism, 188, 189, 191
redundancy, 185, 186, 201, 202, 204–206
referential uncertainty, 19
reinforcement, 101, 113–115, 140
reuse, 5, 7, 86–88, 90, 91, 95, 107, 141, 143, 144, 152–154, 161, 174, 175, 184, 190, 199
RGB-channel, 56
rich-get-richer dynamics, 107
robot, 13, 14, 16, 18, 25
Russian, 13, 167

saliency, 56
scaffold, 5, 14, 15, 51, 59, 60, 70, 108, 127, 152
second-order semantics, 20, 21
selection, 47, 163, 167, 170, 171, 174, 176, 184, 190, 191, 196, 199, 205, 206

utterance-based selection, 12, 169, 170, 176
self-assessment, 51, 52, 93
self-organization, 16, 18, 174, 195
semantic bleaching, 204
Semantic Map Connectivity Hypothesis, 194
semantic maps, 163, 188, 192–197
semantic motivation, 6, 7, 183, 188, 189
semantic role, 6–9, 20, 37, 39–41, 46, 49, 51, 61, 86, 90–92, 95–97, 101–106, 165, 166, 169, 171, 173–175, 196
  agent, 7, 36, 37, 40, 41, 46, 173
  beneficiary, 178, 179, 192–194
  causer, 8
  dative judicantis, 192, 193
  direction, 192–194, 200
  experiencer, 192, 193
  instrument, 25
  patient, 7, 8, 40, 45, 165, 168, 173, 183, 199
  possessor, 192, 193
  predicative possessor, 192, 193
  purpose, 192–194
  recipient, 2, 109, 178–181, 192–194
  source, 4, 25, 36, 40, 41, 43, 45, 150
semiotic cycle, 52–54
semiotic dynamics, 18
semiotic landscape, 18
sensory-motor system, 53, 54, 57
serial verb, 5, 108, 110, 236
serial verb language, 5
Shannon coding, 64
situatedness, 51, 64

Subject index

spatial language, ix, 167, 196
speech population, 5, 7, 12, 14, 16–18, 37, 49–52, 60, 68, 69, 78, 79, 81–85, 94, 95, 97–99, 106–109, 114, 120–124, 126, 127, 129–131, 134, 136–139, 141, 144, 150, 154, 158, 159, 164, 165, 169, 170, 172, 176, 195, 196, 200, 206
stochasticity, 18
structural coupling, 16, 18
structure building
    J-operator, 30–34, 39, 61
Swiss army knife, *see* case
synchronic layering, 112, 116, 205
synchronic, 78, 107, 116, 130, 237
syntactic role, 8, 9, 39–41, 45, 46
    object, 6, 36, 40, 41, 46, 129, 156, 166, 167, 172, 177, 194, 198, 200, 202, 203
    oblique, 36, 39–41, 45
    subject, 5, 8, 12, 36, 37, 40, 41, 45, 46, 109, 129, 156, 166, 167, 172, 177, 178, 198, 200, 202, 203
syntactic space, 188
syntax-lexicon continuum, 116
syntax-semantics interface, 129
systematicity, 50, 111, 125–127, 129–132, 134–136, 138–141, 143, 144, 147, 148, 163, 167, 176, 184, 190, 191, 198

Talking Heads experiment, 18
temporal, *see* tense
tense, ix, 5, 14, 125, 160–162, 188, 189, 202, 203
Thai, 5
thematic hierarchy, 163, 183, 199, 200

to-infinitive, 202, 205
token frequency, 94, 104, 106–108, 127, 142, 170, 187, 190
tool design, 12
transitive clause, 198
transmission, 18, 164, 169, 175
Turkish, 2
type frequency, 90, 94, 103, 107, 150, 153, 156, 187, 190, 199

unification, 20, 27, 29–34, 148, 179
unify and merge, 28, 30, 34, 38, 39, 44, 45, 47, 66, 67, 73, 75, 76, 91, 116–118, 177, 179, 180, 191
Universal Grammar, 156, 164, 165, 169, 198
usage-based model, 92, 114–116, 131, 163, 184, 186, 188, 190, 206

valency
    actual valency, 36, 45, 47, 181, 189
    potential valents, 35–37, 39, 45–47, 61, 92, 180, 189
variable equality, 25, 26, 37, 41, 43, 44, 50, 55, 67, 72, 73, 77–79, 86, 91, 92, 120, 128, 141, 153
variation, 6, 11, 78, 79, 81, 95, 97–99, 101, 102, 104, 105, 107, 109, 111, 122, 129, 137, 143–145, 148, 154, 155, 159–162, 165, 167–170, 174, 184, 199, 200, 206
verb, 14, 19, 25, 35–37, 40, 43, 46, 47, 54, 61, 74, 78, 90–92, 97, 100, 101, 103, 107–110, 112–115, 118, 120, 125, 127, 129, 130, 132, 141, 151, 154, 167, 171, 177–183, 185, 188, 189, 193, 201–206
verbal gerund, 202

237

Subject index

vowel systems, 15, 20, 167

word order, 1, 10, 24, 32, 39, 41, 46,
    66, 165, 168, 169, 171
word sense disambiguation, 60

www.ingramcontent.com/pod-product-compliance
Lightning Source LLC
Chambersburg PA
CBHW081203170426
43197CB00018B/2909